LIVING IN THE VILLAGE

LIVING IN
THE VILLAGE

Build Your Financial
Future and Strengthen
Your Community

RYAN C. MACK

🦁 ST. MARTIN'S GRIFFIN ⚡ New York

This book is intended solely as a source of information for readers and is not intended to substitute for professional advice. If the reader needs advice concerning the evaluation and management of specific legal or financial risks or liabilities, such as bankruptcy or tax matters, he or she should seek the help of a licensed, knowledgeable professional.

LIVING IN THE VILLAGE. Copyright © 2010 by Ryan C. Mack. Foreword copyright © 2011 by Ali Velshi. All rights reserved. Printed in the United States of America. For information, address St. Martin's Press, 175 Fifth Avenue, New York, N.Y. 10010.

www.stmartins.com

Book design by Patrice Sheridan

LIBRARY OF CONGRESS CATALOGING-IN-PUBLICATION DATA

Mack, Ryan C.
    Living in the village : build your financial future and strengthen your community / Ryan C. Mack. — 1st ed.
        p. cm.
    ISBN 978-0-312-64636-3
    1. Finance, Personal. 2. Investments. 3. Retirement income—Planning. I. Title.

HG179.M237 2011
332.024'01—dc22

                                                                    2010037778

First Edition: January 2011

10 9 8 7 6 5 4 3 2 1

To my mother, Carol,

who never doubted me

even when I doubted myself

CONTENTS

CONTENTS

Contents

FOREWORD

PERSONAL FINANCE BOOKS HAVE A SAMENESS TO THEM. THEY TELL YOU THINGS YOU already know and, sometimes, make you feel bad for not having already done those things.

This book doesn't do that. I know a lot about money, but I learned a lot from this book.

I've known Ryan Mack for years. He's on my show regularly and was a particularly calming voice during the most stressful, panicked days of the Great Recession. He's a striking guy with a commanding presence, always immaculately dressed, with a syrupy voice that makes you want to hear more about money. In short, he looks like a million bucks. But underneath that he's a regular guy who has had more than his share of struggles, and because of that, he has an unusual commitment to spreading the gospel of personal responsibility and possibility. Unlike so many financial commentators, he doesn't take a populist—and popular—approach that looks to blame others for the bad things that happen to good people. Ryan believes you can fix your own situation, if you have knowledge and discipline.

Ryan is also deeply compassionate and works hard to share his wealth of experience and knowledge with those who want to make a better life for themselves. He works in communities with disproportionate numbers of disadvantaged people, and in doing so, he helps *and* he learns. Then he shares what he learns with others through his writing and his TV appearances. By the way, he runs a little business on the side.

I always knew all of this about Ryan. Now, after reading this book, I know why. Ryan has really been to the school of hard knocks. He's learned about life, and about money, the tough way. He's learned the value of education and faith and discipline and hard work and opportunity, and now, with this book, it's his time to share that.

Ryan and I have long shared the view that proper financial literacy is crucial to avoiding the type of crisis we've just come through. Ryan and I both believe this should start in school. But Ryan underscores his belief that the *best* thing you can do for your "village" or community is to make sure you are a net contributor, not a net recipient. Keeping yourself and your family financially stable means you won't lose your home and harm the values of your neighbors' homes. It means you can contribute to keeping your neighborhood clean and safe, and you can be a mentor to local youth. You can do well and, ultimately, provide services or make donations that make your community stronger. Want to prevent the next major financial crisis? You can't make government policy. You can't make Wall Street do the right thing. You can't make sure you never get laid off. You can't make sure your house doesn't drop in value.

But you *can* take basic steps to protect yourself, and in the process, you can prosper.

In this book Ryan doesn't just tell you what you need to do to improve your financial situation, but he relates it to your larger goals: a better education, a better career, a good education for your children, a more comfortable retirement. And he tells you *exactly* how to do it: how to budget, how to save, how to invest, how to fix your credit, and how to choose the right insurance. Ryan provides answers to questions many people may not even think to ask.

Ryan's a collaborator. He's always posting interesting, thought-provoking articles on my Facebook page, taking time to talk to people about their struggles. When he sees kids who need a leg up, he puts his neck out to help them get a job or an internship; he puts his good name on the line to help people he believes in. He counsels them, he gives them leads, and on occasion he hires them.

At the same time, he continues to expose himself to successful people and he works hard to get past their outward success and gain access to the "magic" that got them there. Was it discipline? Was it faith? Was it family? Or some combination of all of them?

Ryan is a product of where he grew up, in Detroit, and of his parents, his friends, his mentors, and those he has helped. In this book, you'll hear from many of them, who have made successes out of their lives from the biggest messes you can imagine. This book is a first: personal finance tips peppered with stories from thieves, drug dealers, convicts, all of whom have turned their lives around. Ryan has included writings from his family—not accolades of Ryan, but stories of how they faced challenges in their lives and careers; decisions they made and why they made them. Ryan has exposed himself, his family, and his friends; he's told the good and the bad. The point is that he learned from these experiences, and now he wants to share them with you. Most of us don't have to get out from under a combination of a felony conviction and jail time and near starvation and foreclosure. If the people in this book can lift themselves out of their circumstances, then the rest of us can get ourselves out of bad credit, spending more than we earn, not having the right education, and a myriad of other problems. Ryan makes the things regular folks lose sleep about seem manageable.

A book rarely does this. Either it tells you what to do, or it tells you what others did and you can do the work of transposing their experiences onto your life. The fit is rarely perfect in either case. In this book, I could see myself in Ryan's characters even though I didn't share their backgrounds or experiences. And in case you can't, Ryan finishes the thoughts for you with *specific* tips to improve your own situation.

But that's not where it stops. Ryan's goal is not just to help you do better for yourself, but for you to do better for your "village." For Ryan, the loop isn't complete if you don't give back. He shows you how he's done it, and how others around him have done it. Ryan makes giving back seem so effortless, and he shows you how it can be.

I've looked for a book like this for a long time, a book that explains finances so that the reader doesn't feel scolded. A book that empowers you even if you have never read anything about the stock market, made a budget, bought insurance, or earned anything more than a living wage.

Read it, fix your situation, and help build your village.

Ali Velshi
Anchor and Chief Business Correspondent
CNN

INTRODUCTION

IT IS OFTEN SAID THAT "IT TAKES A VILLAGE TO RAISE A CHILD." IF THAT IS TRUE, THE strength of the child depends upon the strength of the village, and the strength of the village depends upon the strength of each individual village member. If we want to make a better tomorrow, we must strengthen every individual. And if you want to make a better world, you must start by making a better you.

This book will challenge you to understand that each decision we make has an impact not only on ourselves but on the community as a whole. A common law of physics is that "every action has a reaction," and this same rule applies to us as we live in our communities. We continuously see people marching on Washington, D.C., for change, writing senators for more substantive policies, and calling congressmen for action; however, the most powerful way that you can create a positive change in your community is to start right within your household, because change comes from the bottom up.

There are many ways to empower your household, but this book focuses on the importance of fiscal responsibility. One may ask how one financially strong household can make a difference in a community. My response is that by itself it won't; strong communities are not built from just one house, they are built by many houses and families, with each one adding to the total value and empowerment of the community. The recession of 2007 began in part because too many of us in this country were buying things we didn't need with money we didn't have. This book is about you doing your part to empower your community financially by making sure you begin right within the walls of your home.

Your success and my success are linked, as we live in this nation together. If I can help empower you financially and remove the obstacle of the lack of money from your path, then your pathway to success will be that much easier. Forming that new business that you want will be easier, the funds that you need to send your child to college will be more attainable, and your golden years can be spent volunteering instead of working because your retirement is adequately funded. Similarly, if you are a successful business owner, you can provide more opportunity for people in my community to have employment; thereby, my community becomes stronger because of your business. If you send your child to school, he or she could become a doctor and save the life of a family member or a close friend; or he could become a teacher and teach my future children how to read and write; or she could become an architect and help to redesign the skyline of my city, raising my property values. If you retire and donate time or money to a worthy cause such as helping to organize blood drives in the community or organize block associations to address the everyday needs on my block, your individual efforts help empower the entire community.

It would be hard to find anyone who denies the importance of financial literacy. However, many people don't understand exactly what it means to become financially literate. My definition of financial literacy is not quite the same as the traditional definition. As an avid reader of financial books, I have a library filled with those that discuss how to improve your credit score (which this book does), how to invest (yep . . . this book does as well), and how to put together a budget (yep . . . got that covered). However, financial literacy is not just about the impact on our personal pocketbook; it's also about our confidence, our outlook on life, our faith, how we view success, our ability to network, our ability to give back to our community, and much more, because all of these things and more impact our bottom line.

When you ask people why financial literacy is important, they usually provide answers such as:

- "I want to strive for financial independence."
- "I want to be able to retire comfortably without living in debt."

- "I want to be able to leave a legacy for my children."
- "I want to purchase a home, start my own business, and spend my golden years on a beach . . . not working for the Golden Arches."

All these reasons are valid, but I think that the recession of 2007 hit home for a lot of people, and this is a teachable moment involving the true importance of financial literacy: As stated above, the success (or failure) of each individual has an impact on the success (or failure) of others. The recession of 2007 was the direct result of individuals, corporations, and the government making a perfect storm of bad decisions that caused the entire country to suffer. For instance, for many years individual savings declined because people had gotten comfortable with purchasing on credit. As a country we were driven by debt, and the economy finally collapsed and credit slowed to a halt.

However, there is a bright side. America has never failed to always come out on top. No meter can measure the enormous will and the spirit of the American people, which aids in our ability to self-correct. The economy is recovering, slowly, and there will be dips in the future, but the crisis could easily have been avoided if we all collectively were more responsible. The importance of financial literacy, not only for the sake of your own financial house but for the sake of this country, cannot be overstated. So if we can join together to make bad decisions to make the economy suffer, we can join together and make wise decisions to make the economy turn around again. This can be done, one household at a time, each member of the village doing his or her part.

We individually can do many things that collectively can empower the country. If, for example, we as individuals ate healthier, exercised more, and got regular checkups, together we would help lessen the strain on the health-care system. If we collectively got our children to put down the video games and pick up a book, we could improve the intellect of all of our youth and the country as a whole. If we all were much more cautious about how we purchased homes, we could avoid another foreclosure crisis.

To illustrate the power of individuals helping themselves financially and how the community benefits from fiscally responsible decisions, this book is filled with examples of those who have taken control of their destinies and financial futures. They demonstrate how financial literacy has not only helped themselves, but many others. These quiet heroes might be right under your nose and you would never know. They could be the teacher riding next to you on the train, the awesome motivator that you pass in the hallway as you report for work, the parent in front of you in the line at the drugstore, the husband in the next pew over at church, the high school student shopping at the mall, the pastor purchasing a new grill at the local home-improvement store, or the school principal that you may have known all your life but just never took the time to figure out how phenomenal he is. In some form or another they have demonstrated sound principles of financial literacy, and they have all touched the lives of tens, hundreds, or even thousands of people.

Are you among those who want to make a difference in your community but can't because you are too busy thinking about your home being foreclosed? Or your job is in jeopardy and you have no emergency fund? Or you thought you were near retirement but had the wrong asset allocation in your portfolio and now have to work ten to even thirty more years? Or you just can't seem to do anything but endure until you can get your next paycheck? Let me tell you something . . . you are certainly not by yourself and it is *not* too late for you to get a stronger grip on your finances! I contend that the pursuit of money does not make you rich; pursuit of passion makes you rich if you plan well and are able to find it. Money is only a tool, just like any other tool, which if used appropriately can help make your journey easier. If used irresponsibly, money will not be an asset to you, but the lack of money will be a liability, thereby making you less effective in contributing to the overall success of yourself and your community. Your success equals a stronger community, so it is in my interest for you to obtain success; however, your success will come faster and easier with a stronger financial foundation.

Madam C. J. Walker was the nation's first African-American millionaire. When she was asked why she wanted to become rich, her answer was simple: "My object in life is not simply to make money for myself or to spend it on myself. I love to use a part of what I make in trying to help others."

She understood the true meaning of how the village is supposed to work. The aim of this book is to help you, just like Madam C. J. Walker, think of more ways to improve the quality of life not only for yourself, but for others in your village. I hope the tools presented to you in this book will help you in your journey of village empowerment!

PART ONE

WHY IT TAKES
A VILLAGE

CHAPTER ONE

It Takes a Village
to Raise a Child

As I write this, I am watching yet another news story covering the uncertainty of the global economy. Rising food prices, record home foreclosures, closing manufacturing plants, and spikes in unemployment rates are a just a few stories that cause Americans to worry about our economic futures. But if we can learn from our past financial crises, we may be able to avert crises in the future.

Let's start with the Great Depression (1929–39). Ignited by a worldwide economic downturn, it had its beginning in the United States with the stock market crash on October 29, 1929 (known as Black Tuesday). In the United States, consumers cut expenditures because of the losses suffered in the market, and this loss of revenue was compounded by a severe drought that ravaged the agricultural heartland starting in 1930.

Despite the great uncertainty and stress, this country pulled it together for World War II, beginning in 1939, which marked the end of the Great Depression. With no "bright sky" in sight, businessmen and -women didn't allow the massive national debt and heavy new taxes resulting from the large expenditures on the war to discourage them. They worked overtime, gave up leisure activities, and graciously accepted rationing and price controls in full support of the war. Businesses took advantage of the tremendous demand for war supplies and were awarded government contracts, which created a lot of jobs. With 11 million men serving in the military, there were not enough male workers to fill the jobs. So women took those jobs, learning new skills and supporting the country through this hard time with their strength and diligence. The entire country banded together to see America through yet another tough economic time.

More recently, there was the dot-com bubble that existed between 1995 and 2000. In 1995 the United States was coming off one of the most successful recovery periods in U.S. history. This was a period of low inflation, a balanced budget in 1998 (budget surpluses in 1998 through 2000), with relatively less government borrowing leaving more resources available for business investment, low interest rates (which encourage business growth), strong consumer spending, low unemployment rates (4 percent in 2000), and continued gains in disposable income. The gross domestic production (GDP) grew at an annualized rate of 8.3 percent in the fourth quarter of 1999. The strong economic expansion fueled investment in the stock market. Many start-up Internet companies were the beneficiary of this increased investment.

When the country's most followed stock indexes, such as the Standard and Poor 500, hit an all-time high in December of 1999, Federal Reserve chief Alan Greenspan characterized this influx of capital into U.S. markets as unsustainable. He saw that many of these start-up Internet companies were not only *not* making money, but were not even real companies. The public listened to Greenspan and realized that growth was not sustainable at current levels, and the dot-com bubble began to burst.

Companies once valued at $10 to $15 per share were selling at over $100 per share. Yet as the stock market began to retract to fair market valuations, many began to suffer from losses. This caused people to stop spending as much money, and companies found themselves stuck with a lot of excess supply (paid for with a lot of debt). By the fall of 2000, one noticed increased filings of bankruptcy, decreased manufacturing production, and a decrease in employment. Soon after, the entire economy was in recession.

This recession served as a steep learning curve for America. The burst of the dot-com bubble forced companies to better scrutinize their investments. Investors gave up on attempts to make a quick profit in unproven companies and instead sought out long-term growth opportunities in companies with positive financials and a successful history of earnings. A wave of accounting scandals also caused corporations to become more diligent with their records and prudent with their capital expenditures. Investors saw the importance of diversification into other assets besides stocks, which caused significant growth in both the real estate and commodities markets.

The result in 2003 was the beginning of one of the longest bull-market rallies in U.S. history.

Fast-forward to 2010, when once again the economy is slowly recovering from a serious downturn and many are worried about the future. The recession of 2007–8 was caused by a perfect storm of three things:

1. Too many *individuals* caught up in the overhyped real estate market who purchased homes before they were ready.
2. Too many *corporations* that sold mortgage loans that shouldn't have been sold. Too many then packaged these high-risk loans as securities and sold them in secondary markets. This made them more money and relieved them of liability of default of the loans. To help with the sale of these loans, they assured the purchasers that they would "insure" the securities against default through the sale of derivatives. However, they didn't have enough money to provide this insurance. Just think if the auto insurer who sold you the policy to cover your vehicle had no money in the bank to pay if you had an accident but was more than happy to accept your premium payments.
3. The *government* regulated the financial system as if it were 1907, but it was 2007. Wall Street had outpaced the regulations imposed on it by the government, and it didn't help that the government had recently removed many of the most important regulations that could have prevented the crisis.

When those who purchased property through these "subprime mortgage" loans began to default, this set off a ripple effect that crippled the entire economy. First, since the bankers had bundled these loans and sold them, those who had purchased these bundled securities began to suffer losses. Those who began to suffer losses had been sold insurance on these securities and attempted to collect on it. However, those who sold this insurance, called derivatives, never had enough money to cover claims because they weren't being watched by the government closely enough and felt that they could play Wall Street like an Atlantic City casino game. This caused Bear Stearns to have to be bought by J. P. Morgan Chase, then came the collapse of Lehman Brothers because there was no one to save this company from bankruptcy. Billions of dollars left the banks, and the credit crunch of 2007 began.

As we have read from the previous examples, we have been here before. But we can learn from the past to get through these times again. The common thread among every previous economic hardship isn't stocks, bonds, business, or real estate. The common thread that carved a pathway for each of us to reach economic recovery is the resilience, diligence, and sheer will of the American people to survive and overcome.

No matter how hard the circumstances have been, people of all races, genders, religions, ages, and income levels came together to pull this country through. Whether it is African-Americans, who despite discrimination fought to aid this country in the Civil War; women, who despite sexism started a movement that turned this country around after a severe depression; or Jewish immigrants, who in the face of Hitler's tyranny migrated to America and helped to establish strong communities . . . we all have a stake in this country's future. This is what "living in the village" is all about: working together and being able to effectively contribute for the benefit of the community, your family, and yourself despite the odds that you face. The village must be strengthened from the bottom up. Each individual has an obligation to strengthen his or her knowledge, wisdom, and character. We must do this not for the benefit of ourselves, but for the sake of the village. How effectively can I contribute to the cause of my community? What else can I do to empower others around me? Every citizen who assisted in pulling this country out of a recession was able to successfully answer these questions.

We all have a role to play in this society. The purpose of this book is for us to understand that role and how we can provide economic strength to our communities, which will in turn make this country better as a whole. A chain is only as strong as its weakest link; therefore, it all starts from the individual. So we first must make sure that we empower ourselves financially, and then we will look at how we can effectively contribute to the economic empowerment of our communities.

DON'T WAIT FOR THE SMOKE!

There is a story about a man and wife who bought a house. After they moved in, the woman discovered that no smoke detector was installed. She asked her husband repeatedly to install a smoke detector but only got disinterested responses. Soon after, instead of asking about installing a smoke detector, she became worried about her husband's lack of concern.

"Why don't you care about the smoke detector?" she asked.

The husband, in a condescending tone, answered, "Why should we get a smoke detector? If ever there is a fire, we will be able to smell the smoke!"

Sound familiar? This story illustrates a problem in many households across America, and we aren't just talking about smoke detectors. When it comes to personal finances, many fail to prepare for the unexpected. Then, just as for a couple who has failed to install a smoke detector, when the fire hits, it is often too late to respond. Stats show how many Americans have not made proper preparations for their financial futures:

- By their sixty-fifth birthday, 93 percent of Americans require the financial support of family and friends or Social Security *just to provide for necessities*. (U.S. Department of Labor)
- Fewer men are worth $100 at age sixty-eight after fifty years of hard work than at age eighteen. (Denby's Economic Tables)
- Eighty-five percent of all people have *only $250 in cash at retirement*. (Social Security Administration)
- Over one-third of all senior citizens *live below the poverty level* as established by the federal government. (U.S. Census)
- Two and a quarter million senior citizens forfeit their Social Security because *they have to work*. (Social Security Administration)

How you prepare for your financial future depends upon the type of person that you are. Two types of people live in this world: those who are proactive, and those who are reactive. The reactive person lives his or her life and responds to changes as they come. The proactive person lives his or her life by preparing for things that could occur, and making his or her decisions appropriately.

For example, a reactive person says, "I want to treat myself to a new SUV. My budget is tight now, but I have worked hard enough to treat myself."

The proactive person says, "I want to treat myself to a new SUV, but my budget is a little tight these days. If gas prices continue to rise, I wouldn't be able to afford to drive it. Plus, I don't have my emergency fund [six to nine months of living expenses] completed yet, nor have I saved as much as I can within my IRA. I think I will purchase something a little more affordable. Then when my income increases, I will be ahead of the game in my retirement savings and then I might think about splurging."

The reactive thinker becomes the retiree mentioned in the above statistics. The proactive thinker found the situation urgent enough to begin saving earlier to avoid becoming a statistic. Just like the wife who wanted a smoke alarm, the proactive thinker starts saving as early as possible because he has seen what happens to those who fail to see the urgency in planning for the future.

So I ask you, which are you? Do you never have the time to plan for your future? If you ask the 85 percent of the people who have only $250 at retirement, they will tell you what is *truly* important. They will tell you what you should make time for. The dilemma with life is there are no second chances, and those 85 percent will never have the opportunity to go back and begin planning for their future at an earlier age. How many of those 85 percent thought they would never be in this predicament?

So ask yourself: How are you spending your money? Why haven't you started an investment plan yet? Few things are more important than your financial future, your financial independence, your financial freedom. If you tell yourself that you will certainly have more than $250 at your retirement, then I ask you, "What are you doing now to prepare for that future?"

Put the Oxygen Mask on Yourself First

If we are going to become effective contributors to our village, then it is imperative that our financial house be in order. This is rule number one. It is amazing to me how many people attempt to help others without paying any mind to their own financial situations. You should be kind enough to get your financial future in liftoff before working to help others. We have all heard the preflight airplane cautions: "Put the oxygen mask on yourself before you put it on your child." The same applies to how we contribute to the financial future of our village. If we want to create change, we must put ourselves in a position of power to be able to support and sustain making change. You are no good empowering the homeless in your community if you cannot pay your mortgage. That new nonprofit that you were going to form that would have helped children in your community needs you to have a good credit score in case you need to take out a loan for your business. I have been a witness to many failing business ventures because people have failed to take care of things at home. So start a path to join the ranks of the 7 percent of this country who have decided that *nothing* is more important than starting down the road to being financially independent *today*.

The Importance of Personal Responsibility

A few employees in this country have what is called a defined benefit plan. This plan is defined as follows:

Defined benefit plan: A company retirement plan, such as a pension plan, in which a retired employee receives a specific amount based on salary history and years of service, and in which the employer bears the investment risk. Contributions may be made by the employee, the employer, or both.

The key phrase in this definition is "the employer bears the investment risk." This plan is quite a deal for many workers across the country. In many programs, the employee did not have to contribute a single dime to the plan. His retirement benefits were based solely upon salary history and tenure with the company. Even in poor economic times, the employer was still obligated to provide for the employee. Millions who have reaped the benefits of these plans worked in peace knowing that their employer would take care of them in return for many years of dedicated service. However, as time passed and life expectancy increased, so did the financial burden on the employer. This increased financial burden caused fiscal problems for many corporations, and many began to search for ways to eliminate this burden. Enter the defined contribution plan:

Defined contribution plan: An employee-funded retirement plan, such as a 401(k) or a 403(b), that pays benefits based on the amount the employee has accumulated over his or her working life.

With the defined contribution plan, a corporation still provides a retirement plan but does not bear the risk or financial burden of the plan. The employee contributes and bears the risk of the plan. Companies obviously benefit from this, and therefore a dramatic shift in plan offerings occurred across the country. In 1985 the number of defined benefit plans totaled 114,000. Twenty years later, in 2005, they numbered 13,000.

I do not disagree with these actions by corporations. The longevity of many corporations was in jeopardy under the defined benefit plans. However, with the rapid shift toward the 401(k)-type plan, no adequate system was in place to educate the common American about its use and importance. Many will admit to being overwhelmed when faced with making investment selections in their 401(k) or 403(b) plan (if they choose to utilize the plan at all). A common asset-allocation strategy that I have seen is to simply select four or five different investment types and invest an equal percentage in each. As we will discuss in a later chapter, this is an inefficient style of selecting investments and trivializes an extremely critical investment.

We can complain that we want our corporations to take more responsibility for our retirement. However, while we are complaining, we are losing valuable time that we should be using to learn about how to plan for our retirement. Corporations have shown that they are no longer going to bear the weight of our retirement, and it is only right that the brunt of the weight lands mostly on our shoulders. We must bear full responsibility for our financial future.

The Secret to Success

Have you ever wondered what it really takes to be rich? When the Mega Millions lottery jackpot mounts up in your area, do you rush out to purchase a ticket? How easy would life be if someone came along and just dropped $10 million in your lap? The stories below are of those who also had that fantasy, but they actually won the lottery.

- **William "Bud" Post** won $16.2 million in the Pennsylvania lottery in 1988 but now lives on his Social Security.
- **Suzanne Mullins** won $4.2 million in the Virginia lottery in 1993. Now she's deeply in debt to a company that lent her money using the winnings as collateral.
- **Ken Proxmire** was a machinist when he won $1 million in the Michigan lottery. He moved to California and went into the car business with his brothers. Within five years, he had filed for bankruptcy.
- **Willie Hurt** of Lansing, Michigan, won $3.1 million in 1989. Two years later he was broke and charged with murder. His lawyer says Hurt spent his fortune on a divorce and crack cocaine.
- Missourian **Janite Lee** won $18 million in 1993. Lee was generous to a variety of causes. But according to published reports, eight years after winning, Lee filed for bankruptcy with only $700 left in two bank accounts.

All of the above people were handed great amounts of money, only to end up poor. What happened?

Maybe all the millionaires in this country inherited their wealth? Are the rich nothing but a "silver spoon" population living off the fruits of their parents' labor? The statement below implies otherwise:

Of all the millionaires in America, "only 19% receive any income or wealth of any kind from a trust fund or an estate," and "more than half never received as much as $1 in inheritance" (*The Millionaire Next Door*, Thomas J. Stanley and William D. Danko).

Most of this country's millionaires are first-generation rich and created their own wealth. What was their secret?

Half the secret is found in these news stories:

- "GM Buyout Package"—UAW members with at least 10 years of service at the world's largest automaker will get $140,000 if they give up the retiree health care coverage that has become a crippling burden for GM. (CNN News)
- "Enron 401(k) Analysis"—Not only was the company match all in stock, but the corporate environment encouraged employees to put all of their nest egg in Enron . . . In total, 60 percent of the plan was in company stock. (MSN News)

The GM buyout package actually occurred, and today hundreds of ex-employees of GM do not have any health-care benefits in their golden years. If they had *known* that the number one cause for bankruptcy is medical bills, they may have rethought accepting the retirement package.

In the Enron story, hundreds lost the majority of their retirement account in the collapse of this corporate giant. If those who participated in the company stock-purchase plan had *known* to limit their exposure to one stock in their portfolio to 15 percent, they would still have the majority of their portfolio intact.

The first half of the reason for success is knowledge. Knowledge in the two above issues would have saved millions of dollars in unaffordable medical bills and depleted retirement plans.

However, knowledge by itself is not power. It is important to have knowledge, but I know many smart broke people. The second part of the equation is action. Those who acquire wealth become an expert in their passion through study and research. Through diligence and perseverance they then apply this knowledge to achieve wealth. If you think of wealth like a game of sports, you will find that you have offense and defense strategies. Offense is the ability to acquire wealth, and defense is the ability to preserve wealth. Here in America 85 percent of the U.S. dollar is spent on consumption. We constantly go into debt purchasing things that we don't need with money we don't have. We are the richest country on the planet but we are among the worst in maintaining the wealth that we acquire. I have seen $300,000 wage earners who are living check to check, but $40,000 earners who have homes, contribute to retirement funds, and save money for their children's education. The secret to success is both having the knowledge and taking the action to achieve greatness. It is the ability to have great offensive and defensive strategies to plan and save for what is important in your life.

FOUR STEPS TO SUCCESS

Step One: Find Your Passion

The two most important days of your life are the day you were born and the day you know why you were born. Our creator has given us skills and talents upon birth. You can do something better than anybody else. What are you always thinking and talking about? What skills and talents do you have that you can translate into dollars? Your passion will give you the strength to finish a job even though you are tired. Your passion will carry you through the night to do the extra research necessary to create a successful company. Within your passion you will find the excitement that will always grab your attention so as to focus when all around you seems to be in chaos. Volunteering is a good start in your search, for if you are willing to do something for free, then it might just be your passion. Not only does volunteering help the community, but it gives you a chance to experience new and different perspectives. Talk to any millionaires and more often than not they have found their passion in life. What is yours?

ACTION STEP. Take an hour to think about all of the skills, talents, and hobbies that you have and write them down on paper. Try to write at least five things that represent one of the following categories:

- Things that you can do better than or at least as well as others you know.
- Things that you are passionate about. If you find yourself yelling at the TV screen while a commentator provides his or her opinion, what are you yelling at? This could be your passion.
- Things that you are always thinking about.

If you can think of more than five, even better. The more you write down, the clearer picture you will have of your passion.

Step Two: Have a Vision

If you are driving a car but do not know your final destination, how are you supposed to know if you are off course? Within the word *destination* you will find the root of the word, *destiny*. Do you know what your destiny holds? I challenge you today to have a vision of your destiny. Where will you be in ten years and what will you be doing? Twenty years? Thirty years? It might be okay not to have a vision at this very moment, but you should be working toward creating a vision for yourself.

ACTION STEP. Imagine where you will be and what you will be doing in one year, five years, ten years, and twenty years. Write these visions down on a sheet of paper. Try to make them as specific as possible. "I will be rich" is not a vision because it is too broad. "Owning a law firm and having an office downtown" or "Traveling back and forth to Africa as owner of a nonprofit to provide free medical services" is a more appropriate vision.

Step Three: Collect the Necessary Resources for Success

Now that you have a vision, you must collect the necessary resources to make that vision happen. The most important are knowledge, people, and capital.

Knowledge

High School Dropouts. Get your GED. If you can't or don't want to go to college (it's not for everyone), then find the resources to develop a skilled trade so that you can contribute in the building of your community.

High School Students. For those who have visions of higher education, talk to your school counselors to assist you in researching the best school that fits you and your personality. Make sure to research all of the scholarships that are available to you on Web sites such as www.FastWeb.com, www.ScholarshipAmerica.org, and www.Scholarships.com. After you have applied for at least twenty (yes, I said twenty) scholarships, apply for as much financial aid as possible.

Don't limit your search to only local city or state institutions. There is nothing wrong with attending these schools—they are cost-effective, and many students have done a lot with their degrees from these institutions.

However, there is also nothing wrong with believing that Harvard, Brown, Yale, and Princeton are options for you. Don't limit yourself. No matter which school you seek, have the vision and desire to see outside the boundaries of your immediate community. I am from Detroit; however, the world did not start and end for me there. I attended the University of Michigan, where I graduated from the number-one-ranked bachelor-of-business-administration program in the country. I had the vision to leave Detroit to pursue something larger than my surroundings. I urge you to do the same. (At the same time, don't forget where you came from. Use the knowledge that you acquire in higher education and in life to return to your home community and help to build and strengthen it. I try to travel back to Detroit once a month seeking ways to empower my community.)

College Students. Do not limit yourself to just your curriculum. Now is the time in your life to contribute as much as possible to the development of a community. The more you work in the community, the more experience you can add to your résumé and the more attractive you will be to employers. Talk to as many business owners as possible, be a mentor, tutor students at a local high school, organize workshops for the local high school that teach youth about your major, volunteer to work with a nonprofit, create a Web site and write a blog that educates the community about your major (for example, if you are a premed student, write about health tips, etc.), or try to take a semester abroad—use every opportunity possible to live outside your schoolbooks.

College Graduates. Continue to learn and develop your mind. If you are the smartest person in your group, find another group. Always push yourself to find those people who will stretch and challenge you mentally.

ACTION STEP. Go to Amazon.com or your local library and get five books. Three of the books should be directly related to your vision. For instance, when I started my financial-planning company I read many books on how to start one. Two of the books should be related to self-empowerment. Read a book a month, alternating between the vision-related titles and the self-empowerment titles.

People

It has been said that you can tell a lot about people by the company they keep. Loyalty may be important to you, but as you begin your journey through intellectual and spiritual development, some people will no longer be on the same level as you. I am not saying that you should not associate with them, but I am saying that you must recognize the path that you are on. If they are not willing to support you, they may drag you down. It is important to recognize that those who are too timid to follow their own dreams will often spend a lot of their time trying to discourage you from following yours.

I challenge you to meet as many positive people as possible until you meet that one person who catapults you to the next economic level through his or her contribution to your life.

ACTION STEP. Think of five people in your network that you haven't really talked to about your vision, and write their names and numbers down on your vision sheet. Over the next three months, set up a time to talk with them about mutual synergies and opportunities. Do not contact them with the purely selfish intention to only try to pick their brains to figure out how they can help you move ahead. Remember, this is the village and we must help each other, not only seek help from others. Calling with benevolent intentions, or intentions of mutual empowerment, will increase the odds that you will have more of an empowering conversation.

Capital

The bottom line is money, right? Without it, I would not have been able to start my financial-planning company. Nonetheless, looking back, I could have been better prepared. When I started my company, I had barely twelve months of living expenses saved up plus $28,000 for the start-up. So there were many dinners of Cheese Nips, tuna fish, sunflower seeds, or nothing at all. I lasted a year on savings alone, but had I been more diligent, I would have been a little more comfortable during that time.

ACTION STEP. Having a vision that you would like to achieve, such as a business, a new home, a comfortable retirement, or a college education, requires capital. Make sure that you are not placing a higher priority on material items than on your future financial goal. Your actions and your bank statement will tell the story of what you are placing a financial priority on in your life even as your words might state otherwise. I wish I had a dollar for every family that said they wanted to buy a home within a year, but ate out frequently or shopped excessively. Figure out exactly how much money you need to raise for your goal, put together a budget that gets you to your finish line, and be as diligent as possible in keeping it. Before you go and purchase that new clothing item, ask yourself, "Have I met my monthly savings goal for my new home/business/retirement?"

If the answer is yes, feel free to purchase the item. If the answer is no, walk on by.

Step Four: Write a Five-Step Plan of Action

It is a misconception to say that knowledge is power. I know many smart people who are penniless. Knowledge plus action equals power. I challenge you today to write out a plan of action. This plan should be at least five steps and should be specific as possible. ("Working hard" is not specific or actionable enough.) Examples of tangible steps of action include:

- Call the local community center to sign up for a GED course.
- Go to the local community college to enroll in a certification, training, or educational course for a new career.
- Ask your friend who has his own business how he started it.
- Complete a college application and send it in.
- Research scholarships, complete scholarship applications, and send them in.
- Create a budget to monitor your spending habits and avoid over-consumption.
- Read an investment book (or a few) so that you don't have to completely rely on your broker.
- Buy life insurance and write a will so that if something happens to you, your family will be taken care of.
- Learn how to write and then prepare an elaborate business plan to start your business.
- Go on www.inc-it-now.com and fill out the form(s) necessary to incorporate your own company.
- Have regular conversations with your significant other to make sure that you are on the same page about finances.

ACTION STEP. Take some time to write out this plan of action, as it is vital to your success. The odds of achieving your goal increase tremendously if you write the steps down. On your vision sheet, write out a five-step plan of action that starts from today and ends with your achieving your vision. This plan will grow and change as you grow and change. This is fine as long as you keep your eyes on the prize. If you find your passion, have a vision, acquire the necessary resources, and write out a plan of action, it might take six months, one year, three years, or even five years, but . . . you *will* be successful.

Repeat these four steps at least once every three to six months, as you always want to have a firm reminder of what your skills are and if you are on the right path in life.

VILLAGE VISIT

The Power of Finding Purpose:
The Public Speaker

Jullien Gordon is a young entrepreneur whose company is just breaking even. However, one should not measure success in monetary terms. Before the age of thirty he has already written and published two books and has toured the country inspiring thousands to achieve their purpose in life through his DMV (Department of Motivated Vehicles) workshops. In an economy where people are struggling to find employment, he was able to quit his job and run his business full-time. He was able to do all of this through a textbook vision and the execution of a plan as outlined in the previous section. He is the perfect example of someone who has not only found his purpose, but has dedicated his life to helping others to find their purpose as well.

THE PURPOSE FINDER
by Jullien Gordon

I believe that it is not only possible to make a living doing what you love, but that it is essential if you are to become financially free *and* fulfilled. Some people have financial freedom, but they aren't fulfilled. You can be earning $200,000 a year and still be unsatisfied. Yet when you are living a life that is in perfect alignment with your purpose and passions, you will be making your highest contribution to the world and creating extreme value through your career.

The goal of my work is to help people discover their purpose and crystallize their passions into a skill so that they can make a living doing what they love. My own entrepreneurial roots began when I was a little boy. I made my first profit in junior high school selling Now and Laters out of my backpack. My mother bought me a big jar

(continued)

17

of 172 Now and Laters from Costco, which cost about $12, but I sold each Now and Later for twenty-five cents. One jar sold meant $43.

Fast-forward to college, where I came across Robert Kiyosaki's *Rich Dad Poor Dad*—from that moment, my perceptions of money were forever transformed. His book was my first introduction to the concept of financial literacy, and it inspired me to start an on-campus group called S.T.O.C.K.S. & B.O.N.D.S. (Sisters Taking Ownership of their Cash and Knowledge of Stocks and Brothers Organizing Networking Dollars and Sense). Through the collective wisdom of this group, I learned the basics of business. While my business classes taught theory and accounting, my peers and I experimented together, starting on-campus businesses and investment clubs. This training laid the foundation for more significant ventures postgrad.

After college, I went to business school. There I learned about organizational leadership, strategy, general management, operations, marketing, etc. Despite all the talk about money and wealth, few courses, programs, or student groups were focused on personal finance. The implicit assumption was that most people in business school would earn their wealth as consultants, bankers, and managers, but my entrepreneurial roots wouldn't allow me to buy into that story. My focus was financial freedom *and* fulfillment—I felt that it was best and possible to have both at once.

During business school, my goal was to graduate as an entrepreneur. I tried to start two ventures, but both failed.

So I took a bridge job afterward. *Bridge job* is a term I created to describe a short-term employment opportunity whose goal is to position you for your next move. Once you have saved up six months of living expenses or at the eighteen-month mark, you should leave. This forces you to maximize that opportunity, develop skills and relationships, keep your living expenses low, and save money for your transition. I met my savings goal and left my job to start my current business, in the beginning of an economic depression.

Given the times, I fell into a mentality of lack and cost-consciousness, as did the rest of the world. But mine was even more severe because I had no prospect of significant income yet. For the first three months of my business, I didn't invest anything other than time. After a while I realized that if I didn't invest in the things that were

(*continued*)

necessary to grow my business, I would lose it. So I started asking questions like "How can I afford that?" instead of saying "I can't afford that." In a way, I created my own stock market where the currency was my time and money, which I believed would yield short-term and long-term returns. When your livelihood is on the line, you tend to make decisions either rationally or irrationally—fortunately, I made rational ones. Each day I would ask myself, "How can I create the most value possible for others and thus my company today?" The answer guided my goals and actions.

After a year of being in business, I am happy to say that the business has broken even. Though the cash flow isn't great, the company is more valuable than it was a year ago. In the past twelve months, I have published two books, helped over two hundred people discover their purpose through my Driving School for Life course, addressed over a thousand people through various speaking engagements, developed a strong offline and online brand, and created significant momentum for 2010.

Jay-Z said it best when he rapped, "I'm not a businessman, I'm a business maaannnnn!" Value creation should always be at the forefront of your mind. Those who create value will be in the best position to capture it in the form of money, impact, or status.

Ryan Mack's Five Economic Empowerment Tips for Public Speakers

1. Read as much as possible. If you want to make it in this field, you must be knowledgeable about various topics because people will get bored of a topic repeated over and over.
2. Practice speaking as much as possible. When I am at home, at least once per day I find myself talking to myself and giving a speech about a topic.
3. Write a book. Jullien learned that to be taken seriously in the game of public speaking, you must be a published author, which gives you credibility.
4. Build your network as aggressively as possible and flood your network with e-mails about where you will be speaking and your content. People won't call you if they don't know that you are open for business. If you do a small speech at the local library, videotape it, load it onto YouTube.com, and send the link to your network

along with a press release. When I started speaking, I would go to public housing communities and teach audiences of only three people—the community center director, the janitor, and someone who was just walking by. I had someone take pictures of me speaking, posted them in a newsletter, and wrote the press release as if I had spoken to a roomful of people.

5. Public speaking shouldn't be your primary line of work initially. It is a slow gig until you are known in the field. My company was and still is my primary source of income, but public speaking happened because of my media exposure. However, pay attention to how Jullien played his cards to start his journey. He budgeted to save the appropriate amount of money from his "bridge job"; while at his bridge job he established a business with a curriculum that he could teach and charge people to learn; and when he quit his job, he hit the ground running. He now has a business that supports his desire to get out there with his message.

CHAPTER TWO

The Evidence of
Things Unseen

TIMES HAVE BEEN HARD FOR EVERYONE. HOWEVER, AS HARD AS THEY HAVE BEEN, the spirit of the people of America sustains them. More than stocks, bonds, or gold, faith is the most precious commodity that we should all have. Faith has two components: The first is the belief that tomorrow will bring brighter/better days. The second is being able to act on that belief. Having one without the other will not produce the results that you desire.

Imagine a person who has faith that he will own his own home. Not only does he believe, but he begins to act on this belief. He hires a financial adviser to help him put together a home budget, which determines how much he can afford. He hired this adviser because he understood that just because you are preapproved by a lender, who only looks at your income and debt levels, it does not mean that you will be able to afford that piece of property.

After he talks with his adviser, he calculates that he can afford a home with a mortgage $300 more than his current rent. He begins to save that $300 per month in a high-yield savings account and acts as if he were paying that mortgage. He researched the most lucrative high-yield savings accounts online so that his savings will be safe and grow faster than the rate of inflation (to be discussed in a later chapter). He puts another $300 on top of that, for a total of $600 per month, because he knows that when he owns his home, he will need additional funds for retirement and other household expenses that he is not currently paying. Also, whenever he calls the landlord to fix anything around his apartment, such as the plumbing, he puts the same amount as that maintenance costs into his savings account. This way he is getting real-time training in the costs of owning a home *before* he owns the home. He asks his landlord how much property taxes are and finds out that they are $3,000 per year. He takes $3,000 of his own money and deposits it into his savings account to act as if he were paying property taxes. After a year or after he's saved 20 percent toward his home, whichever happens last, he will purchase his home. (Many will argue that it is fiscally responsible to purchase a piece of property entirely with "other people's money" or with nothing down. Those who advocate the nothing-down purchase tend to be in the mortgage industry and can profit from the sale of a mortgage through interest on loans or commissions. If you can put 20 percent down on a piece of property, not only will you avoid PMI payments and/or costly secondary mortgages, but you will know that your fiscal discipline and responsibility ensure that you will not be a part of those dreary foreclosure statistics.)

During this time, he follows the steps to improve his credit to a score of 750 (to be addressed in a later chapter) to receive a prime rate on his mortgage. He also interviews at least six lenders a year in advance of even getting preapproved and asks them what FICO score he must have to get the prime rate. He writes down his goal purchase date and checks his score on annualcreditreport.com one year, six months, and three months before his purchase date. These actions and more represent faith: He believes he will own a home and goes through the necessary actions to responsibly prepare himself for a lifetime of homeownership.

With faith, nothing is impossible. Faith will make your first home become a reality, that new job happen—and any goal you desire come true. Faith is not rainbows, unicorns, and other notions of false realities. Faith is effort, faith is diligence, faith is real, and faith is hard work! You can read all the empowerment books you want, but if you choose to believe that the principles are not for you or that you are predestined to live in lack, you will not be successful. Believe that there is a greater quality of life for you, your family, and your community. One of your most important tasks is to contribute toward making a better world. The best way to do that is to make a better you.

VILLAGE VISIT

The Power of Faith: The Religious Leader

Religious leaders can create a tremendous impact on a community with the right vision and direction. Those religious institutions that are open more than one day per week and stretch their outreach beyond the walls of their place of worship are the most successful in creating change. Every day, those religious leaders will have teams of people providing education, food, and shelter for those in need.

The Reverend Edwin Reed has been CFO of Greater Allen AME since 1996. He is responsible for overseeing Allen's corporations, which provide a multitude of social services as well as operate a school, a resource center for battered women, senior-citizen complexes with 630 units, a for-profit transportation company, several commercial stores, and nonprofit entities responsible for neighborhood preservation, affordable-housing development, and commercial revitalization. He also helped to write a book on church management, entitled The African American Church Management Handbook, *published in 2005. He is the perfect example of a religious leader who uses faith to empower his community financially.*

FAITH, FINANCE, AND FOLLOW-THROUGH
by the Reverend Edwin Reed

The faith community has a unique opportunity to impact its environment. A local church is the "permanent community resident." Empowering churches do not exist in the community only on Sunday mornings; empowering churches change the outlook of the people that they serve. The people who are served by a church are principally from the neighborhood in which the church resides. Thus, the church has the same economic underpinnings as the community that it serves. Given its unique character, the church—by using collective resources, vision, and a God-centered faith—can effectively implement a mission of empowering people and communities by identifying and meeting expressed needs. The implementation of the mission in the broader

(continued)

community enables the church to be a central force in its immediate locale as well as to become a national force for community-based change through collaboration. Sharing ideas and concepts is the foundation for church empowerment, community empowerment, and financial empowerment because in the faith community they share a fundamental principle—managing resources intelligently and effectively.

Managing resources in all three areas depends on lifting the aim of the community. For the church, it is a God-focused ministry that at its core is encouraging each member to have an ever-growing personal relationship with God. For the community, it is becoming involved in maximizing the quality of life and services. For financial management, it is providing tools that support excellent stewardship of all resources.

Religious institutions can successfully run community-based programs such as employment training, after-school tutoring, senior feeding programs, youth programs, foster-parent recruitment, abstinence and self-esteem building, and welfare-to-work initiatives. If there is a need for a certain program, then empowering churches look for resources that can fulfill the needs of members of the church and the community.

Based on its position as a community-focused institution, the church has the ability to develop partnerships with governmental entities, nonprofits, for-profits, and philanthropy entities that participate in faith-based community programs. Being involved by accessing and directing funding streams can be an excellent method for enhancing the mission of the church. For community empowerment, the church should establish a nonprofit corporation that more effectively allows for participation in various programs and fulfills the tenet of separation of church and state. It is important to note that nonprofit organizations flourish with the realization that the power of the church is not just in speaking about faith but rather demonstrating faith in action.

Partnership between faith and finance is a fundamental principle that leverages the benefits of each. The principle of community empowerment is that each party benefits through cooperation. The church has the ability to support the growth of the church while serving the community, and the funding entity has a more cost-effective

(continued)

model for service delivery. The church retains its foundational principles that ensure that community empowerment is accomplished within the context of spiritual revival. One example of leadership that raises the aim of a community and people is at the Greater Allen Cathedral. The Reverend Floyd Flake encouraged the church to get involved in education. He visualized a new building on a dilapidated corner that would have more than twenty-five classrooms with a cafeteria and a gymnasium, serving nearly four hundred students from pre-K to the eighth grade. Faith was buttressed with action, and Allen has blossomed into a church-based nonprofit organization with over $200 million in development projects and a budget of over $14 million for community-based programs.

To be effective at its mission, the church must encourage engagement outside the walls of the church. In finance, the ability to use internally generated funds to support and attract programs will rebuild the economic underpinnings of the neighborhood. Opportunity is ever present. When an outside force takes advantage of the opportunity in historically underserved communities, it is called gentrification. When the indigenous community residents take advantage of the same opportunity, then it is called community empowerment. In finance, if we manage our resources well, it is called wealth. If all our resources flow out of our hands and are managed for the benefit of others, it is called the transfer of wealth. Either can occur, but community empowerment requires action from the principals in a community.

There are a variety of methods for implementing a successful community-empowerment strategy. The two primary models are the single-church development, along the lines of Greater Allen Cathedral, and a consortium of congregations, such as Harlem Community of Community Improvement (HCCI). HCCI consists of ninety interfaith congregations and has leveraged more than $240 million in support to develop more than two thousand units of housing and more than forty commercial stores, including a forty-five-thousand-square-foot Pathmark. Regardless of the model chosen, the compatible principles of managing resources and taking responsibility for outcomes are fundamental for economic development and financial security. Planning and action are critical components for success. For community

(continued)

empowerment, local businesses are owners of the new establishments; the strategy is to attract customers from a broader geographic area as well as from the local neighborhood. God changes the lives of people, while church community empowerment allows that change to be demonstrated broadly.

Any financial success is a reflection of all aspects of your life—spiritual components, time, priorities, talent, and relationships. It is a holistic approach that leaves a person fulfilled, not just financially well-off. Furthermore, an appreciation for personal finance should be an empowering ministry for each member of the church. This concept has been pioneered by the Reverend Buster Soaries of First Baptist Church of Lincoln Gardens in New Jersey. On the fourth Sunday of each month, the congregation celebrates a concept called D*free*—no deficits, no debt, and no delinquencies. The goal is to internalize good financial management by members of the church. Three levels of classes provide budgeting, debt recovery, five-year debt-elimination plans, estate planning, and financial accountability. As members reach levels of success, there is a celebration as part of the worship. The dual benefits of using godly principles regarding finances are that the people *and* the church experience overflow blessings.

The lessons to be learned are that a sense of purpose, a real appreciation of the potential of a community and a people, and an abiding faith effectively direct making good decisions. There should be a focus on success in the present and options for the future. Continuous growth is the focus even through temporary setbacks. Seek and accept new challenges. Strong spiritual bases coupled with effective financial planning along with making a difference in growing a community are the fundamental results of faith, finance, and follow-through.

RYAN MACK'S FIVE ECONOMIC EMPOWERMENT TIPS FOR RELIGIOUS LEADERS

1. Keeping the doors of the church always open should be a critical component of your church mission. Many churches take up space on the block but only operate one day per week. Fill up those empty days with programs that your membership can use to empower themselves.

2. Keep adequate records. You would be amazed at the number of religious institutions that don't keep good financial records simply because they are tax-exempt. What they don't realize is that they are inhibiting growth in their church from the lack of funding that they might have received.

3. Network with local professionals in your community to help to build and provide educational services to your membership regularly. If you need an attorney to help with legal matters, hire from your local community. If you want to teach your membership about the importance of financial literacy (or any other important life skill), choose a professional from your local community as well.

4. If the church owns property, leverage the land for the benefit of the community. Obtain loans to build businesses, purchase franchises, and develop your community. The building of businesses that are run and operated by your membership and/or people in the community creates jobs for the people; so does real estate development.

5. Don't be afraid to partner with other churches in the community. Churches can easily create substantial leverage with collaboration and unity, even across faiths. One of the most productive planning meetings that I have ever witnessed was one at which members of Protestant, Catholic, Jewish, and Muslim faiths met to discuss ideas for the greater good of the community.

THE CORRECT MIND-SET

The mind is the most powerful tool in the human body. The ability to imagine is the best gift given to us. If you start a journey without having the proper mind-set, then the journey is over before it has even started.

If we were to examine the power of the mind, we would constantly be amazed. I once heard a story of a doctor's father who had suffered a massive blow to the head. He injured the portion of his brain that controlled movement and was unable to use his legs to walk. He was so determined to walk again that every day he would roll to a gym in a wheelchair. To the amazement of his son, who was a neurologist, he began to slowly gain motion in his legs. He passed away before regaining full use of his legs, but he did work himself out of the wheelchair and walk with the use of crutches.

After his death, his brain was analyzed and showed evidence that uninjured portions of it had begun to compensate for the injured parts that had controlled motion. This story illustrates that there is no limit to what the brain can do; we just have to unleash our mental visions and let the mind operate at a higher capacity!

So, if you believe it enough, you can do whatever it is that you want to do. You have to believe, have courage, and accept that failure is not an option. If you look at infants learning to walk, it is truly amazing. They learn how to walk despite enormous obstacles. They could easily have the negative mind-set that many of us adults have and make up excuses. Imagine that you are an infant learning to walk and you think like far too many of us adults think. . . . It might look like the following:

- There are too many things to bump into and I don't want to get injured.
- I have never walked before so how can I begin now?
- My mother is carrying me wherever I go, so there is not really a need as of yet.
- I think that I need to get a little stronger or study a little more how other people walk.

Why do some people possess so much negativity toward change? Break out of that rut and be positive! How many goals could be accomplished if you would not let the cynicism of life create obstacles for you? Think outside the box and dare to dream big despite what others tell you and despite what inhibitions have formed within you over the years.

The mind needs to be constantly stretched, challenged, expanded, and exposed to new ideas. You can exercise your mind just by taking the time to notice new colors and flowers that you haven't noticed before. Change your routine, read new literature, and challenge yourself to think differently about your financial future. Let's make it a goal to break out of those ruts of cynicism, negativity, pessimism, and the victim's mentality that hinder our mental growth and success.

Gandhi said, "A man is but the product of his thought. What he thinks, he becomes." Every day, practice thinking positively about every aspect of your life and you can not help but think positively about your financial future. Small minds think about what other people are doing; average minds think about what events are happening; and large, successful minds think about ideas that will not only impact themselves but will empower others. Practice thinking large today!

VILLAGE VISIT

The Power of the Proper Mentality: The Formerly Incarcerated

Nearly 3 million people are in prison in the United States at the time of this book's publication. This year, 650,000 will be released, and 63 percent of those will return to prison within three years. One of the key ingredients of not being part of that statistic is to have the right mentality. I do considerable work helping those recently released to achieve their full potential, partly because I believe in them, and also because I believe that to teach someone how to empower himself or herself economically decreases the likelihood that he or she will go back to jail. Helping the formerly incarcerated is a great way to reduce crime, keep our neighborhoods safe, and increase the economic viability of our communities as a whole.

Damon Jenkins was formerly incarcerated but not only became certified in numerous trades, including as an electrician, but also networked well and started his own company to help others who were still entrenched in the gang life to find jobs. Damon perfectly exemplifies the correct mind-set. He was never discouraged by the question "Have you ever been convicted of a felony?" If there were no opportunities, he created opportunities.

METAMORPHOSIS OF A LOST SOUL
by Damon Jenkins

I was no stranger to hard times, growing up underprivileged in the Breukelen Houses projects in the Canarsie section of Brooklyn, New York. At the tender age of thirteen, instead of playing video games, I was initiated into a notorious street gang. I joined the gang looking for communal support.

I recall being referred to as a "lost soul" because I constantly got into trouble. It started in high school, when I was living with ten people in a two-bedroom apartment and it was not easy. However, we persevered within our environment, and this made us a

(continued)

close-knit family. Given our financial struggles, I had no constructive outlets to express my frustrations. So when in school I would take my frustrations out on the other kids. This resulted in a vicious fight in which I was stabbed in the face, and it nearly cost me an eye. I rebelled and fell deeper into the streets, which welcomed me wholeheartedly.

With my gang affiliation, my life took a deadly plunge into selling drugs, grand larceny, assault, and gangbanging. I soon dropped out of school. My circumstances continued to deteriorate, and street life became the best route to travel.

I was stubborn and hardheaded, so at the age of sixteen I became a high school dropout and was kicked out of my home.

Feeling that I had no other alternative and because I liked the prospect of making the kind of money I saw being made by the "corner boys," I jumped on the next bus to upstate New York to start selling drugs.

Everything ran smoothly for my buddy and me for about three months. We were bringing in large amounts of cash and living "ghetto fabulous" until my friend got caught leaving our apartment with several packages of drugs and all of our money by the narcotics division. As I was coming back from the store, I saw several cop cars in front of the apartment and disappeared without being noticed. So with no food, no clean clothing, and most important, no shelter, I was now homeless in upstate New York.

Knowing that my situation was dismal, I pondered how I would legitimize myself and get financially stable. With no other recourse, I decided to play the streets for another month. I started stealing food daily from grocery stores and bathing in the bathrooms of fast-food restaurants. I became the new "local stickup kid," and I now added robbing people to my criminal résumé. My motto was "If you have it, I will definitely take it!" One day, I came across the sweetest vic [victim] opportunity; I robbed a big-time drug dealer of his drugs and money and got a one-way ticket back to New York City.

Back in Brooklyn on a hot day in August, I was with some of my friends hanging out in the playground (which was in the middle of the projects) showing off my beautiful baby boy. While we were talk-

(continued)

ing, we noticed a guy riding past on a bike. We didn't realize he was a threat until it was too late. He rode past us and pulled out a gun and began shooting. I ran out of the playground with my son in my arms. Anticipating gunshots, I peered over my shoulder and saw that God had saved me because the guy's gun had jammed. That day, I realized that I could have lost my life; but the possible loss of my innocent son caused me to fall to my knees and call on God. I knew that if I continued on this same path, I would certainly end up in the graveyard. This coupled with the tragic loss of my friend who wasn't so lucky was the moment that changed my life forever.

My past indiscretions and offenses eventually caught up to me and I served some time in jail. While incarcerated, I used my time wisely and began to transform myself through Christ, prayer, and perseverance; I learned firsthand anything is possible with God. After I was released, I was placed on probationary monitoring, and I complied with all the rules and regulations. I was now a former street kid who had committed crimes but turned my life around. I began to regularly attend several Baptist churches in Brooklyn, and many pastors began to take me under their wing as mentors. I attended classes at the Berk Trade School, where I graduated at the top of my class and received certification in electrical repair and maintenance. In addition, I created for myself a foolproof "blueprint" plan.

What exactly is that blueprint plan? Now in my late twenties, I am the president of my own construction company, which specializes in providing construction and renovation services. The company is family owned and operated and hires newly released felons. I want to make a difference in the lives of newly released felons because of the adversity and discrimination they face regularly. I believe that empowering them with job training, education, and rehabilitative counseling services is crucial in transforming their lives for the better.

Through my new mission I met and joined the team lead by the author of this book, Ryan Mack, and learned about financial literacy. He was critical in helping me establish my construction company, and since meeting him I have toured with Ryan to public-housing community centers in Manhattan and Brooklyn, where we taught financial

(continued)

literacy seminars to adults in addition to giving inspirational speeches to youth. When talking to them, I emphasize that they can also have positive alternatives; I use myself as a role model. I forged ahead, deciding not to let my tumultuous past experiences and events deter my life's path. My ability to overcome adversity enabled me to convert my life to that of an upstanding citizen, contribute positively to society, and steer clear of the perils that plagued my past. Now armed with new enthusiasm and knowledge, I am giving back to the community by offering programs that empower our misguided youth as well as giving them job opportunities.

I would like to say to those who judge individuals like me who have made some wrong decisions in their past (I am certainly not proud of many things that I have done), please do not judge a book by its cover. While we all are susceptible to hard times, individuals with felony convictions are subject to prejudice because of who they used to be. No matter what obstacles, trials, or tribulations they may encounter, many former felons have worked hard to turn their lives around. Going back to prison is definitely not an option.

RYAN MACK'S FIVE ECONOMIC EMPOWERMENT TIPS FOR THE FORMERLY INCARCERATED

1. Enroll in all available free support programs as soon as you are released. Many might not initially seem beneficial, but any program is only as good as the effort you put into it.
2. Talk to nonprofits, your local politicians, churches, community colleges—as many outlets as you can find that provide free or inexpensive job training, education, and certification courses. The more you can add to your résumé, the faster you will find a job.
3. Do not be ashamed to take that low-paying job that was provided by your parole office or that you found through a connection. Your initial goal is to make enough to keep a roof over your head and provide for necessities. Anything else is a bonus. Once you get on your feet, hit the library and research your next move.
4. Don't hang around those who are still doing the very things that put you in prison. Now is the time to find a new circle of friends who will not pull you down, but lift you up. Remember that those

too weak to follow their own dreams will continuously try to find ways to discourage you from finding yours.

5. Manage your money wisely. The less money you make, the more fiscally responsible you have to be. Budgeting, establishing credit, and growing savings for that rainy day are a few of the things that should be nonnegotiable.

PART TWO

SEVEN STEPS TO
FINANCIAL FREEDOM

Now that we are mentally and emotionally prepared to become financially empowered, here are the actual steps that will help you achieve that. These seven steps are designed to give you a tangible outline to follow toward your goal of financial freedom. For many of you, this may be unfamiliar territory. However, I encourage you to remain diligent. I wasn't born financially literate; it took work. Now that I have that expertise, let me help you understand the fundamentals of financial literacy, keep you out of trouble, and help you accumulate wealth safely and responsibly.

1. Getting your house in order.
2. Eliminating all high-risk debt.
3. Effectively allocating your company retirement plan.
4. Adequately funding your emergency fund.
5. Establishing an individual retirement account.
6. Eliminating low-risk debt.
7. Pursuing a diversified investment strategy.

The first step, get your house in order, is all about making sure that in times of economic hardship you have an adequate plan B. This step has four components, and none of these four deals with investing. There is no individual investment advice until step five of the seven steps. Many people think they should begin investing immediately and fail to lay a proper foundation. Not correct! First, establish a safety net for what you already have. The four components of step one are:

1. Create and maintain a household budget
2. Obtain adequate insurance coverage
3. Obtain and maintain up-to-date estate-planning documents
4. Achieve and maintain a FICO score above 750

Let's get started!

CHAPTER THREE

Step One: Getting Your House in Order—Creating and Maintaining a Household Budget

YOU CAN USE MONEY IN THREE WAYS:

1. Spend
2. Build (saving, investing, etc.)
3. Give

SPEND

The failure to watch what we spend is the primary reason that we are not able to accumulate wealth. I know of a doctor who earns well over $300,000 per year, but he and his family live check to check. They are inundated with debt because they live beyond their means. However, I have a client in New York City who is earning a little over $60,000 (which is not a lot for this expensive city) and has just purchased a home, is saving regularly for retirement, and takes yearly vacation trips. She makes about 20 percent of what the doctor makes but has more money for her retirement.

It all depends on how you handle your income. I have noticed, by talking to many people across the country, that those making $90,000 per

39

year can have the same fiscal problems as those earning $30,000 per year. You would think that three times the income would equal three times the savings. However, we find that as people's salaries increase, so does their spending in most cases.

Individuals of all income levels may have problems with spending for many reasons, including:

- **Lying to Themselves.** They spend money frivolously because they don't want to face the truth about just how much of a mess their financial house is in.

- **Spending Tomorrow's Money Today.** People spend money that they don't have, expecting increases in earnings or windfalls. But when that tax refund wasn't as high as you thought or you didn't get paid as much overtime as you anticipated, you are now on the hook plus interest.

- **The "Big Shot" Mentality.** Many people love to be perceived as financially stable. I have seen people who I know just lost their job pick up the entire dinner tab just to maintain a façade of affluence with their peers.

- **Humble Upbringing.** Many people didn't have a lot of money growing up, and once they get a taste of financial stability, they shower themselves with things that they were once deprived of.

- **Plastic Is Not the Same as Paper.** People spend on average 35 percent more than they would in cash if they have access to a credit card. Holiday season is a perfect example, with people spending themselves into the poorhouse because they are caught up in the moment, purchasing gifts with money that they don't have. Why do you think that casinos have you exchange your money for plastic casino chips? They understand that it doesn't feel the same to spend those plastic chips as it does cash.

- **Instant Gratification.** This is the most common cause of excessive spending. People live in the now as opposed to delaying gratification by saving for the future. The savings rate in America in 2005 dropped to a negative 0.5 percent for the year—the first time the savings rate had been negative since the Great Depression. This means the average American was dipping into savings or borrowing to pay for purchases and spending in excess of what he or she was earning. Many of the purchases were luxuries, not necessities. Budgeting for purchases, saving the needed amounts, and avoiding using credit for nonessentials require following sound principles of financial judgment.

- **Keeping Up with the Joneses.** I know of a person who moved his family into a house that he couldn't afford just because his friend moved into that neighborhood. His wife, a stay-at-home mom who had been taking care of their kids as they originally planned, now had to work for them to afford the home. They upgraded their old 1998 Volkswagen to a Mercedes to match the quality of cars owned by neighbors. Unfortunately, the wife fell ill and had to stop working; they fell behind on bills and the husband had to take a second job; debts and stress began to pile higher, and they lost their home to foreclosure. They also lost their marriage (did you know that money trouble is the number one cause for divorce?).

- **Insecurity.** Many people will spend $2,000 for a designer handbag, $75,000 for a car, or even $1,000 for a simple wool coat. They purchase these items to gain assurance of their status in life. They feel as if these purchases give them a sense of value and purpose that is hard to find anywhere else.

Below is a chart of ratios to show you some general parameters for spending compared to your gross income:

Expense	Targeted % of Total Income
Housing *(rent/mortgage, insurance, real estate taxes, etc.)*	28
Total Debt *(rent/mortgage, car, credit card, etc.)*	36
Savings *(IRA, 401(k), brokerage account, etc.)*	15

I wouldn't advise you to get too hung up on these ratios, as they can vary depending upon your lifestyle desires, your financial goals, where you live, your transportation needs, and more. If you are spending 30 percent of your income on housing, that doesn't necessarily mean that you are on the road to foreclosure; however, if you are spending 45 percent of your income on housing, I would definitely look for places to downsize your lifestyle.

Build

Investing is putting your money into anything that has the potential to go up in value and should not depreciate. Stocks, bonds, businesses, education, real estate, artwork, and gold are all things that can go up in value and are good investments. We will discuss investments more in depth later in this book because they are a crucial component of your road to prosperity, but I want to fill you in here on the basics

Try to invest *at least* 15 percent of your income every year. If you are earning $100,000 per year, you should be saving at least $15,000 per year. If you can afford to do more, please do so, because the more you do, the faster you will be able to achieve those important long-term financial goals that you have always dreamed about.

The secret to achieving wealth is to understand that the more you invest, the more you will have to spend and to give as well. And how you invest is by budgeting.

Budgeting is not meant to constrict your spending, but to organize your spending so that you can do what is responsible with your money for the good of yourself and the community. Why are you spending excessively on entertainment when you are saving to purchase that new home? Why are you purchasing that new car when you want to save to start your new business? You can't be the next person to help revive the economy if you are spending like there's no tomorrow, living check to check, and not prioritizing in your life. It is hard to become the next Bill Gates if you are overwhelmed with worry that you won't have enough to pay the light bill. If you are having trouble paying your bills, stop making extra bills. Thousands of people have items collecting dust under their bed that they are still paying for but haven't used in over a year. The world needs responsible people and households more than ever before; with a sound budget you can be on your way to helping to make paradigm shift away from a consumer-driven mentality.

Give

Giving back is one of the most important wealth-building principles in this book. I am not talking about the giving that you do for that family member who refuses to get a job. I am talking about giving to charitable organizations that do tremendous work in your community, such as giving to a school so it can buy new textbooks, or giving to a family member who can't afford to pay for his or her college tuition. The more that you save, the more you can help somebody else.

Giving is also an important wealth-building principle. When you see that homeless person asking you for money and you clench your wallet as if giving the person a dollar will break you, what does that say about your confidence in earning that dollar back? Are you so insecure about your ability to earn money that you are scared to give it away? I am not saying that you need to give money to every homeless person that you see. Some of the richest people in the world are the most prolific givers because they are confident that they will be able to make back every dollar that they give away. This level of confidence is an essential component on your road to accumulating wealth.

In a perfect world, I would love for you to be able to give away 10 percent of your income. This can be to your church, a charity, or any place that you feel can be empowered by your gifts. It is always the case that the person who has the least and is able to budget and develop the confidence in his or her earning potential somehow finds the money and even starts earning more. I understand completely if times are hard at the moment and you can't give; however, I urge you to set this as a goal for you to achieve in the near term. As with other goals, write this down and work toward improving your financial condition to be able to eventually meet this goal. Giving is one of the most powerful things that we can do to empower our community, and every little bit counts!

CREATING AND MAINTAINING A HOUSEHOLD BUDGET

Failing to plan = planning to fail.

Many people feel that there is a magic wand for accumulating wealth. You wave this wand and *voilà* . . . you are rich! However, at its core, accumulating wealth is simple. Some accumulate wealth by earning more money, which is an offense strategy. They strive to increase their salary consistently. Others attempt to save/invest as much money as possible. This is a defense strategy. I know of an elderly gentleman who never earned over $11 an hour his entire life yet was worth over $2 million by seventy years of age. The wise person increases his or her odds by implementing a little of both offense and defense strategies. To keep accurate control of how much you are spending and saving, you should use the most powerful tool in the personal financial planning arsenal . . . the budget!

The budget is the most important piece of the financial plan. Many underestimate the power of the budget and make light of its use. However, with 60 percent of Americans spending more money than they earn in a given month, we must make a more accurate account of each dollar that is being spent in our households. The first question I ask those who take my courses is if they have some sort of budget in their household. Most say that they do not. However, of those who do claim to have a budget, I then ask, "How much does it cost you to support yourself in a given month?" An overwhelming number of those asked do not know the answer.

USING THE BUDGET TO CALCULATE YOUR FINISH LINE

I have never met someone who has not said it would be nice to eventually be financially independent. This means to be able to afford to never work again without worrying about supporting your family or yourself. While I am a strong opponent of the traditional form of retirement—I believe that we should always be working to fulfill something while we are alive—the traditional retirement age is sixty-five, when we are to resign our jobs and seek out a beach on which to spend our "golden years." When you go to a McDonald's, whom do you see as their employees? You typically see many young individuals and many elderly, right? For many teenagers, it is their first job, and they are ecstatic to get their first paychecks. However, do you think that for those who are elderly McDonald's is their dream job? More often than not, they are working because they did not adequately prepare financially for their later years in life. There is a difference in your golden years between working because you want to and working because you have to.

Try this exercise: What is the "magic number" that it will take for you to become financially independent? How much money will it take so you can quit your job if you want to and still be able to support yourself for the rest of your life? Everyone has a different number, and it depends upon the amount of living expenses that person has to provide for. Many guess at this number, but there is a way to find out a more precise estimate. This estimate can best be achieved through a budget.

In appendix B we have placed a sample budget for you to fill out so that you can do this exercise for yourself.

Step One: Complete your budget to discern your estimated monthly living expenses.

Let us say that after you have completed your budget, your household expenses totaled $3,000.

Step Two: Multiply your monthly living expenses by twelve to obtain your estimated yearly living expenses.

In our hypothetical example, our estimated yearly living expenses would total $36,000 (12×$3,000).

Step Three: Divide your estimated yearly expenses by a reasonable rate of return that you could earn on your investments throughout the duration of your golden years. I usually select a conservative return of 5 percent at most.

Note: It is better to underestimate your return on investment (say 2 to 3 percent) than to aim too high and run out of savings. In addition, remember that these savings will be in your retirement account and should be invested in more conservative investments with lower risk (risk as it relates to return will be explained in greater detail in later chapters).

In our example, we would arrive at a figure of $720,000 ($36,000/.05 = $720,000). This means that we would be required to save $720,000 to become financially independent.

Step Four: From the figure derived in step three, subtract the total amount of savings that you have already accumulated from the total amount that you need.

Assuming that you have $25,000 in cash saved and $50,000 in a company retirement plan, you would subtract $75,000 ($25,000+$50,000) from $720,000 to get a savings goal of $645,000.

Step Five: Calculate how long it will take to save the amount derived in step four by using the surplus that you arrived at with your budget. Your surplus is your total income earned during the month minus your total expenses during the month. This is also called your disposable income and is the most important figure in your budget. The larger your surplus, the faster you will be able to achieve financial independence. To reiterate an earlier point, you can earn more, spend less, or do a little of both to achieve a higher surplus.

In our example, John Smith has a surplus of $500. Below is a chart of how long it will take him to reach $645,000 if he takes this $500 and invests it in the market monthly.

	Dollars Invested Monthly	Rate of Return (%)	Years to Reach $645,000 Goal
Scenario A	500	7	31
Scenario B	500	8	28
Scenario C	500	9	26
Scenario D	500	10	25

Note: To calculate the length of time with the various interest rates, I simply used a financial calculator. Below is a list of Web sites that contain savings calculators into which you can insert numbers pertinent to your own financial situation.

www.bankrate.com
www.greenpath.com
www.fincalc.com
www.moneycentral.msn.com
www.mint.com

To some of you, $500 is not a lot of money, but to the 60 percent of this country spending more money than they earn every month, it is a lot of money. Let's just see what happens if this surplus is only $200 per month.

	Dollars Invested Monthly	Rate of Return (%)	Years to Reach $645,000 Goal
Scenario A	200	7	43
Scenario B	200	8	39
Scenario C	200	9	36
Scenario D	200	10	33

As you see, the time gets a little longer, but the goal is still attainable. We have to concern ourselves with long-term goals and not with short-term gratification. In the second example, $200 per month equates to only about $50 per week. Fifty dollars per week equates to only $7 per day. We all have seen the news around the holidays when hundreds beat the door down to purchase the new PlayStation, the new Xbox, or the latest phone that has unlimited capabilities. All of these gadgets cost more than $200. What does it say when we have a country that has closets and garages full of out-of-date toys and gadgets (if they haven't already been donated to Goodwill) but over 90 percent of the country is financially dependent after the age of sixty-five?

A budget is crucial in determining how much we are able to save monthly, how much is required to support the household, and how long it will take to achieve financial freedom. What you earn is not as impor tant as *what you do* with what you earn. We can control the dollars spent and saved in the house with the proper use of a budget.

THREE STEPS TO A BUDGET

While the concept of a household budget, monitoring how much you spend and save in the house, is pretty simple, it isn't easy at first when it's new to you. However, as with most habits, the more they are implemented, the easier they are to follow. Here are three easy steps that you can follow to establish such a budget.

Step One: Fill out an estimated budget.

Pull together any check stubs you've received from your job, old bills, grocery receipts, and anything else that will give you a history of what you have earned and spent in your house. Do not get discouraged if you do not have any of that information handy; this is an "estimated" budget, so just give your best estimate of your financials.

Step Two: Complete the thirty-day-diary exercise (see Appendix D).

After you have completed the estimated budget, make a journal for the next thirty days to write down all of your cash inflows and outflows. If you throw a penny in a well, write it down. If someone gives you a penny, write it down in your journal. This sounds tedious, and it can be at times. However, just keep in mind that you won't have to do this monthly . . . only long enough to get an accurate picture of your spending habits. Most are amazed at how much they spend on certain items. Also, it would prob- ably not be wise to do this exercise during December or any other month in which you have untypical spending patterns. If you do the exercise once and find that too many unforeseen events caused irregular expenditures, do it for another month.

Step Three: Fill out an actual budget.

Now that you have completed your diary, you have the information to fill out a more precise budget. This budget will be your guide going forward, as you have now successfully created a household budget. Hopefully you will have a surplus in your budget. If you don't, it is time to make some cuts. A major wealth-building principle is that one has to live beneath one's means. Many times individuals are not able to distinguish between needs and wants, necessities and luxuries. We must all fight the tendency for our luxuries to turn into necessities as income rises. Did you ever consider Starbucks coffee a luxury but now, after your raise, you are having it every morning? We must keep our expenses reasonably the same even as our income rises if we are to achieve a consistently increasing net worth and financial independence.

Budgeting Strategies

No particular strategy is best for budgeting, for it really all depends upon the individual. You can use the envelope method, where you set aside a certain amount of money for a specific purpose in an envelope. For instance, you may have a problem with eating out too frequently, so every month you place $200 into an envelope and label it *Eating Out*. Every time you go out to eat (even for a lunch break at work) the money must be taken out of the *Eating Out* envelope. If the envelope runs out of cash before the month is up, you are not allowed to go out to eat until the following month. For example:

John has a problem with eating out, so he places $200 in an envelope labeled *Eating Out*. Every time he wants to eat out, he must take money from the envelope.

Month One: During the first month, John went out quite a bit for lunch, and a few times on the weekend. By the third week he had exhausted all $200 in the envelope. For the rest of the month he didn't pick up the phone when his friends called him to hang out for dinner, and he packed a bag lunch.

Month Two: Learning from the first month, John began to pack his lunch regularly after realizing it was cheaper. He didn't go out as much, and by the end of the fourth week he had only spent $150 of the $200 in the *Eating Out* envelope.

Month Three: John placed $150 in the envelope (as the envelope is never to exceed $200) and allocated the extra $50 toward his credit card debt.

You can use the envelope method with as many categories as you like. If you do not like to carry around cash, you can use the spreadsheet method. This is the same as the envelope method except that you write down the dollar amount on a spreadsheet, deduct it from the appropriate category, and, just as in the envelope method, when you hit zero, you are not allowed to spend more in that category until the following month.

So whether you use the envelope method, purchase some money-management software, or simply monitor your budget with a pencil or pen, what is most important is that you select a style and strategy that is comfortable for you and that will encourage you to form the best budgeting habits possible. Each of us must select a strategy and a style that fits our personality and allows us to achieve the main objective of a budget: to monitor our cash inflows and outflows to minimize our expenses and maximize our savings.

AVOIDING TRAPS THAT WILL SABOTAGE YOUR FINANCIAL GOALS

Consumer Traps

It wouldn't make sense to write about budgeting without writing about consumption. Anything labeled an item of consumption is worth less or is worthless immediately after you purchase it. If you purchase a new car, it is worth 25 percent less as soon as you drive it off the lot . . . this is called depreciation. Depreciation is a noncash expenditure that reduces the value of an asset as a result of wear and tear or age. This explains why most millionaires only purchase pre-owned cars. Cars depreciate the fastest in the first one or two years, so it makes sense to purchase a vehicle that is a year or two old and has already undergone this initial stage of depreciation. According to *The Millionaire Next Door*, half of the millionaires in America have never spent over $30,000 for a car in their *entire* life.

Why? The main reason is simple: They understand that as long as they spend money on items that lose value instead of things that gain value, they are less able to maintain and increase their economic status. This is why you will hear stories about Jim Walton, heir to the fortune created by his father, Sam Walton (founder of Wal-Mart). He still drives a fifteen-year-old Dodge Dakota pickup despite being number 23 on the 2007 billionaires list. You may also have heard about Ingvar Kamprad, also a billionaire. He still drives a fifteen-year-old Volvo. Before he attained his fortune, his father gave him a modest reward for doing well in school, and what did he spend his money on? Investing in a "modest" furniture company named IKEA, which he founded, which reported revenues of $17.7 billion in 2005.

Food, clothes, cars, and taxes are all examples of consumption. A key principle to building wealth is to maximize investments (stocks, bonds, businesses, real estate, etc.) and minimize consumption. This is easier said than done. The United States may be in the middle of a recession, but Jordan shoes are still selling off the shelves at $190 per pair. Is there ever an economy that is good enough to justify paying $190 for a pair of sneakers that won't be worth 10 percent of the purchase price one week after you buy them?

The answer to this question is the essence of successful retail marketing: Companies use tried-and-true sales tricks to get into our pockets. It doesn't happen by accident that in the middle of a recession people line up ready to rush a store to get their $190 sneakers. I want to outline a few of these sales tricks so you can be aware of them.

The "Bogus" Sales Strategy

Why is it that people feel that they have somehow won something if they find a sale? Retailers are completely aware of the psychological motivations of consumers—they are always trying to get more for less.

How many times have you been walking down the street, not shopping, only to be stopped in your tracks by a 50% OFF sign? Let's look into how it's possible for retailers to slash prices so much.

A store owner purchases a shirt from a supplier for $10, slightly above what it cost the supplier to make the shirt. The owner marks up the shirt 300 percent to $40 and puts it on the rack. After some time, sales of the shirt slow and he cuts the price by 50 percent to $20, and he puts a huge 50% OFF sign in the front window on bright red paper with white letters for the world to see. He still sells his shirt for 200 percent of what he purchased it for and is making a 100 percent profit on every sale. I am not saying that you shouldn't purchase clothes, but only purchase clothes that you have decided to purchase and don't be influenced by seemingly amazing deals and buy something you don't need.

The "Guilt" Sales Strategy

Why is that store clerk so nice to you? Why does she offer to let you try on so many pairs of shoes? Is it because she feels kind or got up on the right side of bed that morning? Well, actually, it is more than likely that she recently had some mandated sales training. This training gave her tips and strategies on how to more effectively make a sale. One of those tips? Allow the customer to try on as many shoes as possible. The more shoes the customer tries on, the more likely the customer will feel guilty about walking out of the store without purchasing something.

Have you ever said or thought to yourself, "Well . . . I guess I did have her going back and forth a lot, and it would be a huge waste of her time for me to not purchase something. Let me at least purchase one pair of shoes"?

If you have thought anything that sounded remotely like the above quote, then you have been the victim of the guilt sales strategy. To avoid this trap, keep in mind that the salesperson is getting paid to service you.

Don't ever be influenced by guilt—there is nothing wrong with changing your mind, even if you seem to be at the point of purchase. Too many times people allow themselves to feel pressured by the misconception that they are "bad" if they decide to walk out without making a purchase.

The "Impulse Creation" Sales Strategy

Ever walk around a store and observe that an item you saw last week is no longer there? You might think that it was sold and merchandise must move quickly in this store, so much so that the next time you see something you like, you decide not to waste time and purchase it right on the spot. You just fell victim to one of the oldest strategies in the game . . . the "impulse creation" sales strategy.

This strategy was created by those in sales who had a firm grasp of the psychology of the human mind. People tend to want even more those things that they cannot have. Ever see a child who has thrown a toy to the side with indifference only to want it again after it's picked up by a sibling or a friend? That toy suddenly becomes his favorite toy again.

Stores play off our instincts of wanting what we can't have. In the above example, although it was no longer on the rack, that item wasn't necessarily sold. Chain stores understand that people are creatures of habit. They know that habitual shoppers of Store A Uptown will not necessarily frequent Store A Downtown. Understanding this, they will move that coveted hat from Store A Uptown to Store A Downtown after a week to make it seem to shoppers as if the merchandise is really moving! This creates an impulse within shoppers to make sure that they don't miss out and thus to purchase items of interest as soon as possible.

There is also the trick of supply and demand. Those long lines outside a store the morning of a new release are not an accident but rather a clever sales trick. When a new shoe is released, stores purposefully do not hold as many in stock as they normally do. This causes a great disappointment for Little Johnny, who had his heart set but just missed the last size 8! However, never fear, because the savior parent is here who says, "Don't worry, Little Johnny . . . next time we will be the *first* in line when some new sneakers are released, and this won't ever happen again!" Sucker! Over and over this occurs within the sneaker market until you can find a new pair of sneakers costing more than $200 because of the increased demand.

The "Credit Card Discount" Strategy

Does this sound familiar? "Would you like to save ten percent on today's purchase by signing up for a credit card?" It is said that average Americans will spend an additional 35 percent just because they have a credit card in their pocket. This is why stores are asking you to sign up for a credit card when you get to the front counter. They know that with that additional access to the capital, you are likely to spend much more money than that 10 percent discount amount.

Have you ever heard of someone getting rich because they earned frequent-flier miles? These perks and bonuses are only there to entice us. Nothing is free. If they are giving you a discount in one area of service, it is coming from another area, and that usually means higher interest rates or fees on the card. Credit cards should be chosen with extreme care. (Two of the most popular choices of credit cards by millionaires are Visa and MasterCard.)

The "Lure" Sales Strategy

Have you ever asked why your favorite song is being played when you walk by a store? Or why it always smells so good? Everything from displaying your favorite clothes in the window to that salesman who grabs you to tell you about the super "specials" . . . retailers have done studies on what attracts potential shoppers and are pulling out all of the stops to try to get into your pocket.

Check Your Emotions

Before you go shopping, check your emotions at the door. Many things may be going on in our lives that influence our spending habits. Let me give you a few scenarios.

Happiness and Celebration. A lawyer has been working on an important case for quite some time. He finally has a breakthrough and closes a deal. He calls his wife to announce that they are "going out to celebrate." This done in moderation is not so bad; however, the human tendency is to not just stop there. Before long, if they're not careful, the lawyer and his wife will begin to find more reasons to celebrate. I have worked with many people who have not fulfilled their financial goals because every month or even week they were not consistently saving, but consistently celebrating.

Going out and having fun is essential in life. In no way do I want people not to have a good time. Have as much fun as you would like as long as you don't exceed your budget and sacrifice important financial goals. Just ask yourself these questions:

- Do I have enough in my budget for this dinner/vacation?
- Am I neglecting to pay any bills because of this unexpected expense? (This includes money that would otherwise be saved for that new house, retirement, children's education fund, and/or your new business that you have always dreamed about.)
- According to my budget, when was the last time that I had a celebration dinner? Am I frequently finding reasons to go out to eat?
- Can I think of another way to celebrate that does not require me to spend so much money or any money at all?
  - A celebratory picnic at the park is a great way to enjoy the weather and is really romantic.
  - A celebratory ice cream cone is a great way to feel like a kid.
  - Get the guys together and go play some basketball. It is a great way to get exercise and bond with the guys.
  - Have the girls over to rewatch that movie that you all loved and haven't seen in years.

Sadness. Let's say a woman has been going out with a man for a few months and begins to feel that he is "the one." But one day she sees him out with another woman. She confronts him about it later with the "What are we doing?" discussion. His answer is not favorable, and she is hurt by his response. Immediately she calls her best friend for consolation. What is her friend's response to her grieving? "Girl . . . we are going to get the ladies together and we are going shopping!" Famously called retail therapy, shopping may feel good at the time, but you may feel differently when your credit card bills pile up. I am not a psychologist, but it is easy to see how when people turn to alcohol or other more severe drugs in times of depression, they can become hooked. The same effects can be seen in someone who turns to shopping as a quick fix.

So before you you agree to go shopping with the girls, here are a few alternatives to consider:

- **Exercise.** Jogging in the park, a regular routine at home, swimming at the local YMCA, or playing sports at the park are great remedies for stress and depression.
- **Meditation.** Prayer is my favorite remedy because it helps me to clear my mind of negative thoughts and focus on the positive. Even if you do not follow a religion, you can practice meditation by going into a room and taking thirty minutes to visualize/focus on the positive in your life.
- **Renting a Movie.** There is nothing like renting a movie at home to allow your mind to drift to fantasyland for less than $5 for two hours.
- **Work.** Is there a big project at work that you could focus on that will help you pass the time?
- **Community Service.** This sounds strange to some, but one of the greatest remedies to a sad disposition is to help others in your community. I started my youth organization as a result of breaking up with my girlfriend. I was extremely depressed, but instead of shopping I went to an elementary school and asked if they needed a volunteer. Working with those kids, I soon forgot all about my problems and was focused on becoming a mentor to them.

Boredom. A young woman gets off work an hour before she has to pick up her son from day care. The center is directly across the street from a shopping center, so to her it only seems natural that she spend that time shopping before she picks up her son. One can easily see how this can become habit-forming. Boredom is one of the most common causes of excessive consumer spending.

My solution? The easiest and most effective remedy I have found is to *always* carry a book with me. No matter where I go, I always have reading material for times such as these. Not only does it prevent me from frivolously spending money, but it helps me continue to read at least one book per month to enhance my intellectual capital. Knowledge is one of life's most valuable commodities, and one should always have literature in his or her possession.

Anxiety. A man is sitting at home flipping through the channels when he sees a brand-new television and home-theater system on the Home Shopping Network that really catches his attention. He hadn't planned on purchasing anything and didn't even know that he wanted it until he heard the extremely low price being yelled from the screen. He is wavering about purchasing it until he sees a clock appear on the screen stating that he only has three minutes to make a decision to purchase this limited-edition television. He can't pull out his card fast enough and runs to the phone to make the call! Anxiety is a key driver of impulse buying. People begin to feel so strongly that they are suffering without a certain product, they become extremely anxious to purchase it, and they begin clumsily fumbling to grab their credit card or money to make a purchase.

We must try hard to remove the impulse buy from our daily purchases. If you feel the need to purchase something on an impulse, whether you are watching television or you are at the shopping center, give yourself a two-day test. Write down the number or tell the clerks to put the new jacket to the side (if they are able to do so). Wait two days, and within those two days think of all of the things that you could be doing with those funds for that new item. Think of whether you really *need* this item and what you were doing to cope in life before you saw that brand-new leather jacket that you never thought about before. If after two days you feel that you have it in your budget and don't have any more important needs than that jacket, feel free to purchase it.

Below are simple demonstrations of how excessive spending on things can cause us to miss out on a lot of savings that we could have used for other purposes.

Excessive-Consumption Demonstrations

Designer Suit

If you purchase one suit per year, how much would you pay for that suit? A designer suit might cost you as much as $2,500 if custom-tailored. The average millionaire has never paid more than $399 for a suit in his lifetime (*The Millionaire Next Door*). The yearly savings that you could attain by following the purchasing habits of the average millionaire would be $2,101 ($2,500 - $399) on your suit purchases. If you invested the annual savings of $2,101 in the market, after thirty years at an average return of 8 percent, you could have collected $238,008.

Shoes

Many people will pay as much as $575 for a pair of shoes. The average millionaire has never paid over $140 for a pair of shoes (*The Millionaire Next Door*). This equals a $435 savings on the less expensive shoe that probably looks just as good to the naked eye. This annual $435 invested at an average rate of return of 8 percent over thirty years would equate to $49,278 saved.

Coffee

If you purchase coffee every morning, my first suggestion would be for you to buy a coffee machine and make it yourself for less. However, let's analyze how much that cup of Starbucks coffee costs you over time versus your making it yourself.

The Starbucks cup of coffee costs you $5 per day to purchase. If you purchase a thirty-nine-ounce can of Folgers coffee that costs roughly $10, it can make you over two hundred cups, which averages five cents per cup of coffee. Granted, Folgers does not taste as good as Starbucks, but if you calculate the amount that you are saving, perhaps you will make an exception on taste.

The savings per cup of coffee is $4.95, which if invested daily at an average 8 percent return on investment, over thirty years would equate to $226,301.

Lunch

One of the biggest ways that we spend money is through the everyday lunch break. Instead of bagging lunch, many of us like to spend as much as $10 every day to purchase lunch at a nearby restaurant. So as opposed to spending as little as $10 to pack a lunch for the entire week, many spend as much as $50 for the week. Monthly, that is $160 that we could be putting toward saving. Over thirty years, at an average rate of return of 8 percent, $160 per month would equate to $238,458.

AVOIDING FINANCIAL TRAPS

Wherever financial illiteracy exists, you will find opportunies that seem too good to be true. Many creative products and services prey upon our need for instant gratification—all the while filling their sellers' pockets with profit. Some are more benign than others, but all take advantage of your wanting something fast. How do you not fall into one of these traps? Research, research, and research. It is up to us to educate ourselves as much as possible to avoid being taken advantage of. Here are just a few traps to steer cleer of.

The Prepaid Debit Card

The value of the prepaid debit card has caused a long-standing debate in many communities. I remember when bottled water first became a commodity that one had to pay for. I used to pay for it until I decided that it would be cheaper to purchase a filter to use at home. I remember when they started to charge for air to fill your tires. I have yet to find an alternative, so when I need to fill my tires, I grudgingly pay the fifty cents. I pay for water, I pay for air . . . but I will never pay to use my own money!

A prepaid debit card is tied to an institution that allows you to make electronic withdrawals from funds on deposit with that custodian, as in purchasing goods or obtaining cash advances. You can find many of these cards being offered online, at the checkout counter at your corner store, or at your local bank. You give this institution money, they give you a card that links to your funds, and you can make purchases with this card until you have exhausted the funds you deposited. These cards are particularly targeted at those who do not have a checking account, have problems with overdrafts of their accounts, find it hard to open an account, or want to have easy access to their funds. Then they find out all the fees that are attached to using this card.

The prepaid-debit-card industry has always been built upon a lack of knowledge within the community. More efficient means exist to empower those in our communities than prepaid debit cards and other financially destructive establishments such as check-cashing facilities. The typical bank offers debit cards that if used properly do not charge any fees and can be used for the same purposes as the prepaid debit cards.

One of the most famous of these cards is the RushCard, which is sponsored by Russell Simmons. As he is a nationally known celebrity, his name pulls a lot of weight in many communities, and his name on this card probably dramatically increased its sales. If we compare the fees charged by the RushCard to those of the typical bank debit card, we can clearly see the advantage of the conventional bank cards.

RushCard vs. Typical Bank Card
(RushCard fees taken from RushCard site as of 5/7/10)

	RushCard Monthly Plan	RushCard Pay-as-You-Go Plan	Typical Bank Card
Activation fee	Free with direct deposit	$19.95	Free
Monthly fee	$9.95	$0	Free
Convenience fee	$1.00	$1.00 (capped at $10/month)	Free
ATM cash withdrawal	2 free withdrawals $2.50 after first 2	$1.95	Free (at branch)
ATM balance inquiry	$.50	$.50	Free
Bill payment enrollment	$2.00	$2.00	Free
Bill payment fee	$1.00	$1.00	Free
Maintenance fee	$0	$1.95/month	Free
Replacement card	$9.95	$9.95	Free

As you can see, there is no financial reason to choose the RushCard over a typical debit card offered by a banking institution as a part of its services. With the continuous onslaught of technology and programs by banking institutions/credit unions that target the underserved and unbanked people in various communities, it is becoming increasingly easier to open a bank account. If individuals put $100 on the RushCard under one plan, they immediately have to pay $19.95 and their account reads $80.05. Over the next three months, if they make five trips to an ATM, that will cost another $9.75. If they hold the card for three months, they will pay $5.85 in maintenance fees. These very reasonable actions result in $35.55 in fees just to have access to your own money!

With 85 percent of all dollars in America spent on consumption, the unnecessary, excessive fees charged on prepaid debit cards do nothing but compound the problem by eroding crucial capital that could be used for important activities such as retirement, entrepreneurial endeavors, higher-education costs, homeownership, and/or building a sound financial legacy for our families.

Many ask, "If someone owes two thousand dollars to their bank because they have bounced checks and/or overdrafted their account, wouldn't the RushCard or other prepaid debit cards be useful?" The answer is yes, it would be useful. However, other alternatives would be much wiser, such as:

- Open up a bank account and use a debit card that has no fees attached to it. For some, this may require some work as they are considered "not bankable." The solution to not being bankable is not to find a solution that will allow you to continue to live and operate in a world where you are not bankable. If I have a cavity on the right side of my mouth, is the solution to chew on the left side? *No!* I must fix the cavity.
- Join a credit union that has a loan-builder program that actually allows you to establish credit and will supply you with a debit card.
- Go to bankrate.com and select a secured credit card that has no fees. Anybody, even those with poor credit, can get a secured card. A secured card actually has a credit line, so when you use it, not only do you not have to pay a $1 convenience fee, but when you pay back what you immediately used, you help to restore your credit. (Secured cards and restoring your credit will both be discussed in more detail in later chapters.)
- Find a bank that has a "second chance" account option. These accounts are specifically for those who are in the Telechex,

CrossCheck, or Chex Systems as having overdrafted or bounced checks in their account in the past and are now finding it hard to open a regular bank account. Be careful, however, of a "second chance" account that is not at an established bank, as they may come with high fees and are no better than the prepaid debit card. You might not be able to write checks on this account, nor will you be provided overdraft protection; however, if you choose the right bank, you will be provided a debit card with a Visa or Master-Card logo that you will be able to use in the same manner as the RushCard without the fees attached.

The Refund-Anticipation Loan

Every year around tax time many people get excited to get their refund. They envision a multi-thousand-dollar check coming in the mail to make their year that much brighter. Sadly, many people begin to spend extravagantly before and upon the check-arrival date. What too few realize is that a tax refund is money that you should have received during the year but elected to give to the government to invest and earn interest on (interest that you could have been earning on your money) throughout the year, so I will refer to it as an "interest-free-loan principal return." It is longer to read and write, but I think that it communicates the point more effectively.

In waiting for this interest-free-loan principal return, many begin to spend haphazardly. So much so that they find themselves in financial straits and want to get an "advance" on their refund. But this "advance" isn't really that; it is a loan. And you know what that means—interest rates are attached. The refund anticipation loan, or RAL, is a high-interest, short-term loan secured by a taxpayer's "expected" tax refund. It is supposedly designed to offer customers quicker access to their funds. Yet quick access is really the only benefit. Consider these consequences:

1. High Fees/Interest Rates. Many companies such as Jackson Hewitt and H&R Block make a strong pitch for your quick access to this cash. However, a hefty price is paid for this access. In 2007, according to IRS figures, approximately 8.7 million Americans got refund anticipation loans. Altogether, according to estimates by the National Consumer Law Center, these 8.7 million Americans paid almost $900 million in interest and fees. Many of the loans, when you calculate the fees and interest charged as an annual percentage rate, ran from 100 to 500 percent interest.

2. Time. Those who are receiving these loans believe that they are drastically cutting the time before they will receive their return. However, technological advances such as e-file and direct deposit have virtually eliminated all waiting time. It can take up to ten days to receive your refund anticipation loan, and you can receive your tax return in the same amount of time or in only a few days more.

3. Risky Assumption. There is no such thing as a guaranteed return. The return that you believe you will get is only an estimate, while the RAL is a loan against what you think you will receive. If your return comes in a lot lower than you expected, you are still on the hook for the entire RAL, which includes heavy amounts of additional interest and fees.

4. Slanted Marketing. According to IRS data, of the 8.7 million who received an RAL in 2007, 67 percent received an earned-income tax credit (EITC), while only 17 percent of the entire U.S. population received the EITC. The EITC program is designed to assist the working poor, so when you see that two-thirds of those who received an RAL came from only 17 percent of the population, it is clear who those in the RAL business are marketing to.

So, even if you have to pay a few bills late, do not take on the additional risk and expense of an RAL. The interest rate is too high, you don't save on time, and there is no guarantee that you will ever receive your estimated return in full. So when you see Magic Johnson trying to get you to take a trip to Jackson Hewitt to get your RAL, praise him for his basketball skills but not for his ability to select products that benefit the community . . . and say no!

Rent-A-Center

Many people in this country are not yet ready to purchase their first home, but what about a sofa or a television set? Are your sights set so low that you feel you do not have the ability to own your own DVD player? If the answer is yes, then Rent-A-Center has built a business model especially for you . . . those who have a desire to underachieve.

Rent-A-Center, based in Texas, is a furniture and electronics rent-to-own company. They do exceptionally well, with more than thirty-five hundred stores nationally, and are repeatedly being listed in the Fortune 1000 list of the largest one thousand corporations. They provide an answer to the question "Why do I need to wait and save to purchase a TV for my apartment?" With Rent-A-Center you do not have to wait, you can purchase a TV right now! However, you will have to pay a hefty price in interest before you own that television.

To see just how much interest Rent-A-Center charges, I called them and acted as if I were a customer wondering about their terms. I asked how much it would cost to purchase four items, which included a regular sofa-and-love-seat set, a leather sofa-and-love-seat set, a twenty-six-inch television set, and a fifty-two-inch television set. For each I got the price that it would cost to rent it from Rent-A-Center weekly and how long it would take to own the product. Then I found the retail price of a similar product from Amazon.com. The results were amazing and are listed below.

THE RENT-A-CENTER WAY

Item	Weekly Payment	Retail Value	Weeks to Own	Interest Rate	Interest Paid	Total Paid
Sofa and love seat (regular)	$19.99	$900	78	80%	$659	$1,559
Sofa and love seat (leather)	$30.99	$2,000	78	26%	$417	$2,417
26-inch Sony Bravia	$17.99	$550	104	163%	$1,321	$1,871
52-inch Sony Bravia	$59.99	$1,900	116	159%	$5,059	$6,959

THE SMART PERSON WAY

Item	Weekly Savings	Retail Value	Weeks to Purchase	Savings Rate	Total Paid	Money Saved	Weeks Saved
Sofa and love seat (regular)	$19.99	$900	44	3%	$900	$659	34
Sofa and love seat (leather)	$30.99	$2,000	63	3%	$2,000	$417	15

THE SMART PERSON WAY

Item	Weekly Savings	Retail Value	Weeks to Purchase	Savings Rate	Total Paid	Money Saved	Weeks Saved
26-inch Sony Bravia	$17.99	$550	30	3%	$550	$1,321	74
52-inch Sony Bravia	$59.99	$1,900	31	3%	$1,900	$5,059	85

As you can see from the charts, those who choose the Rent-A-Center way pay a lot more than those who are prudent about how they purchase the same items. If you take the fifty-two-inch Sony Bravia television, which retails for $1,900, you could use the $59.99 that you would be giving to RAC and put it into a savings account for purchase of the product. Doing it the smart way would allow you to purchase this TV in just thirty-one weeks. However, through RAC you would be paying on that TV for 116 weeks before you actually own it. Over that time you would pay a total of $6,959. When you subtract the total paid ($6,959) from the retail value of the TV ($1,900), you would have paid over $5,000 in interest at a rate of 159 percent. Being prudent saves you eighty-five weeks of payments and over $5,000, which you could have used to put toward retirement, a new home, a business, or some other more meaningful use. Doing it the smart way, you could almost purchase four TVs of an equivalent price in the time that it takes you to purchase just one TV doing it the RAC way.

If you ever feel the urge to use Rent-A-Center, please consider paying a visit to your local Salvation Army and purchasing a temporary inexpensive piece of furniture. Put the money that you would have been paying to RAC in weekly rental payments in a savings account until you can purchase the product that you truly wanted for your home.

Quick Cash Loans

Growing up, I used to watch a TV show called *Good Times*. Many of you might be familiar with it. One of my favorite characters was Sweet Daddy. He was the neighborhood loan shark, who would allow many in the community to borrow funds from him at an interest rate of 50 percent or higher. He would always show up dressed in the fanciest of threads. He didn't have an official collections department for his operation; what he had were two oversize men who would be sure to break a leg if payment was not made in a timely manner.

In neighborhoods around the United States, many loan sharks are still in operation. However, they don't all appear the same. They are legal institutions that you have probably seen in your community, or learned about on television, on the radio, or in your e-mail in-box, claiming that you do not have to wait to receive "fast cash." They prey upon uninformed consumers, hoping that they will find it attractive to obtain funds through a quick loan. However, they usually neglect to inform consumers of the abnormally high interest rates that are attached to these types of loans.

These loans can come in many forms. There are check-advance loans, postdated-check loans, cash-advance loans, credit-card cash advances, payday loans, or even deferred-deposit loans. The interest on these loans has been reported as high as 750 percent on an annualized basis when you include their exorbitant fees. As reported by Credit Info Center (creditinfo center.com), these loans can be quite damaging:

"Payday loans, also known as deferred presentment, are currently available in 20 states plus the District of Columbia. They are short-term loans, generally 7 to 14 days, against a post-dated check. In Arizona, this loan against the paycheck you haven't yet earned carries a 15% fee. On the average payday loan of $300 for eight days, this 15% fee equates to an APR of 459%!"

The companies use advertisements to give the false impression that their product/service is the best solution for your desire to get quick cash. Below is a list of strategies to avoid falling prey to these traps.

- **Ask for Time.** If we are proactive and up-front about our financial situation, companies are more likely to work with us. You should be able to foresee if you might be a little short on a bill before the bill is actually due. *Do not* wait until the bill is already late before you call them. Give them a heads-up and see if they can give you more time to pay or can work out a payment plan with you. Calling them before they have to call you increases the odds that they will be willing to assist you.
- **Employer Advance.** Many employers will grant employees with a compelling enough reason an advance on pay. Some will provide small loans with low interest rates. This will be a much cheaper alternative to a payday loan or a cash advance.
- **Family and Friends.** It is never a good idea to borrow from family and friends, but if the alternative is going deeper into debt with

high interest rates and fees, it doesn't seem as bad. Nonetheless, if you are forced to ask for money from a loved one, make sure that you devise a promissory note to force you to be accountable. Be professional about it: This promissory note should have specific terms; make sure that you communicate your understanding that the person can pursue legal action if you fail to pay him or her back.

- **Budget.** The best way to prepare for a fire is to take the proper precautions before it strikes. This is what a budget does. You would be surprised how $20 to $30 per week can add up to aid you in a time of need. In this consumer-driven society where we are constantly spending money on things we do not need or for people we do not like, it is time that we started planning for disasters.

- **Credit Counseling Service.** There has been a huge push for nonprofits and credit unions to assist individuals to work out debt-repayment plans, improve their credit scores, or put together effective budgets. Many of these programs are at low to no cost. Check with your employer, local credit union, housing authority, politicians' offices, or the Internet for credit counseling programs in your area. Below are a few groups that can help:
  - GreenPath Debt Solutions: www.greenpath.com
  - Crown Financial Ministries: www.crown.org
  - National Foundation for Credit Counseling: www.nfcc.org

Multilevel Marketing Companies

When the going gets tough, those who are not tough try to find a way to make easy money. Okay . . . so maybe the saying doesn't go quite like that, but that is what I think of when I think of multilevel marketing companies, or MLMs.

I have nothing against MLMs. Many are built upon a great business model with a lot of promise for those who get in early or build the model around something that they have a passion to sell. A multilevel marketing company has a pyramid structure. All goods and services are sold with the distributors/sellers on the top of the structure recruiting others lower down in a chain to sell in return for a commission. The more people you recruit to sell in your "down line," the more money you can make.

The problem that I have with MLMs is not the business model; it's their selling of a false bill of goods implying that your joining will get you easy money. We have all heard the exaggeration that has been told over and over:

"This is the easiest way that you will ever be able to earn money from the comfort of your own home! Join the movement of the *many* who have reported large incomes!"

The truth: Nearly everyone who signs up with an MLM will *never* see a profit. Over 90 percent of the time, only those at the top ever reap any substantial benefits, unlike those who have gotten in at the bottom.

Automatic Teller Machine (ATM) Withdrawals

ATMs are everywhere, but we pay dearly for that convenience. Institutions such as Bank of America and Chase charge as much as $3 per transaction for cardholders using their services outside of their network. Many banks also practice what I call double-dipping. This is when you go to a bank outside your network and are charged $3 for using their ATM machine *and* charged another $2 by your own bank for using that out-of-network machine. Doesn't that seem like a lot to you? Consider this: Consumers spent more than $4 billion on these fees in 2006 alone.

And consider this: If you avoided using out-of-network ATMs (at a rate of $3 per transaction) four times per month over ten years, you'd save $1,440. If you invested that same $3 per month, four times per month, for ten years, at an 8 percent rate of return, you would save $2,387. Every little bit counts!

So, bottom line: You shouldn't spend money to get your money, and the best way to avoid doing so is to walk a few extra blocks to the nearest branch of your bank. Become familiar with where these are located in your neighborhood. If you find yourself in an unfamiliar area, here are a few tips on what to do:

- Look on the reverse side of your ATM card for a logo that indicates which network your bank belongs to. Using an in-network ATM will at least save you from paying an out-of-network fee.
- Internet banks (banks that don't have branches but do their banking primarily online) often reimburse you for fees up to a specific dollar amount. Just make sure that the bank that you choose, whether it is an Internet bank or any other bank, is FDIC insured (to be described in a later chapter when we discuss an emergency fund).
- Join a bank or credit union that participates in a network that does not levy surcharges and won't charge you when you take out

money from the ATM of another bank. This should be one of the first questions you ask when opening an account.

Check-Cashing Facilities

These companies cash your check right before your eyes—convenient, right? Well, it's less convenient when you find out that they charge a fee to cash that check. According to a 2008 report by the Financial Service Centers of America, check-cashing facilities charge between 1.5 and 4 percent of the check amount for cashing payroll or government checks. Over a year, many people pay as much as an entire paycheck's worth of fees just to collect their money. So why not keep your money for yourself and avoid these facilities? As convenient as these facilities can be, it is much more fiscally responsible to seek out a bank or a credit union that will allow you to directly deposit and cash your checks without any fees.

VILLAGE VISIT

The Power of the Budget: The Parent

The parent is arguably the most integral part of the village. Learning begins in the home, and no one in the village has a stronger impact on the development of a child than the parent. It is hard for a parent to teach their children about the importance of financial literacy, or any important life skill, if the parent is not versed in this information. Stronger parents can produce stronger children, and stronger children can produce stronger villages.

Carol Mack-Wells is my mother. If she had not taught me, through her actions, the importance of financial literacy, you wouldn't be reading this book right now. Her sensitivity has driven me to work to improve not only my own life, but the lives of others. I owe a lot to her, and those whom I have helped to empower themselves are in her debt as well. I placed my mother's words after the budget section because she was able to stretch a dollar better than anybody else I knew. She made a way out of no way and mastered the principles of fiscal responsibility with conviction to empower our household.

(continued)

LIFE LESSONS FROM A SINGLE PARENT
by Carol Mack-Wells

It was 6:30 P.M. Christmas Eve 1980 and I sat alone looking at the sparsely decorated Christmas tree, knowing that there would be only five gifts beneath the tree in the morning. Three large gift-wrapped boxes—one for each of my two sons, Richard and Ryan, and one for me—were from my parents and undoubtedly had several gifts in each box. There were also two smaller gifts from me to Richard and Ryan. In years past, the tree was always surrounded with presents, but this year was different. It was the first year that I was divorced from the boys' father, and finances were, to say the least, extremely lean. I had only enough money to buy them one item each, even though they both let me know in no uncertain terms what they wanted Santa to bring them.

While this night was not the first time that I'd felt the impact of not having money, it was certainly the saddest. The phone rang, and believing that it was either Richard or Ryan, I ran to answer it. But much to my surprise and dismay it was a bill collector, calling me on Christmas Eve! After my shock came anger. I thought, "How dare he call me on Christmas Eve!" I completely lost my composure (I'm not sure that I ever really tried to keep it), and the words that came out of my mouth would have put a sailor to shame! Now, thirty years later, I am in a much better position, with a successful career that compensates me well. The journey from then to now has been filled with many ups and downs, and I thank God every day that I have been able to get to this place of financial stability with His help and with the wisdom to take advantage of and learn from those "life lessons" that allowed me to survive.

Have Your Pity Party, but Then Pick Yourself Up

Most of us, even those who are wealthy, have been in financial difficulty. It is not fun and most often it required us to make choices that we did not want to make. During the early eighties my sons and I had only a black-and-white TV (long after most people had a color TV). I decided to put money aside to buy a color television, and after

(continued)

68

almost a year I had enough money to finally buy a small used one. I was excited, as this was the first major purchase I would make. On the day that I planned to buy the TV, I received a call that a check had bounced and the day-care school wanted their money in cash, just a little less than I planned to pay for the TV. I was devastated, and this was one of the many times I sat down and cried. Why couldn't God see that I needed to feel that I could buy something nice for my sons? Why couldn't I just once spend money on something that I didn't *need*? I began to feel sorry for myself. I felt sad and spent a couple of days going from sad to angry. After several days I began to see even more clearly that things had to change. I decided then and there that I had to get a job that paid more—there was no choice.

While I did eventually get the color TV about six months later, the most important lesson was that I became even more determined to make a change in how I managed my money so that bills would never be a surprise again. I began to keep better records of my expenses so that I would not be disappointed by unexpected bills and, more important, so that I would not bounce any more checks.

Lesson: Have your pity party. Get angry and feel sorry for yourself, but know that this must be temporary and that it must end with a resolution that things will change. Whether it is to get another job that pays more or to save more money, leave your pity party knowing that something different must happen as you move forward.

Make Life Fun—No Matter What the Circumstances

I believe that it is not healthy for any individual to walk around with self-pity all the time. Therefore, I tried to inject fun and humor into most of what we did. Since money was always limited, I could not buy as much food as we needed to eat three good meals every day. At times I went into my "gourmet" cooking style and made "pizza" out of slices of white bread and cheese (my sons say they remember us eating "government cheese," but perhaps this is one of those memories I have repressed!). Nonetheless, we all had a good laugh whenever we had "pizza." Then at times we enjoyed watching

(continued)

movies on TV and eating a box of plain popcorn purchased at the theater around the corner. We would pretend that watching TV was much better than seeing the movie at the theater. And of course our vacations were always fun, as we looked for free sights to see within driving distance of Detroit.

Lesson: Put humor into most of what you do. Sometimes you have to look hard to find the humor, but trust me, it's there and can always make a dire situation look ten times better than it actually is.

Make Changes That Make Life Easier

Being poor is no fun (even though we can always find something to laugh about). When I made that decision to make more money, I quickly began to look for opportunities. I heard about a job at a local university for more money and got it. However, after about a year I realized that we were still struggling. While Ryan was still in day care, Richard was going to a Catholic school. Even with financial aid, I could not afford his tuition. As much as I didn't want to, I decided to move to the suburbs. This change allowed both my sons to go to good public schools and made our lives easier.

Lesson: While it may require some research on your part, there is a way to make changes that will make your life easier and your dollar go further.

Be Persistent

I recall that when looking to purchase our first home, I looked for about two years to find a home that I could afford. Along the way I had at least one two-day pity party when I submitted a bid on one house only to have the owners select another bid. The real estate agent, however, told me that the couple's mortgage would probably not be approved. Armed with that information, I began my campaign of persistence. I called the agent every day to find out if the other bidder's mortgage had been approved. Finally, after two months he called to tell me the other mortgage had indeed fallen through. I

(continued)

was able to buy the house, and I attribute this purchase to my persistence.

Lesson: Never giving up is not a bad way to live.

Make Provisions for Possible Shortages

It is inevitable—at one time or another, money will be limited, and some months there will not be enough money to cover all the bills, no matter how much you plan.

I learned that the best way to avoid being hassled by bill collectors is to take the offensive—*call them before they call you!* Every month when paying bills, I determined if there would be any bills left unpaid for that month. If there were any, I would call the company (e.g., Detroit Edison) to let them know that a payment would be coming—in time. I was surprised at how understanding they can be if they know that they're dealing with someone who actually intends to pay the bill. After doing so, I was rarely hassled by any collector.

Lesson: Plan for days when money will be exceptionally short by letting others know that you intend to pay them. Then stick to your promise.

What About Me—Don't I Deserve Something?

You work every day and try to make ends meet. We always take care of our children while we do without. I got through these times by going shopping.

Yes, I have always been a shopaholic, even when my money was extremely limited when my children were young. My career taught me two valuable lessons about life: (1) If I wanted to make more money, I had to work hard and demonstrate my competence to get promotions; and (2) if I wanted to be a vice president, I had to dress like a vice president. I had no problem with the first, but having little or no money made the second a dilemma. So I learned how to shop at thrift shops. First I went to the upscale shops (e.g., Saks, Neiman Marcus, etc.) and saw what they were selling: classic clothes, traditional clothes (after all, I couldn't afford to change my look every

(continued)

year with each new fashion trend!). I then went to the thrift shops and found designer clothes that were both classic and traditional. Rather than splurge on a restaurant lunch one week, I took the money and went shopping. Doing this allowed me to buy two or three suits per month, and my self-confidence was given a major boost! Dressed for success, I worked harder than ever and the promotions followed.

Lesson: Yes, you do deserve something for *you*. Treat yourself, but do it so that it doesn't hurt your budget. You can look good and be dressed for success by shopping for good bargains at the right stores.

Being a single parent is an experience that I will never forget and do not want to ever forget. The life lessons were many and have helped me even to this day. I have two beautiful sons who are now successful adults, and I am certain that their success is due in large part to their experience as children in a home where money was scarce. To watch them develop and to see how far they have come is my biggest blessing of all. I am convinced that they can survive the most difficult circumstances because of their past. They are both strong, independent young men who also recognize the value of nurturing relationships and taking advantage of opportunities. I have no question that they have learned the life lessons we experienced while they were growing up. This makes all that we have gone through and survived worth it.

Ryan Mack's Five Economic Empowerment Tips for Parents

1. Talk with your children about money regularly. Don't just give them an allowance, but set up three boxes in the house marked SAVE, SPEND, and GIVE; have a conversation about what they are going to do with the dollars that you give them.
2. Demonstrate with your actions the importance of financial literacy. Involve them in developing a household budget so that they know money doesn't grow on trees.
3. Start them working early in life so that they learn the value of a dollar.
4. When they are as young as seven years old, occasionally purchase

a toy and have them sign an IOU. Assign dollar values to chores around the house so they have money to pay you back. When they earn the dollar value of the toy, have a debt-burning party and celebrate to give them a sense of debt.

5. Plan "empowerment trips" with your children where you take them to visit local colleges, jobs of professionals in your network, or a local food bank to volunteer to feed the hungry during the holiday season.

CHAPTER FOUR

Step One: Getting Your House in Order—Obtaining Adequate Insurance Coverage

THE MAIN QUESTION THAT PEOPLE SHOULD ASK THEMSELVES WHEN CONSIDERING how much life insurance they need is:

"If I were to die today, is there someone that would be negatively impacted by the loss of income that I was earning?"

For instance, do you have a child that is dependent upon your income? Are you married and would your spouse suffer a financial setback by your premature death because of debt and other bills that would have to be paid? Do you have a parent that will depend upon your income in the future? If the answers to these questions are yes, then perhaps you could use some life insurance.

The many different types of insurance policies cover an almost infinite number of scenarios. Arm yourself against predatory insurance practices by using your head. Insurance companies use scare tactics to try to create a need when you hadn't thought about that need ever in your life. Did you know you can purchase a policy to cover you if you are hit by a meteor? It's true. I know that this is an extreme example, but I am sure that at least one agent has scared someone enough into thinking that he or she had better guard against the huge risk that a meteor might hit him or her in the head on the way to the office. Life is full of risks, and your job is to discern which of those risks are worth your actually paying to cover.

You must determine what is important to the needs of your household and family.

Conduct Your Own Life Insurance Needs Analysis

The easiest way to figure out exactly how much insurance you need is to do an "insurance needs analysis." This is a calculation that determines the total amount of life insurance you should purchase, taking into account the three areas outlined below. If you are married, you should have this conversation with your spouse to make sure that your house is in order.

1. How Much Assets and Insurance Do You Have?

I can't tell you how many people have fallen victim to what I call insurance piling. If people have life insurance policy, on top of policy, on top of policy, more than likely a few agents have paid them a visit and convinced them of the need to purchase more insurance.

You should take these things into account when you are conducting an insurance needs analysis:

- Liquid assets—cash, CDs, money-market accounts, and any other investments.
- Disposable assets—rental property, business assets, cars, and anything of value that can be sold.
- Total amount of existing insurance policies—group insurance, personal insurance, mortgage insurance, etc.

Total Amount of Assets = _____

2. What Is Your Total Amount of Liabilities and Cash Needs?

A common saying is that many people don't leave wills, they leave bills. In my hometown of Detroit, Michigan, bodies pile up in the city morgue because their families do not have the money to provide a proper burial and the city lacks the budget to provide a basic service. The bills that we leave behind do not vanish, and below is a list of cash needs and liabilities that you might want to take into account in your insurance needs analysis:

- Total amounts of mortgages that you owe
- Total amount of other loans and debt that you owe including credit cards, bills, monies owed to collections, etc.
- Expenses that occur at death including lawyer fees and other estate-administration expenses; funeral expenses; and income and capital gains taxes
- An emergency fund of six to nine months of living expenses if you don't have one
- A college education fund for your children—you should prepare for at least $12,500 per year of college per child, although costs of college can go as high as $35,000 per year. Keep in mind that the more costs accounted for, the higher the costs of your coverage
- Costs for the care of aging parents
- Costs for child care through college

Total Amount of Liabilities and Cash Needs = _____

3. How Much Income Will Be Needed by Your Dependents/Survivors in the Event of Your Death?

With your debts taken care of, there is still a need to replace the income for all the years that survivors would have been dependent upon it. You must consider:

- Annual income provided to survivors: This figure should be approximately 70 percent of what you are currently earning. It is not 100 percent because many of the bills that you are paying for, such as mortgage payments and child care, are already accounted for.
- Years of that income that are to be provided: This number should come with much consideration because the more years you choose to replace income for, the more coverage you will need, and the higher your premiums will be. It might be nice to provide income replacement for your spouse for twenty years, but does she need that many years? Won't she be able to recover before then? It might be nice to provide replacement for your children for thirty years, but will they need your income after they graduate from college? Won't they be financially independent when they start working? Remember, we are only focused on what you feel you

need, not what you want. I am sure that the insurance agent that you see will feel happy that you want to replace income for twenty years because he or she sees a hefty commission check in the near future.

Annual Income Provided × Years of Income Provided = _____
(Note: This value *does not* take into account the time value of money or inflation. The actual amount of this figure when taking this into account will be less.)

To get a rough estimate of the amount of insurance that you need, you should add the final values in 2 and 3, and subtract 1 from this figure. To get a more precise estimate before you head to the insurance agent, you can find an insurance needs analysis at www.fincalc.com or search for "insurance needs analysis calculator" on Google. Going through this exercise above, especially with a loved one, will help you to get a firmer grasp on your finances and become more organized.

THE BEST LIFE INSURANCE STRATEGY FOR YOU

There are many types of insurance and you should become familiar with most of them before you purchase your policy. Thus you can determine what is best for you and your family without breaking the bank. Let me give you some sample scenarios.

Scenario One: Single Parent with Limited Income

If you are a single parent with limited income, the last thing that you would want to do is to add another bill to your household. However, if you don't have adequate life insurance through your employer, and something happens to you, your child is left behind in a bad predicament. If you are already living check to check but still need insurance coverage for your child, term life insurance could be the best bet for you.

Term Life Insurance. This is the simplest form of life insurance and is only provided for a term of your life (e.g., five, ten, twenty, thirty years). After the term has elapsed, you are no longer covered and the policy expires. With this coverage you can generally purchase large amounts of coverage for little money. These policies are well suited for families on a limited budget as it is not atypical to be able to purchase $250,000 worth of coverage for as little as $30 per month depending upon age and health.

Scenario Two: Newly Married Couple with Discretionary Income and No Children

This new family might be concerned about what will happen to his or her spouse in the event of an unlikely incident. Since they have more discretionary income, they might be able to consider something more permanent than term life insurance. They can choose between universal life insurance and whole life insurance.

Whole Life Insurance. This coverage lasts throughout your life as long as you continue to make timely payments. If this family elects to get $250,000 worth of coverage, that is guaranteed to remain in force their entire lives. Unlike term life insurance, whole life has a guaranteed cash value that, if they surrender the policy, would be available to them or that they may borrow against at the current policy interest rate. Whole life also pays dividends that can be returned to the policy owner as a reduction in premium or as cash or be applied to the policy to increase the payout. The biggest drawback to whole life insurance is its price . . . it is by far the most expensive insurance policy to purchase. That $250,000 worth of coverage that cost $30 per month for term can cost up to $250 per month for whole life insurance or more depending upon age and health.

Universal Life Insurance. The compromise between pricey whole life insurance and cheap term insurance is universal life insurance. This policy has a flexible premium and an adjustable benefit that accumulates in value. This policy is cheaper than whole life but the cash value is not guaranteed. A $250,000 universal policy might cost as much as $150 per month depending upon age and health. However, the premium is flexible, so if the family does not have the full $150 for the month and can only pay $100, the policy will draw the $50 they are short down from the cash value to keep the policy in force.

One good strategy that the family can implement is to purchase the cheaper universal life insurance policy, which will remain in force for the duration of the lives of the spouses. When they have a child, they can purchase a twenty-year term policy. The policy will expire when the child is twenty years of age, near when the child is close to being independent. If you have another child, purchase another twenty-year term policy that will be solely for child-care expenses if something happens to you. This cost-efficient strategy can maximize coverage while minimizing costs during the years when you need it most.

INSURANCE TIPS AND STRATEGIES FOR OTHER INSURANCE TYPES

In putting together the best strategy, you don't want to spend too much and get coverage beyond what is needed by your loved ones. However, you don't want to spend too little, putting your loved ones and/or your pocketbook at risk of being tapped out if a tragic event occurs. Also, it is perfectly acceptable to say that you do not have the funds to purchase a policy or are willing to accept the risk of not being covered. If you have substantial savings, then you may not need disability insurance; if you are single with no children, you may not need life insurance; or if your savings are substantial and your retirement fund is adequate, you may be willing to bear the risk and live without long-term-care insurance. *You* must make the decision, not the insurance agent. The point of this section is *not* to get you to go out and purchase insurance; it is to make you aware of a few of your options to mitigate financial risk in your life. If you read this book and decide not to purchase insurance, which many people may do, it isn't because of lack of knowledge but because you made an educated risk assessment and decided that you were comfortable with the additional risk and cost savings from not purchasing a policy.

That being said, if you decide to forgo any policy, I hope that you are aggressively saving to compensate for the additional risk in your life. If you do not purchase long-term-care insurance, what is your financial plan if you have to pay for a nursing home, outside of spending down all of your assets until you are poor enough to be eligible for Medicaid (i.e., taxpayers pick up your bill, thereby further bankrupting the Medicaid program)? If you decide not to purchase disability insurance, what is your financial plan if you become disabled besides trying to live off of supplemental security income (SSI) and moving back in with your mother? If you decide not to purchase health insurance, what is your financial plan if you get sick besides checking into the emergency room and getting treated for free, while the American taxpayers have to pick up your bill? If you cut corners, make sure that the corners you cut don't hurt somebody else financially. This is a crucial empowerment principle of the village . . . if you don't pay for it, somebody else will. Below are a few tips for various areas of insurance that should assist you to maximize quality and minimize cost of coverage.

Car Insurance Tips

Everyone who drives must have car insurance. Therefore, if you are a driver, it makes sense to make sure that more money is going into your pocket and not the pocket of your insurance company. So below are a few tips that you can implement to make sure you are saving money on car insurance.

1. **Shop around.** You should get a least three quotes before you purchase your insurance. Don't shop on price alone, and ask your friends and relatives for recommendations. Here are a few questions that you should ask about your insurance carrier:
   - What is the financial stability of this company? Check out its ratings with companies such as A.M. Best (www.ambest.com) and Standard & Poor's (www.standardandpoors.com).
   - How do others like this company? Ask friends and relatives for their opinions on car insurance. Also, contact your state insurance department to find out whether they provide information on consumer complaints by company and provide a record of claims payments.
   - How receptive is your agent? You want an agent who is receptive to answering your questions and addressing your concerns. You should have plenty if you have done your research.
2. **Increase your deductible.** The more money that you have to pay when you have an accident, the less you have to pay each month to maintain your insurance. Remember, insurance should not replace the need for financial planning.
3. **Choose your car carefully.** The type of car you drive has a lot to do with the amount you will have to pay for coverage. You may want to purchase that speedy sports car or that fancy new SUV, but the insurance company could charge you much more to protect you while driving it. This is the hidden price that you don't see in the sticker price. All of the following determine the price of the insurance that you pay on a vehicle:
   - Sticker price
   - Repair cost
   - Overall safety record
   - Likelihood of theft

Many car insurance companies will give you discounts for features that reduce the threat of theft or injury, such as antitheft devices or daytime running lights. Resources are available, such as the Highway Loss Data Institute (www.iihs.org), to help you obtain industrywide information on injury claims, theft rates by vehicle model, and collision repair costs.

4. **Know the policy.** Many components make up the cost of car insurance. They include:

   - Bodily injury liability—If your car hits and kills or injures someone and it is your fault, this protects you against claims.
   - Property damage liability—This is required in most states and covers claims for property that your car damages in an accident.
   - Uninsured motorist protection—For you or someone in your car who is hit by someone who does not have insurance in a hit-and-run.
   - Underinsured motorist protection—For the driver who hits you who does not have adequate insurance to cover all of your injuries.
   - Medical payment liability—If you live in a state that is "no-fault," personal injury protection replaces medical payments as a part of basic coverage.
   - Collision coverage—This covers the car up to its book value and comes with its own deductible. If you have an older car that is worth less than ten times the premium you are paying, purchasing this coverage may not be effective, though lending institutions usually require collision coverage. You can check out auto dealers or banks or visit Kelley Blue Book at www.kbb.com to learn the value of your car.
   - Comprehensive coverage—For if your car is stolen, vandalized, burned up in a fire, or damaged by wind. This also carries a deductible, so if your car is older, you could consider dropping this coverage as well.

5. **Buy from same insurer.** If you have a home and a car, you could get a discount if you purchase coverage for both from the same insurer. This can also work if you have more than one car and purchase from the same company. However, don't let this take the place of shopping around.

6. **Improve your credit score.** Yes . . . it really does affect your premium if you have poor credit.

7. **Use the low-mileage discounts.** A few companies provide discounts for motorists who drive less than the average number of miles per year. Carpooling not only helps the environment, but can also save you a few dollars on your premium.

Health Insurance Tips

Over half of all of the bankruptcies filed in the United States are due to illness and medical expenses. At the time of the writing of this book, Congress recently passed one of the largest reforms of the health-care system in the history of this nation. However, we must still continue to be sure that we are doing what we can to get the best coverage for ourselves and our families. The government does play a role in society, but the most important role must be played by the individual to prepare for his or her financial future. In no area is it more important than in purchasing health care. Below are a few tips.

1. **Choose group insurance if possible.** Group insurance through your employer is likely to be much cheaper than any individual policy that you will purchase for yourself. This is because of the multiple premiums being paid to the insurer by employees; the insurance company receives more money, spreads the risk of policy payouts over more people, and charges each individual less than he or she would have to pay if he or she had an individual policy. It is not unusual for people to pay $100 per month in premiums for their employer's insurance versus as much as $1,000 per month for an individual policy. However, obviously these savings are not possible if your employer does not offer health coverage.

2. **Know the laws.** Do you know the laws in your state on purchasing individual policies? As you travel from state to state, the laws may change, and it is important to know the laws in your area.

3. **Write out your priorities.** Before you spend a dime, you need to know what is important to you in obtaining your medical coverage. Write down your top five priorities and take this list to your broker or insurance company. Some of your concerns could be the following:
   - Do you want to be able to continue to see your current doctors?
   - How much are you able to pay in premiums?
   - Do you like good customer service?

4. **Pick the right broker.** The right broker can help do the legwork in finding you the right company and rates and can explain the logistics of your health-care plan.

5. **Read the plan thoroughly *before* purchasing.** If you find a plan that fits your needs and your budget, before you pay a dime be sure to get a complete copy of what the plan looks like. Determine if any exceptions or clauses in the plan will deny you health coverage in a time of need. Many companies will give you a short trial period to allow you to test-drive the plan. If you do ask for this "free look," be sure to obtain the exact terms of the trial period in writing and stay within the guidelines of its terms.

6. **Be careful and honest.** Filling out the application, you should be very cautious. Be sure that you are completely honest about *everything* and make no mistakes. The last thing that you need is to be denied coverage because you put down your date of birth incorrectly.

7. **Find the deal.** Once you have your plan, you can still try to save money on your health care. Shopping around for generics whenever they are available, ask your doctor to write out a longer prescription period to pay the same copay but get more drugs (e.g., a ninety-day versus a thirty-day supply), or negotiate with the doctor for a price if you have to pay out of pocket.

Disability Insurance Tips

You have a larger chance of becoming disabled than you have of dying prematurely. According to the American Council of Life Insurers, nearly one-third of all Americans between the ages of thirty-five and sixty-five will become disabled for more than ninety days. Many mistakenly think that disability comes only from accidents; however, the majority of long-term disabilities are caused by illness (e.g., cancer and heart disease). If your job does not offer disability insurance, you should definitely consider it. In choosing a policy, you should ask yourself:

Do They Offer It at Your Job?

Your employer, because of group policies, is usually the best place to purchase disability insurance. So when they give you that thick benefits book that normally ends up collecting dust under the bed, in the basement, or at the home office . . . read it! Many times you will get cheap, short-term insurance, so you will want to financially prepare yourself for a disability.

This is a great time for married couples with both partners working to compare which package is best between their two employers. However, purchase with caution from your employer because most of the time this insurance is not transferable, and if you leave your job, you will be without coverage.

How Much Insurance Do You Really Need?

This all depends upon what you would like to pay for. If your spouse is a stay-at-home mother, would you like for her to be able to stay at home and not work? Would you like to continue saving for your retirement? Is your teenager in private school or college? Do you feel you can eliminate any monthly expenses? Obviously, the more expenses that you compensate for, the more premium you will be paying; therefore, a budget of your needs versus wants is definitely in order.

How Long of an Elimination Period Do You Need?

The elimination period is the amount of time that it takes for your insurance benefits to begin. This period can be as short as one month (or shorter), or it can be as long as a year. Why would someone elect an elimination period as long as one year? Simple . . . the policy is cheaper, and you may have been able to save up enough money to cover your expenses during this time. Remember, insurance should never take the place of financial planning. So, just because you can get a policy with benefits that begin immediately does not mean that you should opt for this so you can avoid having to build a savings fund. The ideal scenario would be to opt for a long elimination period (perhaps six months to one year), save an emergency fund that will cover at least the amount of the elimination period or six to nine months of living expenses, and obtain a disability policy that has a lower premium.

How Many Years Will You Need to Receive Benefits?

Some policies are designed to pay only two years of benefits, other are designed to pay out benefits until the age of retirement. The longer you elect to receive benefits, the more expensive the premium you have to pay.

What Is the Maximum Benefit Level That You Need?

Most insurance companies are reluctant to provide over 70 percent of your current income. As your income increases, that figure decreases. This is because if you received 100 percent of your income for the rest of your life, what would be your incentive to go back to work? Furthermore, the benefits are tax free, so you are receiving pretty close to 100 percent of your take-home pay if you were not disabled, perhaps more.

Have You Read What the Policy Says?

Many people read the company brochure, which constitutes the depth of their research on an insurance policy. Keep in mind that sales literature is meant to entice you to purchase the insurance, so they will only put in it the most attractive components of the insurance. Do not sign anything until you have read the contract, which is legally binding, in its entirety. Not to say that agents cannot be trusted, but they have a vested interest in having you sign on the dotted line because of the commission that they earn. Have your family or close trusted friends look over the contract with you, as they can provide an unbiased and objective viewpoint that does not have any conflict of interest.

Also, make sure that you know exactly what you are paying. You might want to add some things to the policy that would make it much more beneficial to you, such as the following:

- Waiver of premium: This allows you to stop paying the premium if you become disabled. Most policies have this, but some do not; be sure to ask for it.
- Noncancelable clause: This can be an expensive option to add, but it prevents the insurance company from being able to cancel, change the terms of, or increase the premiums of your policy for any reason.
- Inflation rider: This can cost extra as well, but it can't hurt to ask for it to be throw in there for free. In the event of a long-term disability, your benefits will keep pace with the cost of living.

Long-Term-Care Insurance Tips

Long-term-care insurance is a great way to protect the assets you have worked so hard to accumulate. A great time to start to think about purchasing a plan is when you turn fifty, or to qualify for cheaper rates, start your search at forty-five. According to the AARP (www.research.aarp .org), there's a 68 percent probability that people age sixty-five and over will become disabled in some of the activities of daily living or that they will become cognitively impaired. According to Americans for Long-Term

Care Security (www.ltcweb.org), more than half of the U.S. population will require long-term care at some point in their lives. Furthermore, one out of five Americans over the age of fifty is at risk of needing long-term care in the next twelve months.

With costs for long-term care on the rise ($75,190 annually for a private room, $13,000 annually for adult day care, and $25,000 annually for assisted living), long-term care insurance is become more and more necessary. However, we must be careful to buy the appropriate amount of insurance.

Here are some tips on how to purchase long-term-care insurance:

Shop Around. Make sure that you get comparison quotes. You should have a long-term-care specialist explain the differences in benefits and premiums. Try not to purchase benefits that you won't need.

Cheap Is Not Always the Best. Be sure to do your research on the company's experience in the market. Many companies have a history of rate increases, which can be detrimental during a life of fixed income within your golden years. Many companies offer rate guarantees, which can be a plus. Just because a policy is cheap doesn't mean it is the best for you . . . check the company's rating.

Know What You Are Purchasing. Some policies don't offer coverage for home health care, but do offer coverage for care in a long-term facility. Also, there are many various definitions for the word *facility*. What is the policy's definition, and how comprehensive is the policy? Again, make sure that you are aware of exactly what you are purchasing with your hard-earned dollars.

Avoiding Predatory Insurance Practices

In every industry, some are ethical and some are not. The insurance industry is no different. I would think that it is safe bet that, for the most part, if you meet someone in the insurance industry, they probably got into that industry for the right reasons and have every intention to make sure that you are treated fairly. However, some care more about their own well-being than about being fair to you. Also, some have the best intentions to be equitable toward you but fall short because of error. As much as we would love to meet only those who are fair and free from error, we must prepare ourselves for those who do not have our best interests at heart. We must prepare for the worst but expect the best in all situations.

A saying often related to the insurance industry is "If I have a hammer, you must have a nail." This means that many insurance agents will attempt to fit their products into their "victim's" or client's life regardless of expressed need. As the owner of an insurance agency myself, I have attended many industry sales conferences. These conferences always discuss either how to sell more insurance or review new insurance products agents will be able to market to potential clients.

Who is a potential client? you ask. *Everybody!* Regardless of whether you have a need or not, some insurance providers view their job as that of a salesperson to create the need in all people. If you are twenty-five, single, with no kids . . . then the need created might be to purchase life insurance while you are young to avoid higher premiums. If you are forty-five, single, with no kids . . . the need might be for you to purchase life insurance on yourself and name your aging mother, who might need your income if "God forbid" something happened to you. If you are forty and married, then there is never too much insurance that you can purchase for your spouse. I can go on and on creating a need for each scenario. At these conferences, the goal is not to get the agents excited about finding those who have a need for insurance . . . the goal is to motivate the agents to get on the phone and call everyone they know to get them to purchase insurance. If there is not a need . . . create one!

Please do not get me wrong. I firmly believe that in many instances life insurance, or any other insurance, could prove important in a financial plan. My point is that *you* must determine whether there is a need. The days of going to a financial professional without a strong foundation of knowledge are over. We should educate ourselves about insurance, and other financial topics that impact our lives, before we walk into the office of the insurance agent. You could walk into the office of an agent who seems to have your best interests at heart—or not. As long as we are in a capitalist society, there is the potential for a conflict of interest, and the potential for the agent to put his own financial needs ahead of yours. So we must educate ourselves.

I would like to introduce you to a term: *predatory insurance practices*. Almost everyone has heard of predatory lending practices, when a lender uses deception to convince borrowers to agree to unfair loan terms. This, as we discussed earlier, was a major cause of the recent recession. However, predatory insurance practices are actually more prevalent than predatory lending practices; we just don't hear about them. This is because the insurance industry is still not highly regulated and its effects aren't as obvious. If a real estate agent sells you a home that you cannot afford, you may be forced to go into foreclosure, which is a life-changing financial bind. Your credit suffers, you potentially go deeper into debt, you are displaced from your home, and an entire litany of financial issues confronts you. However, predatory insurance practices frequently go below the radar, unnoticed by all except the insurance agent and your savings account.

So how do you spot a predatory insurance practice? It happens every time an insurance agent convinces someone to buy more insurance than is needed. Here's an example. A thirty-five-year-old man—let's call him Bill—wants to purchase life insurance to provide for his family in case, God forbid, something happens to him. He goes to Mr. John Crooked, the life insurance agent, and Mr. Crooked tells Bill that he should purchase a $5 million policy. Bill immediately thinks that is an exorbitant figure, that he doesn't need that much insurance for his family. He thinks about what his family would really need if he passed away. He thinks about his funeral, costs to care for the children, paying off debt, and other expenses that he would not want his wife to worry about if he weren't here. He doesn't know much about the process and expresses this concern to Mr. Crooked, and Bill is definitely unfamiliar with how the amount of the coverage increases with the premiums. Mr. Crooked goes into full sales mode, saying things like the following:

- "Don't you care about your family?"
- "Is there ever too much that you can give your family after you are gone?"
- "This is the best deal ever . . . you pay a little and get five million! Hurry and jump on it now because as you get older, the price goes up!" (Mr. Crooked combines the best-deal-ever strategy with the strategy that creates an impulse to purchase now.)
- "This is how the rich take care of their children." (This strategy plays upon how most in America, even if they are not considered rich, want to do the things that the rich do.)

How do I know that this goes on? I own an insurance agency and have sat in *many* sales-strategy courses across the country that teach how to make the sale. They drill making the sale into your head so much that you soon forget that you are providing a service for the client. You hear it so much, it is entirely possible that Mr. Crooked actually believed that he was doing Bill a great service. When you leave those sales meetings, your first inclination is to get on the phone and sell some insurance.

Lesson learned: Before we go into the insurance agent's office (or any financial consultant's office), we must arm ourselves with the knowledge that will lessen the odds that we will be victims of predatory insurance. Had Bill, in the above example, been properly informed, he would have known he may only have needed $1 million of coverage to provide for the basic needs of his family.

Let us look at some real numbers using the above scenario. Mr. Crooked wanted to sell a $5 million policy to Bill. For the sake of argument, let us say that Bill only needed to purchase $750,000 worth of coverage to provide for the needs of his family should something happen to him.

Predatory Insurance Example

Bill—thirty-five-year-old male, nonsmoker—twenty-year term—$5 million policy
Monthly-cost quote—$483

Adequate Insurance Coverage Example

Bill—thirty-five-year-old male, nonsmoker—twenty-year term—$750,000 policy
Monthly cost quote—$88

Excess cost of predatory insurance—$483−$88 = $395

As we see from the above example, if Bill falls victim to this scam, he would pay an additional $395 per month because he didn't do enough research before going to see Mr. Crooked. The savings could go toward retirement, college education, a new business, or any other financial goal of his. How much would that $395 each month be worth if invested for the twenty years of the term policy? At a 10 percent rate of return, that would be close to $300,000.

You may be thinking that $300,000 is not as much as $5 million. Let me ask you this question: Are you preparing to live or are you preparing to die? If you are preparing to die, then maybe that $483 per month is the best price for you. However, if you are like most proud Americans that I know, you are preparing to live! If so, insurance should be used to cover our needs and not our wants. I am sure that it sounds nice to think about your family receiving a tax-free $5 million check if you die within the twenty-year window. However, your family needs those funds for day-to-day living expenses today. If yours is like most households in America, an extra $395 per month is a lot of money. For every extra dollar that you spend on insurance, that is one dollar that is not going for your bills, retirement savings, savings for a new home or a new business venture, or any other financial goal of yours. Insurance was never meant to be a replacement for financial planning, and it is important that you only use insurance to fulfill your needs in case something, God forbid, should happen to you.

Now, this is not your cue to cancel all of the policies that you have. We need to be smart about this. Some policies you should have, and some are excessive. That is up to you to determine.

VILLAGE VISIT

The Importance of Insurance:
The Construction Worker

If you walk outside in any city across America and look around, you will see their work. The beautiful skyline that you see as you fly into New York City, the high skyscrapers of Chicago, or the modern buildings of Los Angeles would not exist without construction workers. As you ride down a smooth highway, thank them; cross a fancy bridge, thank them; or marvel at how they built that long tunnel deep under a river, thank them as well. They build America with blood, sweat, and tears. In no other industry will you see the importance of insurance more than in the construction industry.

I have never seen a more hands-on jobs program than the one led by Darnell Canada. He has a knack for finding employment for hundreds of workers in the field of construction. Darnell has trained, certified, and placed into jobs close to two thousand people from 2006 through 2009. Darnell is the perfect example for this insurance section because one of the primary concerns that he has had to deal with is making sure that the workers are properly insured. In construction, insurance is critical because of liability issues.

(continued)

Have You Ever Seen an Angel?
by Darnell Canada

A twenty-eight-year-old man once asked me a question that gave me tremendous pause. He asked, "Did you know that you would have the level of success that you have now when you were my age?" I eventually told him that at age twenty-eight, I didn't believe I would live to be twenty-nine years old. I sure didn't think I would reach age fifty with any degree of success. I then explained to him that at age twenty-eight I couldn't read or write.

In fact, at age twenty-eight I had gained a reputation as a drug dealer, a drug user, a stickup kid, a thief, and muscle for hire. Most people looked at me as a street thug who was no good for himself or anybody else.

Here's a brief summary of my life to that point: I was arrested for breaking into a store and sentenced to three years of probation. Later I was arrested for possession of a controlled substance and a firearm; this led to a sentence of five years of probation. I continued along the same path until finally I was arrested for assault one and was sentenced to seven and a half to fifteen years in prison. It's not hard for people to perceive you as a bad person with a past like that.

Yet, despite all the evidence of my negative behavior, I was not a bad person then, and to this day I firmly believe that I have never been a bad person. Yes, I take full responsibility for all my past negative behaviors, and I paid a dear price for them by losing my freedom for a number of years. I spent many years in jail, and rightfully so. But my lack of education and lack of a moral and spiritual foundation played a big part in my delinquency.

When I was sentenced to seven and a half years in prison, I was sent to Downstate Correctional Facility, for orientation into the correctional system. This was my first time in a state correctional facility. I had always thought of myself as a person who could handle any situation. But once I reached Downstate Correctional Facility, the reality of having to do so many years in prison sank in!

I found myself afraid of being away from my family and living in a small cell. I told myself that this was no way for a man to live. I began going to medical call-out as often as I could, and I hid the

(continued)

91

pills they gave me until I felt I had accumulated enough for me to escape the reality of being in prison.

I remember the night I took the pills. It was late and everybody was locked in his cell. (There was only one man to a cell.) I took the pills and drank some water. I remember feeling drowsy, and then it seemed like I was falling into the ocean and was being pulled down deeper and deeper. As I went deeper, I heard a voice that I recognized as the voice of my deceased grandmother. I heard her say, "Darnell, go back, it is not your time yet." The voice was getting louder. I then woke up and there was a corrections officer at my cell door yelling, "Get up, it's not your time yet." I jumped up off the bed and went to the cell door and the officer said, "Don't worry, the truth will come and set you free. Don't worry about doing the time that was given to you, because the truth will set you free."

He told me not to worry "because as you walk in this valley of darkness called prison, there will be light. The light will be those men that seem to have a glow around them. Listen to their words for in them you will be given life and freedom." He told me not to worry about what religion they might be: "You will know them by their word and their glow." Then he prayed the Lord's Prayer and left.

As I went to lie down, I realized I no longer felt any drowsiness from the pills. In fact, I felt as if I had not taken any pills at all.

The next morning when I woke up, I asked the corrections officer on duty the name of the officer that worked the night before. He said he had worked a double shift and was the only officer that worked my cellblock that night. To this day I have never seen the officer that spoke to me that night. I often think he was my guardian angel!

No matter what really transpired, I wholeheartedly believe this was God's way of giving me another chance. Ever since then I have been moving toward being the best moral and spiritual person possible. As I continued my journey through prison, I found a few people with a word and a glow to help me on my way.

I made an important decision to go to school and earn my GED. This was probably one of the most important decisions I have ever made. After obtaining my GED, I entered a college program and received a two-year degree in sociology and a four-year bachelor's

(continued)

degree in psychology. Education opened up a whole new world to me. There is no question that traditional education played its part in helping me become a thinking human being, an intellectual creature.

After leaving prison, I began working in community-building organizations to help people find jobs. Most recently I created a program called Real Economics for Building Unity and Innovative Local Development (REBUILD) to place hard-to-employ people in construction jobs, but this proved difficult. While billions of dollars were being spent in downtown Brooklyn for new construction, we could not obtain jobs for residents who lived within a ten-block radius of this construction. We were told that the people who lived in the community were lazy and incapable of handling the work safely.

I am happy to say REBUILD has lived up to the challenge, responding to the negative feelings that some contractors and developers have had concerning not just the people in the immediate area, but also certain classes of people—formerly incarcerated individuals, people on public assistance, and those who are homeless. We responded by creating training programs that helped teach over two thousand individuals safety on construction sites. Our program has graduated thousands of individuals with fifteen or more city, state, and federal certifications, many of which are required for any individual to work on a construction site.

After going through an at least six-week course, a participant must be at one of our pickup points by 6:30 A.M. and ride in a sixteen-passenger van until three P.M. for two weeks before being considered for a job. This lets us know that each individual will show up to work. We have placed over a thousand people on job sites in the downtown Brooklyn, as well as around New York City. Yes, we proved that although people may have gone through negative circumstances in their lives, they can get beyond those things, they can change and become productive individuals.

I would be remiss not to talk about my relationship with Ryan and how we met. I was telling a friend about some financial problems I was having with REBUILD and she told me about Ryan Mack. I told her that based on what I was hearing, his services were probably too expensive. She suggested that I at least meet with him and hear what he had to say. I agreed.

(continued)

I remember the first time I met Ryan. He was articulate, but to my amazement he explained complicated subjects in a way that any child could understand. I told him that I didn't have much money and asked him how much his services would cost. Ryan told me that as long as I continued to help those who could not help themselves, he would help me for free.

Ryan not only helped me financially with his advice, he also became an active board member of REBUILD and has helped members change their lives, too.

As I seek to help people take care of their families, by helping them get a job, a feeling of comfort comes over me when I realize that I am not out here alone. It brings joy to my heart to know that there are people like Ryan Mack out there ready to give us advice, give us insight on our plight, an understanding of how to better use our resources, while giving us the tools to do something about it. Continue to glow, Ryan, continue to give us a word on how to be financially stable. Continue to do God's work!

RYAN MACK'S FIVE ECONOMIC EMPOWERMENT TIPS FOR CONSTRUCTION/BLUE-COLLAR WORKERS

1. Fiscal responsibility for you is extremely important. In good times, save up for the slow times. The less money you make, the more fiscally responsible you have to be. Budgeting, establishing credit, and building savings for that rainy day are a few of the things that you should be focusing on.

2. Make sure you are legit. If you are independent and not with a firm or union, form your own LLC or sole proprietorship and make sure your company is licensed properly. Also, get the proper amount of insurance to be a general contractor. In construction there is a lot of liability, and you want to make sure your personal assets are protected as much as possible. If you start your own business, be sure that you advertise in your community. There might not be any jobs on the larger sites, but Ms. Smith around the corner might be looking for some work to be done around the house. You can never become certified in too many areas. This makes you more diverse and obviously more attractive to developers, who are looking for specific types of skills on their site.

3. The economy is very sporadic, so that means jobs and income could also be sporadic. For that reason, having a personal and business budget is that much more important to help provide stability to your life.

4. If you are a new company, locate the larger companies in your area that have the most capacity for work, form relationships with them, and seek subcontracting ventures. At the time this book is being written, billions of dollars of stimulus funding are being given out. Go to www.recovery.gov to see the businesses in your community that have received funding for construction projects; they may be willing to pay you to assist them.

5. Many people get into construction because they feel that they are not suited to enter any other field. This could be a good bridge job, a job that gets you where you need to go, but make sure that you are networking, learning, and looking at *all* your options. You may have a felony on your record, you may not have that much education, or you may not think that you are skilled in any other area because you haven't been exposed to much. But the only limits that apply to your life are the ones that you place. Find a way!

CHAPTER FIVE

Step One: Getting Your House in Order—Obtaining and Maintaining Up-to-Date Estate-Planning Documents

YOU HAVE WORKED HARD ALL YOUR LIFE. YOU HAVE ACCUMULATED THOUSANDS, perhaps millions, of dollars after years of hard work and wise investments. Maybe your property has soared in value and you now have a sizable estate for your heirs. How to manage these assets? Today millions of Americans are faced with the problem of properly organizing their estate. No matter what our personal circumstances may be, we each should have a proper plan in place that protects us against unforeseen life events.

A key wealth-building principle is to know when to invest in the right professional who will help you excel. After you have reviewed the following information, I urge you to talk to a qualified estate planner to assist you to make the proper arrangements. To find a good estate planner, you can log on to the National Association of Estate Planners and Councils Web site at www.naepc.org. Make sure that you talk to an "accredited estate planner" (AEP) or an "estate-planning law specialist" (EPLS) in your area to assist you in putting together the right plan for you. Many try to do it on their own but often regret it when critical errors result in thousands of dollars paid in penalties, fees, and excess taxes. I cannot tell you how many I have seen suffer financially because they are too cheap to get it right the first time.

Now, with that said, here are some basic tips for setting up your estate plan. Remember, this is *not* to replace advice from an estate-planning professional. However, I do believe that it is important to educate yourself as much as possible before you see any adviser.

THE ESTATE TAX

A key wealth-building principle is to minimize taxes at all costs. With a thorough understanding of how your estate is taxed and proper planning, you can be successful. Everyone should know what is considered an estate asset for tax purposes when you pass away. Retirement plans, the face value of insurance policies, and everything that you own are usually put into this equation and considered to be an estate asset. The estate or "death" tax has been a topic of major debate in Congress for many years. This estate tax is essentially the amount the government can tax your estate upon your death. It is highly disputed because it is viewed by many as a penalty assessed just because you passed away . . . as if you had any choice. For those who are married, the entire value of your estate may be passed on without taxes to your spouse upon your death. However, some high penalties could result in your children receiving far less then you would want them to have after the death of the other spouse.

As of 2008, the first $2 million of your estate is exempt from estate taxes. However, every dollar of your estate above $2 million could be taxed at the highest rate of 45 percent. Below is a table that demonstrates how the estate tax will impact your estate within the next four years.

	Estate Tax Highest Rate	Exemption
2008	45%	$2,000,000
2009	45%	$3,500,000
2010	0%	Repeal
2011	55%	$1,000,000

As you can see, the estate tax expires in 2010; however, in 2011 estate taxes are set to return to the same rates as they were before 2001.

The Gift Tax

An efficient way to bequeath assets is to "gift" those assets to your heirs. As of 2010, one can give up to $13,000 ($26,000 for spouses splitting gifts) to any number of persons within a year without incurring any tax. If you decide to give more than that, you must report the taxable give on a Gift Tax Return (IRS Form 709). Spouses who split gifts must file a Form 709 even if a taxable gift is not incurred. It is a great idea to give a tangible gift of education because one can make unlimited payments directly to educational institutions on behalf of others and not incur a taxable gift. The same unlimited-gift rule applies if payments are paid to medical providers on behalf of others.

Also, each donor has a lifetime exemption of $1 million that they can give before any out-of-pocket taxes are due. When transferring wealth, these gifts have significant advantages over testamentary gifts. When you are ready to reduce the size of your estate by using distribution, it is wise to take advantage of the annual $13,000 exclusion, make payments directly to medical and educational institutions, and consider effective use of your $1 million lifetime tax exemption. However, when considering making gifts, remember:

- Each gift has to be irrevocable.
- Never give so much that you don't have enough to live on.
- Don't hesitate to request assistance from a qualified professional.
- Never make a decision based on what *you think* Congress will do regarding estate tax repeal. Your financial needs and goals should be the primary consideration when determining the proper estate strategy.

Four Key Components of an Estate Plan

Last Will and Testament

This is a written or typed statement that declares a person's intent for asset distribution at his or her death. I have seen cases where families were torn apart without this simple document. *Every* adult needs a will; however, seven out of ten adults in the United States pass away intestate, or without a will. Without proper planning, weeks of court battles and high expenses can significantly reduce the size of your estate. As much as 20 to 30 percent of all legal fees are earned by lawyers in probate court in lengthy battles that should and could have been avoided. The distribution of your estate will be left to the courts without the implementation of this simple document. The best way to prepare yourself is now while you can.

When writing your will, you become the *testator* if you are a man or the *testatrix* if you are a woman. Be mindful of all the things that can compromise the integrity of this document. For instance, if you are not of sound mind, then you should not be writing your will. If, according to your state, you are not of majority age, then you should seek a guardian to assist you in writing your will. Did you and your two witnesses sign the will? This sounds simple, but many times the smallest of avoidable things causes lengthy court battles postmortem.

You must also think carefully about whom you will name to be the *executor* or *executrix*. This person inherits the fiduciary duty to carry out the terms and conditions of your will. The person will also have to settle all of the debts that you have left. You must make sure to choose someone who has proven to be competent, and it wouldn't hurt if the person had some degree of financial knowledge. Ask yourself how comfortable you are with that person taking an inventory of your assets, collecting your assets, paying off all taxes and debt, and managing what you have worked all of your life to accumulate. More than likely, the executor will be paid a percentage of your estate as a fee.

Many people ask me if they can save some money by writing their own will. This question is becoming more prevalent as information becomes more available through resources such as the Internet. The answer is absolutely not! I cannot say it enough that it is worth the small investment to pay for a qualified adviser to assist with these financial matters that if handled wrong have tremendous repercussions. Why risk it?

When you have a will in place, it is important that you review it at least once every two years and make amendments if needed. Amendments are usually needed whenever you have a major life-changing situation such as a birth, divorce, significant increase in income/assets, or even if there is a change in tax law.

What many have failed to understand is that with or without a will, your estate has to undergo probate court. If you have no will, then the courts will have to decide the best way to disseminate your assets. However, even with a will you still are subject to probate so that a court can be certain of various things, such as if the will is the most recent copy, that there are no other copies, that the will was written when you were of a sound mind, and that the will was not written under duress. However, you circumvent your will and avoid probate when leaving certain assets to your heirs. For instance, your 401(k) or company retirement plan, your individual retirement account (IRA), and your insurance policy have a section for designating your beneficiary. Whether you pass away intestate or testate (without a will or with a will), your chosen beneficiary will receive the funds as outlined in the retirement or insurance plan.

Another means to circumvent the will and avoid probate court altogether are *payable on death* (POD) or *transfer on death* accounts. In many states, laws allow you to designate a postmortem beneficiary of your bank and investment accounts. This is easy for you to establish at your local bank. Upon your death your beneficiary will simply have to produce proper identification and a proper death certificate to access the account. If you establish a payable on death, be sure that you designate all of the beneficiaries that you want on your account, that you update your beneficiaries constantly (e.g., if one dies, you should make necessary changes), and that you are aware of any consent that you may need to obtain from the beneficiaries if you make changes to the account.

The easiest way to circumvent the will and avoid probate is to have a joint account. This method is most commonly used between married couples, but is not limited to them. If an account is owned by two or more individuals jointly and it is designated "with right of survivorship," when one account owner dies, the surviving owners will simply continue to own the account. Surviving owners will only need to show proper ID and a death certificate of the deceased owner, and he or she will be removed from the account.

The IRS has heightened scrutiny on these accounts to deter people from making secret gifts. In some cases an account owner would add a new owner to an account who did not make any contributions to it but inherited the funds after the death of the original owner. For instance, an elderly mother on her deathbed adds her son to her bank account with a million dollars in it. Upon her death the son automatically inherits the funds. If no contributions are being made by the new account owners, the original owner may be deemed to have made a gift of the account to the new owners for tax purposes.

Make sure that you add owners to these accounts with care and a lot of careful thought to not disinherit anyone. If you make a minor a joint owner, a court-supervised guardianship will need to be established for the account to be used for the minor's benefit.

The living trust is another method/document that can eliminate the need for the court system to plan your estate affairs. This is a technique of titling your deeds and assets in the name of a fictitious entity. For example, the Ryan Mack Trust can hold ownership of those assets and, after the death of the grantor (the person who made the trust, which is usually you), can distribute those assets according to the wishes of the grantor through the use of a "successor trustee." This is a person whom you have appointed because you trust him or her to be competent with the planning of your estate upon your death or incapacity to do so yourself. If your estate is over $1 million, this could be a great option. However, you should not do this yourself but should use a qualified estate planner, as this is not the only option and may not be the most appropriate for you.

Durable Springing Financial Power of Attorney

This document gives an agent power to act in financial matters on your behalf should you become mentally or physically ill and are judged in a court of law to be incompetent. Without this document your family will have to hire an expensive attorney to go to court and have someone appointed as your conservator to make decisions on your behalf.

It is important to have a "durable springing" financial power of attorney because this only takes effect if and when the principal becomes incapacitated. If you grant a power of attorney, then the appointed agent retains control over many of your financial matters whether or not you are incapacitated. I do not trust anybody that much. However, I would want to have a document that "springs" into action if I am unable to make these financial decisions for myself.

The appointed agent has a lot of power and control. The agent has the authority to administer many responsibilities, including the following:

- Use your assets to pay your everyday expenses and those of your family
- Buy, sell, maintain, pay taxes on, and mortgage real estate and other property
- Collect Social Security, Medicare, or other government benefits
- Invest your money in stocks, bonds, and mutual funds
- Handle transactions with banks and other financial institutions
- Buy and sell insurance policies and annuities for you
- File and pay your taxes
- Operate your small business
- Claim property you inherit or are otherwise entitled to
- Transfer property to a trust you've already created
- Hire someone to represent you in court
- Manage your retirement accounts

As you can see, the agent has a lot of control, so it is important that you give this authority to the right person.

Living Will

The living will is a document instructing physicians, relatives, or others to refrain from the use of extraordinary measures, such as life-support equipment, to prolong one's life in the event of a terminal illness. The Terri Schiavo case demonstrated the importance of this document.

On February 25, 1990, Terri Schiavo experienced respiratory and cardiac arrest. These horrific events left her with significant brain damage, and she was diagnosed as being in a persistent vegetative state. For the next fifteen years she lived in an institution where individuals could not tell if she was coherent or incoherent. Her husband wanted to remove her feeding tube after the eighth year. However, her parents opposed this, arguing that she was conscious. For the remaining seven years of Terri Schiavo's life, politicians, advocacy groups, her husband, and her parents went through a rigorous back-and-forth judicial process. Terri Schiavo passed away on March 31, 2005, at the age of forty-one. This entire process could have been avoided if there had been a living will and she chose to be terminated earlier.

Health-Care Proxy

This document provides specific instructions and also designates an agent to make decisions for you in case you are unable to do so. The living will outlines certain wishes, and the health-care proxy appoints an agent to carry out the wishes. This person should not be a close friend or relative, but someone who you feel will be objective enough to "pull the plug" should that time arise. (My mother is not my health-care proxy because she loves me too much to pull the plug on me.) The best person to choose as your agent is your physician.

In all areas of estate planning, I must reemphasize the importance of hiring a qualified professional to assist you. How you own your home, the way you would like to be treated if you are in a vegetative state, who will handle your financial affairs, and other estate-planning issues are all important matters on which you should receive appropriate counsel. Also, be careful that you put great care into *whom* you select to receive certain assets. It has taken you a lifetime to build your wealth. If you do not take proper care to plan, or you leave your assets to someone who is not responsible, these assets could be squandered and your lifelong efforts be for naught.

VILLAGE VISIT

The Power of Proper Estate Planning:
The Married Couple

What is the biggest cause of divorce?

If you said money, then you were correct. Over 50 percent of all marriages end in divorce. Of this 50 percent, 80 percent end because of financial issues. If this is true, then how come this is the least talked about issue among couples? I have talked with many married couples who did not know how each other felt about certain financial issues.

I think that we all need to step back and face the truth that money in a relationship does make a difference. You can turn over your body, heart, and soul to someone, but the union will never be complete unless you link your fortunes together as well. This is for better, for worse, and forever. If you have met the person of your dreams, I can promise you that if you do not discuss how your potential mate feels about money, it will be an obstacle down the road. There are bound to be arguments related to financial issues, but these can be greatly reduced if both individuals discuss money honestly before any vows are made. This is important to the village because marriage is a powerful union that can contribute a lot to it.

Richard Mack, my brother, is married to Pamela Mack. Both are attorneys. They live in Detroit, which at the time I am writing this book is suffering from a severe depression while the rest of the country is in a recession. However, Richard and Pam seem to be impervious to the hardships of the economy, as if they are living in their own economic bubble. They own their home, have two investment properties, invest regularly in their retirement accounts, just adopted a child, can travel whenever they please, and are diligent about their estate plans. I think that much of their success starts in the home because they are such a strong team.

(continued)

Two People, One Bond, Infinite Power
by Richard Mack Jr.

Pinching pennies until the copper rubs off! God blesses us with various talents and characteristics, and that is one of mine. That may not seem like a blessing, but it gets you through those tough times. My wife and I have been married for more than a decade, and we have a handsome boy. We are both lawyers, but we have not always had financial stability. I do not pretend that we got it all right, and we have been "pound-foolish" with some investments, but the concept of penny-wise has, thankfully, developed in our household.

I think I learned frugality from my mother. As a child, I remember seeing her take instant oatmeal to work for lunch, so that she could avoid having to buy a $3 sandwich (remember when sandwiches were $3?). In high school, I learned to cut my own hair to avoid the cost of a barber; I still do to this day. By the time I hit college, I was bragging about being able to survive on $5 a week—of course that did not include the board expenses (three meals per day) that my parents paid for. But I knew that the University of Michigan's tuition was a huge burden on my parents, so I learned to stretch every dollar.

Upon graduation from law school I met and married my wife, Pam. I was frugal, she was not, so money could have been a constant battle. We were able to do what many married couples can't—talk about money openly. I thank God that He has kept our marriage strong and enabled us to develop habits that prevent finances from causing irreparable rifts.

Habit-Forming

God has been central in our relationship and has shown us how to develop financial habits that are long lasting. One day I heard a bishop preach about being a strategic thinker—and taking care of your household spiritually and financially. My brother Ryan had also given us a book, *The Word on Finances* by Larry Burkett, which quotes passages from the Bible that speak to financial matters.

(continued)

After researching and reading financial guides, I realized that my wife and I needed a financial overhaul. One of the common recommendations is to have six months' savings, and I saw we had none (other than retirement). So several years into our marriage, I insisted that we do a budget, at least every other week (every payday). We have an Excel spreadsheet, and at the top we list all of our income for that pay period. We then list each and every bill that we must pay throughout the month—this includes onetime incidentals or recurring items such as a car note or mortgage.

The habit is easy to break. Even today, when we get paid, our initial reaction is to spend. But faith to endure keeps us going. We know that God would have us be wise stewards over what He has blessed us with. We know that in the future we want to buy another house and have enough money saved for our son, Jeremiah, to go to college—without having to stretch $5 for the week. We want to pay off all credit cards and be debt free. We want to be a blessing to our church and to those in need. So keeping those long-term goals in the forefront of our minds, we persist in reconciling each pay period.

The routine discussions we continue to have about our budget have been the key to our financial success. These discussions help us to establish our goals—monthly goals and annual goals—and therefore allow us to enjoy a life that is debt free and fun. Now that we have our son and have had to pay for day care, clothing, and his other expenses, I have really seen the value of establishing a monthly budget.

Without long-term goals, the short-term work becomes a boring routine. I suggest that you set long-term, reasonable goals and remind yourself of them. Post them on the refrigerator and continue to dwell on them. Each day will seem much more relevant, and not a disconnected chore.

Communication

The Bible states that husbands must dwell with their wives according to knowledge (1 Peter 3:7). The word *knowledge* signifies a deep understanding. I could not understand Pam unless we communicated, and we do talk openly about money.

(*continued*)

This budget system was not easy to develop, especially given that Pam did not have the history of frugality that I had. When Pam graduated college, she began to work for the auto industry and made good money. She was used to spending what she wanted, buying expensive clothing and enjoying the finest dining. When we got married, our histories collided somewhat. When this infamous budget came about, the struggle continued. We fought, and discussed, and reasoned about whether this was a good idea. But God touched both of our hearts to establish and maintain this system. It is also not easy to live by, and we are far from perfect. But the system works; the challenge is just our working the system.

I have also learned not to be excessively rigid. When I see Pam come home with another purse, or more clothing, I smile (after asking how much she spent), then meditate on "according to knowledge." . . . But she and I enjoy going out. So as long as I am open with her about our not spending so much, and she is open with me when I get too "cheap," we balance quite well.

There can be no secrets. We do not lie to each other about financial matters. When she buys clothing, she doesn't sneak it in the house and hope that I don't notice. She tells me. When I buy something on the credit card (when I should have used cash), I tell her. When we had less money than what we have now, knowing exactly what was in the bank and exactly what needed to be paid was crucial. Once we listed all of the bills, we had to call some creditors and ask for a reprieve on that month's payment. But if we did not know all of those we had, we would not have known which bills we could pay.

Openness is essential to any financial plan within a marriage; openness about your feelings and openness about your spending. All too often, couples break up because of their lack of candidness, not because of their finances.

Community Involvement

My wife and I believe in the principle of reciprocity—we reap what we sow. We both are involved in several community organizations. It is taxing and time-consuming. The hours that we spend away

(*continued*)

from our family home and each other grow when we contribute time to other projects. But giving to others is part of our modus operandi. We do it because it is a blessing to others. But also, it enhances our relationship, which helps us fine-tune our financial planning because we are working together as a team.

I can't say that I am no longer frugal—I am. However, my frugal mind-set is often offset by our vision of what we both want as a quality of life for ourselves and our son. In the years ahead we must begin to incorporate into our budget an education for Jeremiah and perhaps even a new home with a larger backyard (and more grass to cut!). There will be new goals and new desires, but as we look ahead we now know how to accomplish what we want. It may take just a little longer, but we will enjoy what we get with the confidence of knowing that what we have is the result of sound financial decisions.

RYAN MACK'S FIVE ECONOMIC EMPOWERMENT TIPS FOR MARRIED COUPLES

1. Fill out a budget with your mate and regularly monitor your spending. There is nothing wrong with one of you splurging to go shopping every once in a while; just be sure that you put this splurge in the budget.

2. There is no right or wrong way to feel about your finances. What is most important is that you communicate so that there are no surprises. Nothing is worse than finding out that your spouse has an account on the side without your knowledge. It might have been perfectly fine to have the extra capital if it was discussed, but since it was kept secret, it becomes an issue. Make a list of individual and couple goals that you would like to accomplish in life and discuss this list once or twice per month to monitor the progress on these goals. The beautiful thing about marriage is that you don't have to do these things by yourself; you have an in-house helpmate. It is important that you don't let financial matters be a barrier between you in your relationship. If done right, finance can be used as a tool of bonding as opposed to separation.

3. Prepare your estate by filling out estate workbooks together such as "Set Your House in Order," which you can order at www .crown.org. These workbooks are great because you can compile

all your important financial and personal information and items such as checking, savings, investment accounts, mortgages, insurance policies, birth certificates, marriage certificates, jewelry, and safe-deposit key in one place. These workbooks also provide a place to outline final wishes and arrangements. The last thing that you want your mate to have to do if something should happen to you is to run around looking for important information while in mourning.

4. Review your insurance coverage every year to be sure that you are both adequately covered should something happen to the other. This includes health, life, disability, renter/homeowner, personal liability, and auto coverage.

5. Never let a week pass when you don't sit and talk. Plan outings to force you to stay in constant communication with each other. Perhaps you could go to church on Sundays and go out to brunch afterward.

CHAPTER SIX

Step One: Getting Your House in Order—Achieving and Maintaining a FICO Score Above 750

A WOMAN WANTS TO PURCHASE A HOME AND IS DENIED A LOAN; A YOUNG COLLEGE graduate is denied an apartment; a husband is told that he has to pay much more than he has budgeted for a life insurance policy; a young man has his dreams crushed when he doesn't get a job . . . what could be the common thread in all four scenarios? They all had a low FICO score.

A FICO (Fair Isaac Corporation) score is a three-digit number that determines the interest you will pay on your credit cards and even determine's whether you will get that new apartment or home mortgage. Knowing how to improve your FICO score is one of the most important factors in clearing up your credit. Approximately 11 percent of the U.S. population have a FICO score above 800, 29 percent have a score between 750 and 799, and over 30 million have a score under 620. Your goal should be to be above 750.

FICO Score	Rating
750+	Great—should qualify for most prime-rate loans
720–749	Good—might not qualify for prime rates
680–719	Average—should be built up ASAP
620–679	Below average
619 and under	Poor

Five elements determine the FICO score. They are listed below along with their weight of importance.

1. Record of paying bills on time: 35%
2. Total balance on your credit cards and other loans compared to your total credit limit: 30%
3. Length of credit history: 15%
4. New accounts and recent loan applications: 10%
5. Mix of credit cards and loans: 10%

Number One. Always pay your bills on time. There are no excuses for late payments. As soon as I receive a bill, I pay it. This was a difficult habit to establish because instinct says to hide a bill on the dresser under a pile of other envelopes and avoid it like the plague. Another bill-paying strategy is to designate a day of the month to pay every bill. No matter what you are doing, stop and pay your bills. The only downfall to this is that if sometimes you miss that day, it leaves room for procrastination. If the fixed monthly cycle is your preferred strategy, designating two days a month might be more appropriate. Better still, just pay bills as they come. It feels better, and you don't feel the stress of the buildup of unpaid bills on your dresser.

Number Two. Your debt-to-credit-limit (D/C) ratio accounts for a high percentage of your FICO score (30 percent). Let's say you have a $3,000 balance and a total credit limit of $6,000 among all of your credit cards. Your D/C would be 50 percent ($3,000/$6,000). If you pay off a $1,000 balance on one of your cards (Card A), with a credit limit of $2,500, I would advise you to *not* cancel Card A. If you cancel Card A, your credit limit will decrease from $6,000 to $3,500 (remember, you had a $2,500 limit on the card). Since you just paid $1,000 of your total balance owed, that balance decreased from $3,000 to $2,000. Your new D/C ratio would now be 57 percent ($2,000/$3,500), an increase from 50 percent. The result of your presumably responsible behavior of bill payment and debt reduction would be an increase in your debt-to-credit-limit ratio and a decrease in your FICO score. The best move after paying off a credit card balance is to simply cut up your card and leave the credit line open.

Number Three. Your credit history is important as well. If you must cancel a card, make sure you cancel the newest ones first. The Fair Isaac Corporation has more points of data to determine your FICO score the longer your credit lines have been open. Protect those cards you have with the longest history. If you must cancel a card, cancel one card, then wait three months. At the end of the three months, see if your score was negatively affected. If it wasn't, do the same for each additional card you want to cancel.

Numbers Four and Five. Be careful not to apply for too many cards at once, which sends a red flag to lenders. Steer clear of too many retail cards as well. When you are at the sales counter at Nordstrom, it can be tempting to allow the checkout clerk to talk you into a credit card that will open the door to "extreme savings," although it should really be called extreme spending. In their book *The Millionaire Next Door,* Thomas J. Stanley and William D. Danko mention the most popular credit cards of millionaires. The top five credit cards of millionaire household members, and the percent of millionaires who own these cards, are:

1. Visa (59%)
2. MasterCard (56%)
3. Sears (43%)
4. JCPenney (30.4%)
5. American Express Gold (28.6%)

Why? you ask. The truly wealthy realize the lack of need for retail credit card traps. They use cards responsibly and with caution so as not to accumulate unnecessary, overpriced debt.

Lenders like to see a good mix of installment loans along with your credit cards. Installment loans, such as those for your car and house, show just how reliable one can be, especially if payments have been made for an extended period and are timely as well.

CLEANING UP YOUR CREDIT REPORT

As many as 75 percent of all reports have errors on them, such as a wrong address, wrong amount owed, an old debt that was already paid but not updated, etc. It's easy to rid your credit reports of errors. You first have to obtain your credit report. You can get them online at www.annual creditreport.com or you can call 877-322-8228. The three biggest bureaus are Equifax, Experian, and TransUnion. You want to make sure you get all three since many lenders report to only certain bureaus. If you get these three, you have the bases covered.

Once you have your reports, you should call and challenge any error you see on them. This usually takes a while to complete. The bureau has thirty days from the time they receive your report to investigate the challenge. They will contact the company to verify that the information is correct. Upon doing so, they will report back to you that the information will either stay on the report or be taken off. If it is to stay on, and the information is not erroneous, it is up to you to deal with the company directly to pay or negotiate the debt. (Back in December of 2004, legislation was passed that made companies liable to respond quickly to all challenges with all pertinent information.)

Disputing Claims

Under the Fair Credit Reporting Act (FCRA) you are provided protection and have the right to the accuracy and privacy of the information within the files of the nation's consumer reporting agencies. Disputing claims is a great way to clean up your report. Here are three steps on how to do that:

Step One: Sending a Dispute

If you find an error, tell the consumer reporting company what you feel is inaccurate. Do this in writing so that you can make copies for yourself and begin to build a record. Below is a list of items that you may want to provide to the consumer reporting companies to dispute the claim on your report:

- A letter that clearly identifies each item that you dispute in your report. The following questions should be answered within this letter (see also the sample letter on page 114):
  - What are the facts?
  - Why exactly do you dispute this information?
  - Would you like this information to be removed or corrected?
- A copy of your report with the items circled that you would like to be removed or corrected.

Be sure to keep copies of your dispute letter and all enclosures. Send the letter by certified mail with "return receipt requested" so that you will know exactly when the consumer reporting company received your information. If you ever have to defend your reputation to the consumer reporting companies, to credit bureaus, or in court, your paper trail and records will come in handy.

Unless it considers your dispute to be frivolous, you will get a response from the consumer reporting company within thirty days. Upon receiving your dispute, it will forward that information to the organization that originally provided the information to the consumer reporting company. If you are disputing a claim from Macy's, say, upon receipt of your complaint from the reporting company, Macy's must then investigate the dispute and provide all relevant information about it to the consumer reporting company. If Macy's finds your records to be accurate, they must send a notice to all three consumer reporting agencies immediately to update their files.

Step Two: After You Receive a Response

If you got the correction on your report, that is great news, but the work doesn't stop there. Have the consumer reporting company send notices of *any* corrections to anyone who received your report within the last six months. If you were declined for a position because of your credit—which is happening more frequently these days as employers use credit as a means of judging your responsibility—you can have a corrected copy of your report sent to any potential employer who received a copy of your report within the past two years.

Did the dispute return unchanged or unresolved? Don't be discouraged. Ask the consumer reporting company to include a statement of the dispute in your file and for future reports. You might not want to at this point, but if your dispute is unresolved, you can, for a fee, request that your report with an updated statement of dispute be sent to any person who received a copy of your report in the recent past.

Step Three: Send Your Dispute to a Creditor or Information Provider

In addition to disputing the claim through the consumer reporting company, you should also send the same letter and enclosures, through certified mail with "return receipt requested," to the creditor or information provider. If you are found to be correct, the creditor may not report the item again.

Sample Dispute Letter

Date
John Smith
John Smith's Address

Complaint Department
Company Name
Company Address

To Whom It May Concern:

I am writing you to dispute some information in my file that I have found to be incorrect (or want removed). I have taken the time to circle all of the items I am disputing, and you will find them in the enclosed copy of my most recent report.

The following item(s) are disputed:

- Name of source as seen on credit report
- Type of item (judgment, credit account, etc.)

The item(s) listed above is (are) incomplete (inaccurate) because (use this section to describe what is incomplete or inaccurate and why in as specific language as possible). I am requesting that the item be removed (or changed) to correct the information.

I have enclosed copies of documents that support my position, including (use this space to describe which documents you are using in support, such as payment records, receipts, judgments, etc.). Please investigate this matter (these matters) and delete (correct) the item(s) disputed as soon as possible.

Regards,
John Smith

Reporting Identity Theft

If you see errors on your credit report, you may have been a victim of identity theft. Below are four easy steps to follow if you feel that you have been a victim.

Step One: Contact all the three credit bureaus and ask that an extended fraud alert be immediately placed on your account. After this is completed, all creditors will be required to contact you directly before any new credit in your name is granted. Technically, if you only contact one bureau, it will immediately share this information with the other two; however, I would call all three to be sure. Below are the numbers for the fraud divisions of the three credit bureaus.

Equifax: 800-525-6285
Experian: 888-397-3742
TransUnion: 800-680-7289

Step Two: Close all accounts that have been fraudulently accessed or opened by calling the security department of the appropriate creditor or financial institution. When setting up new accounts, make sure that you also create different passwords for them. Be sure that all new passwords have a good mixture of letters and numbers to ensure their security.

Step Three: File a criminal complaint with your local police department. Even though you may never be able to catch the crook who stole your identity, that criminal complaint document will go a long way when cleaning up your reputation with creditors.

Step Four: Report the theft at the ID Theft Clearinghouse at 877-IDTHEFT (877-438-4338). You will be advised by professional counselors on how to deal with credit-related problems that could result from ID theft. This hotline, as well as the ID Theft Web site (ww.ftc.gov/idtheft), provides you with a place to report the theft to the federal government as well as to receive helpful information. They will direct you on how you can fill out an ID theft affidavit as well as provide you with other useful information.

Seven Steps to Clean Credit

Some companies promise to improve your credit score in nine to twelve months. That sounds great until you find out they will charge you $700 to do it! To be in debt and pay money to raise your FICO score is like trying to drink water to stop from drowning—it only makes things worse.

In the hopes of saving you $700, here are seven steps to cleaning up your credit yourself.

Step One: Conduct Basic Housekeeping of Your Credit Report

- Seventy-five percent of all reports have errors on them. You are allowed to obtain one free report per year from each of the credit agencies (Equifax, Experian, and TransUnion). Go to www.annual creditreport.com and obtain your free copies of your reports.
- Get rid of any small balances that you have forgotten about.
- Dispute all claims that you feel are incorrect. (See page 112 for further explanation.)

Step Two: Pay Your Bills on Time

- Thirty-five percent of your FICO score is your record of paying bills on time, and it is the most important component of the score.
- Use autopayment to assure that the money is automatically taken from your account to pay bills. Make sure that you have an efficient budget to have enough funds to cover all payments.
- If you are apprehensive about autopayments, then designate *two* Saturdays per month when you will wake up early to pay bills. Make sure that the Saturdays not consecutive (i.e., aim for the first and third Saturdays or second and fourth Saturdays). You want to have two Saturdays each month because this assures that you will not be late on any bills that have fluctuating grace periods, such as credit card bills.

Step Three: Pay Down Debts

- Carrying balances on your cards serves no purpose. Eliminate all balances on your credit cards as soon as possible.

- Avoid being seduced by credit card companies with their special offers. You will never hear of someone becoming a millionaire because their credit card company offered them frequent-flyer miles.

Step Four: Do Not Cancel Old Accounts

- Thirty percent of your FICO score is your debt-to-credit-limit ratio. If you already have the account open, canceling that account can lower your FICO score as described above.
- Fifteen percent of your FICO score is your length of credit history. The older the account, the more weight is has on your FICO score. For instance, if you have a credit card that has ten years of history on it, you would want to keep that account open versus a card that has less than one year of history. Creditors like seeing a long track record, with which they can more effectively evaluate performance.

Step Five: Don't Fear Credit Counselors

- Going to a credit counselor or a credit consolidation agency is not viewed negatively by FICO.

Step Six: Steer Clear of Bankruptcy

- Bankruptcy is even harder to file for as a result of new legislation passed by George W. Bush.
- Two hundred points can be deducted from your score.
- This will stay on your report for ten years.

Step Seven: Be Patient!

- Nothing happens overnight. This process will take time.

In addition to the seven steps above, here are some extra tips for you to implement as you are improving your credit.

Clean Credit Quick Tips

- Always ask potential lenders if they subscribe to credit bureaus. You want credit for paying on time.

- When paying off delinquent bills, get something in writing stating that you have taken care of the problem. Make copies of the letter and the canceled check and send them to the credit bureau.
- Clean up any liens immediately.
- Carefully close inactive accounts if you have too many. Make sure they are labeled "closed by consumer" on credit reports.
- Pay off as many bills as possible to reduce debt load.
- If you can't get approved for a loan, think about coming up with a higher down payment.
- For any black marks with good explanations, write a letter concerning them to the credit bureau and have them affix it to your report.

Your credit score is your ticket to many things in your life. Whether you can buy a house, the interest rate on your mortgage, your car payments, your ability to get business loans, whether you get that new job, and even the amount of insurance coverage you can get can all be negatively affected by a low FICO score and bad credit. Start today and get your credit in order.

VILLAGE VISIT

The Power of Good Credit: The Nonprofit

A nonprofit organization does the work that the government would love to be able to do, but doesn't have the size, infrastructure, or ability to do. Nonprofits provide humanitarian efforts to society simply because of the need for them. Organizations that feed the hungry, clothe the homeless, educate the poor, train the formerly incarcerated, and empower youth are extremely valuable to the village. I urge everyone to find at least one nonprofit in the community and support that organization through volunteering or funding consistently; or, create one that you feel can address a need that is not being met.

Steve Loflin is the founder of the National Society of Collegiate Scholars (NSCS), an organization that recognizes academic excellence, fosters leadership, and creates service opportunities for students to be

(continued)

able to give back to their communities. Some seven hundred thousand students around the world belong to NSCS. I placed Steve's section in the credit chapter because he got funding to expand his organization because of his great credit score at a young age.

ONE MILLION LEADERS FROM ONE MAN
by Steve Loflin

It all started with an idea.

In 1993, I was director of campus activities at George Washington University and couldn't help but notice that there were no honor societies for first- and second-year college students. I thought that there should be an organization that would not only recognize their academic excellence, but also foster leadership development and service opportunities, as well as provide a host of other benefits for members.

I invited two students to help brainstorm on what such an organization might entail. We decided that it would, at least eventually, be a national society, and the society's three pillars would be scholarship, leadership, and service. It should also be an organization of, for, and by students. This organization would be called the National Society of Collegiate Scholars (NSCS). With the basic concept in place, the question became "How do we start this?"

I used my good credit to secure a credit card for the organization. I was good with my own finances, and that stability carried over to financing NSCS.

In February 1994, invitations were sent to all first- and second-year students who had achieved a GPA of 3.4 or higher on GW's 4.0 scale. Upward of 120 students chose to join, paid their dues, and were inducted on April 30, 1994, what is now known as Founder's Day. The new members were recognized for their scholastic achievement and were given hand-signed certificates of membership. NSCS was officially alive.

As it is an organization of, for, and by its members, I firmly believed that NSCS should have member representation on the board of directors. I recruited applicants for the first NSCS student representative

(continued)

to the board. Susie Albrecht, the chapter president from the University of South Carolina, became the first person to serve in that position. Only two others would fill that position, as it would eventually be replaced with the National Leadership Council (NLC), a much more comprehensive means of connecting chapters and members with the national office and with the board of directors. The NLC has fifteen members, selected each year. The president and the executive vice president sit on the NSCS board of directors. The president of the NLC is a voting member of the board.

Change and growth were on the horizon for NSCS, as 1998 saw the organization go from volunteer to having five full-time employees. On July 1, 1998, the new NSCS offices opened, with the mission of developing new chapters, supporting existing chapters, and developing opportunities and benefits for members. By May 1999, forty-three NSCS chapters were on the roster. Students from around the country and from all walks of life were joining NSCS and forming active chapters. These chapters were hosting Halloween parties for underprivileged children, sponsoring families for Thanksgiving dinner, and visiting nursing homes during the holidays. Indeed, NSCS members had begun to make a difference around the country.

In the years since, the full-time staff has continued to grow and is currently at twenty-one. The number of chapters has grown to more than 240. After the opening of a chapter in Alaska, we now have a chapter of NSCS in every state, the District of Columbia, and Puerto Rico. Members have an array of opportunities and benefits from which to choose, including a host of scholarships and discounts. Chapters are given resources and encouraged to use these funds for activities and service projects. Members and chapters alike benefit from the national organization's many partnerships with other groups, such as Teach For America, America's Promise, National Youth Leadership Forum, and the Semester at Sea program, to name a few.

I remember the value of finding creative ways to make educational opportunities a reality. NSCS currently provides the most undergraduate scholarship dollars—nearly $250,000—of any honor

(continued)

society. I am working with NSCS staff to grow this fund, and it is our goal to provide $750,000 in scholarships by 2012.

It's been an exciting experience watching NSCS grow from an idea to a small group of students on one campus to having a national office staff and more than 240 chapters in every state, all in fifteen short years. As our early alumni are now well into their professional lives, we are looking at developing opportunities for NSCS alumni.

I remember being told when I originally shared my idea for creating NSCS that it would never work. I am proud to say that I did not listen to those folks. I am eager to see where we end up in another fifteen years. After all, it all began with an idea and the belief that anything is possible. Our amazing members have made that possibility into reality and have formed one of the greatest higher-education honor societies.

NSCS now generates more than $5 million annually, and we are on track to be a $7.5 million organization by 2012. I was recently told that I didn't just start an honor society but a movement of high achievers. Because I believed in what could be, we are now positioned to reach our goal of 1 million NSCS members by 2012. It has truly been inspiring, and an honor, to watch it grow.

RYAN MACK'S FIVE ECONOMIC EMPOWERMENT TIPS FOR NONPROFITS

1. If you are starting a nonprofit, understand that it is not just like a business, it *is* a business. Most of the same rules still apply, except for how your business will be taxed.

2. Are the programs that you created able to run without outside funding? How? If you can answer yes, you are many steps in the right direction in being able to obtain private and public funding, as both individuals and government entities are becoming more concerned that the programs they fund be sustainable and replicable.

3. If you aren't good at keeping records, work for another already established nonprofit in your community. If you can't provide records of how your money is being spent, nobody will want to give you any money.

4. Have you taken care of all of the legal requirements of the nonprofit? Have you received your article of incorporation, filed your bylaws, and registered to raise funds?

5. Make sure that you build an effective board. I know that your mother and father agreed to help you out and serve, but if you have too many family members on your board and not enough who are unrelated, the IRS might mistake your nonprofit for a foundation, which receives different tax treatment.

CHAPTER SEVEN

Step Two: Eliminating All High-Risk Debt

DEBT IS LIKE A SLIPPERY SLOPE—YOU CAN SLIDE DOWN EASILY, BUT IF YOU WANT TO climb back to the top, it can feel dang near impossible. High-risk debt is such a slope. What exactly is high-risk debt? It's any debt that has an interest rate that can go sky-high if you don't pay it back. Examples are cash advances, payday loans, monies owed to the IRS and collections, and credit card debt (the most common type and the primary focus of this chapter). These debts and their high interest rates that give consumers a headache are the primary reason that most Americans operate their household at a deficit. It is hard to get ahead in your savings if all of your capital is going to fill the pockets of your credit card company through your interest payments.

USING AND SELECTING THE RIGHT CREDIT CARD

Once, I was coming home from a trip and was walking through the airport. An airline sales rep was handing out applications for the airline credit card. I was annoyed and was about to walk away until I noticed in the crowd two young college students. I was sure that they didn't know that, as we just discussed in the previous chapter, 10 percent of their

FICO score was related to additional credit inquiries. They didn't know that as soon as they filled out that credit card application, their FICO score would immediately decrease.

I walked over to the two young men and whispered to them, "Did you know that as soon as you fill out this application, your credit score is going to go down? I know that you don't know me from Adam, but I just couldn't help myself to not come over here and let you both know."

At first, the two young men looked at me as if I were crazy, but after I showed them my business card, they listened to what I had to say. As I was speaking to the two young men, a few others joined in for a lively discussion, albeit under our breath, so that the airline rep didn't hear us. It was quite a funny spectacle!

Many people believe that obtaining a credit card is as simple as filling out any application that you come across without any research. Because credit cards can become a major part of your budget and are so dangerous if used inappropriately, each decision to apply for a credit card should be deliberate and made with tremendous care. Below are what I feel are the most important things to keep in mind while selecting a credit card.

Whichever card you choose, do *not* use this card for everyday purchases. When you get a card, store it in a safe place in your home, where you are not tempted to utilize it frequently. The purpose of this credit card will be twofold:

1. To establish a credit history.
2. To give you extra protection in case of an emergency.

Establishing a good credit history gives lenders clear evidence of your being a responsible borrower and increases your ability to take out a loan to purchase a home, car, or many other things that are necessary, as we discussed earlier in the credit-improvement chapter. You want to be extremely careful. NEVER spend money, outside of an emergency, that you can't reimburse immediately. If you want to purchase a book and want to use your card to establish a credit history, don't buy the book if you don't have the funds to immediately pay off the bill. When I use my credit card, I charge the item, then no later than the following day I pay off my credit card. If you can't do that, then you do without the item (unless it is a serious *need* such as food, water, lodging, or clothing).

Second, make sure that you are able to get a sufficient line of credit. Ideally, the credit limit of the card should be able to cover at least three months of expenses barring an emergency. This card as an emergency fund should not replace your building of an emergency fund (you ought to be saving to establish six months of living expenses, and we will discuss this later in the book). Save, and use the card as a standby to whatever amount of emergency fund you have left to establish.

QUICK TIP: If you are not eligible to receive a credit card because of a poor or no credit history, you should apply for a secured card. This card is linked to a savings account that may be claimed by the issuer if the borrower fails to make the necessary payments. This arrangement provides collateral to "secure" the loan and allows the issuer to take on riskier clients. The issuer gives you a line of credit for the amount that you have deposited. You can then use your card as you would any normal credit card, and it will help you to establish a credit history. Go to www.bankrate.com and seek out the best secured cards with no fees and good rates.

Here are a few tips when looking at various cards:

1. Make sure that there are **no hidden fees** for having the card.
2. **Check the interest rate.** If you have a decent credit history, you should be able to get an introductory rate below 10 percent. This rate typically lasts for six months to a year. You might even be able to get a 0 percent rate for this period. Your FICO score is a key number in this situation. If your score is above 750, then you should be able to get an excellent rate. If it is below 750, you might benefit from getting your score above 750 and then applying for a card. You will be able to demand lower rates with such a high score and will be in the driver's seat.
3. **Figure out how they calculate the minimum due.** Cards calculate the minimum due by charging around 1.5 to 2.5 percent of the outstanding balance. The lower the number, the less you have to pay back per month. This can make a difference if you need the cash. However, the less you have to pay off, the more interest is allowed to build up. I strongly urge that you always pay off more than the minimum due when you can.
4. **Pay on time!**
5. **Look out for mistakes.** Many times credit cards double-charge you for items purchased, fail to record a payment, or charge too much interest on your balance.

NEW LEGISLATIVE PROTECTION FOR CREDIT CARD USERS

During the writing of this book, new legislation was passed for the benefit of those who use credit cards. This was the Card Accountability Responsibility and Disclosure Act of 2009. As of February 22, 2010, all credit card companies must:

- **Keep all due dates the same on your credit card.** Allows you to plan for your credit card payments each month without fear of being late because they have arbitrarily changed the grace period.
- **Provide you forty-five days' notice before they raise rates.** Allows more time to prepare for rate increases.
- **Implement stricter eligibility for adults under the age of twenty-one.** Eliminates much of the fear of college students being targeted for credit card offers as soon as they enter school their freshman year.
- **Not retroactively increases rates.** Credit card issuers are no longer allowed to raise rates on an existing balance unless the promotional rate has expired, the variable rate indexed has increased, or you have paid late by sixty days or more. Also, if you have a late payment on an unrelated account, issuers are no longer allowed to penalize you on your other current account balances. Furthermore, if you are more than sixty days late and your rates are raised, issuers must lower your rate to the preexisting rate after six months of on-time payments.
- **Get rid of double-cycle billing.** The practice of basing finance charges on the current *and* previous month's balance is no longer allowed. This allowed issuers to charge interest on balances that were already paid during the previous month.
- **Eliminate overlimit fee transactions unless previously approved.** There used to be a fee for going over your limit. For example, if you had a $500 limit and purchased an item on the card for $505, you were usually charged a fee. Under the new law, you must now give consent, and issuers cannot charge more than one of these fees per billing cycle.
- **Do away with "paying to pay."** In general, credit card companies are no longer allowed to charge a fee for cardholders to make payments on their cards. Previously, credit card companies took advantage of the ease with which you can pay your debt if you

use the Internet or the phone. It never made sense to me to have to pay a fee just to pay my debt. This practice is now ended, unless you are trying to expedite a payment, for which card companies are still allowed to charge a fee.

- **Provide longer notice.** Companies were required to send statements fourteen days in advance; they are now required to send statements twenty-one days before a payment is due.

Credit card companies are for-profit companies. The more you pay, the more money they make. The more irresponsible and uninformed we are, the more money they make. Most Americans spend more money than they make, and this is partly because of inflated debt from the misuse of credit cards. The buck should stop with you!

NEGOTIATING BALANCES OWED WITH CREDITORS

In every one of my workshops, at least five attendees will have concerns about dealing with creditors. With more than 700 million credit cards in circulation and an average credit card balance owed of $7,000, it is not hard to guess why so many people are having these concerns. Here are a few steps that you should take when negotiating your debt balance with your creditors, so they will be a little easier to deal with.

Step One: Take a Deep Breath . . . *Relax!*

Whenever I get a question about debt, it usually comes with this look of great despair. Listen, you are not the first to get into debt, and it is *not* a reflection of poor character. You have done nothing so wrong that your confidence should be shattered—as long as you are doing what needs to be done to handle the situation.

Step Two: Develop the Strongest Weapon

The strongest weapon is a good FICO score. Those who have the highest FICO score, 750 or higher, have an easier time getting their rates reduced and annual fees waived. Make sure that you are doing an all-out blitz on every step mentioned in the earlier chapter about improving your FICO score.

Step Three: Learn Your Rights

Debt collectors can usually sniff out an uninformed consumer, so make sure that you know your rights. Here are a few resources that will help you find how the most current laws impact you.

- **The National Consumer Law Center.** Call them at 617-542-9595 and ask for a "What You Should Know About Debt Collection" brochure. Their Web site is www.consumerlaw.org.
- **Your State Attorney General's Office.** Many laws pertaining to debt collection differ from state to state. Make sure that you know yours.
- **The Federal Trade Commission.** The Web site is www.ftc.gov. This site will provide you the rules that the debt collectors must abide by. They have a click-through labeled "Debt Collection" on the home page; this link will provide many rules that will assist you to become more knowledgeable.

Step Four: Lay Out a Plan of Attack

Before a climber scales a mountain, he will make sure to know exactly how high the mountain is, where the campsites are located, what the weather will be like, and everything else he needs to know to make sure that he reaches the summit. Can you imagine how frustrating it might be to just start climbing the mountain and not know how far you have to travel? The same goes for negotiating with creditors. Writing out all the debt that you owe is a crucial part of laying out your plan. Below is a sample table of the headline categories that you should put together before you begin negotiating:

Company Owed	Phone Number	Mailing Address	Due Date	Minimum Due	Balance Owed	Line of Credit	Interest Rate

If you haven't done so already from reading the previous chapter, you can go to annualcreditreport.com and get your credit information to obtain the amount of your debt owed. You should go to all three credit bureaus because they are each likely to have different information. Once you have written down all of the debts you owe, you are ready to begin negotiating.

Step Five: Play Hardball!

When negotiating, here are some rules to follow:

- **Your family is always first.** Never let a debt collector talk you into paying a bill that causes you to fall behind in paying for necessities for your family. If it is a choice between appeasing a nagging bill collector and feeding your family or paying your rent, the bill collector will just have to wait.

- **Always offer less than you can afford to pay.** Let's say that you owe $2,000, and after you do your budget you find out that you can afford to pay $1,500. Offer to pay less than that amount. Understand that usually after six months, the credit card company will write your debt off before the end of the year so they can declare it as a loss on their income tax. That being said, if they have sold the debt already, they have sold it for far less than you owe. Because the bank has already written off the debt as a loss, they might have sold your $2,000 debt for as little as $500. This is why many people are able to settle their debt for half of what they owe. In this case, if you offered $1,000 to the collection agency, they still would make a $500 profit. Always shoot low!

- **Keep your stories brief.** Just think about what it would be like to hear down-on-your-luck stories all day every day. This is why many times the people on the other end of the line seem cold and heartless . . . they have heard it all before. Save your lengthy explanations and stick to what you can afford to pay.

- **Keep private information private.** Debt collectors are going to try to obtain as much information as possible about you. The address of your job, your mother's home phone number, the phone number of your significant other, anything that you offer, *will* be used to contact you!

- **Tape the call if it is allowed in your state.** In most states, you are allowed to secretly tape the phone conversation. In the other states you are allowed to tape the call with the permission of the other party. No matter what, you want them to know that the call is being taped, as it will keep them honest.

- **Keep an accurate record of the call.** Make it a point to get the creditor's first and last name in such a way that he or she knows that you are taking note of it.

- **"Paid in full" is better than "settled."** Debt collectors can remove any negative items from your report, and this should be a part of the agreement. If you weren't able to get them to budge on terms, try to get them to state on your report "paid in full" as opposed to "settled."

- **Know *when* to negotiate.** Debt collectors are paid each month a percentage of the amount of debt they are able to collect. This is an incentive to have them call you frequently . . . the more they collect, the more they get paid. If you negotiate at the end of the month as opposed to the beginning, the debt collector will be more apt to want to give you a good deal to boost his commission check.
- **Be the squeaky wheel that gets the grease.** Many times negotiating depends upon not when you call, but whom you talk to. I have helped many clients by calling two or three times because the first person was having a bad day and wasn't willing to work with us. Don't get discouraged if the first person says no; never be afraid to call multiple times; and sometimes it is good to ask for the manager.
- **Get the agreement in writing before paying a dime.** If the creditors say that they will accept a $250 payment on a $1,000 debt, make sure that they send it to you in writing. While they are sending a letter, you send a letter to them as well outlining the full agreement of payment. Yes, you should also send them a letter, because you want to have a record of what *you understand* the terms of the new agreement to be and not leave it in the creditors' hands in case they make an error. Send the letter via certified mail so that you can get a delivery confirmation. No matter how much the debt collector pushes and pushes, nothing gets done until the agreement is solidified in writing.

None of these steps are guaranteed to work, but done together and aggressively, they will highly increase your chances of getting a better deal.

Debt-Elimination Strategies

A common question I get when discussing paying down debt is "Should I pay off my debt completely before I start investing in my emergency fund or saving in my 401(k)?" The answer to that is "It depends." Mathematically, a major wealth-building principle is to make sure that interest is always working for you and not against you. If you are earning 2 percent in an emergency fund but paying 15 percent on credit card debt, it makes numerical sense to pay off that credit card debt first.

However, if we spend all of our days paying down credit card debt and continue to see a big fat zero in our savings account, we can suffer what I like to call fiscal fatigue. Seeing growth in your savings account gives you motivation to keep going.

So when determining whether to pay down your high-risk debt or to invest in your emergency fund and 401(k), the answer is probably to do a little of each. After you have done your budget and determined that you have a $200 surplus (money left over after all expenses are paid), a 50/25/25 percent split could be appropriate. That means 50 percent ($100) of your funds going toward your credit card debt, 25 percent ($50) going toward your 401(k) (or possibly more if your company matches), and 25 percent ($50) going toward building your emergency fund in a high yield savings account (see Chapter 9).

The Snowball Method

One of the best ways to pay down your debt is the snowball method. This method uses all or the majority of your budget surplus to "attack" the smallest item of debt owed. After you eliminate this debt, your surplus is increased by the minimum payment of the recently eliminated smallest debt, and you use your newly enhanced budget surplus to pay down the next smallest debt owed . . . and so on. This method essentially allows you to build momentum as you pay, gives you motivation to continue, and forces you to organize your debt efficiently.

Ideally, by now you've organized all of your debt. Write out all of your debt on a sheet of paper from the largest amount owed to the smallest. Here's a sample:

Company Owed	Phone Number	Mailing Address	Due Date	Minimum Due	Balance Owed	Line of Credit	Interest Rate
Bank 1	XXXX	XXXX	1/15	$50	$4,200	$5,000	13%
Bank 2	XXXX	XXXX	1/15	$75	$2,500	$3,000	7%
Bank 3	XXXX	XXXX	1/15	$100	$1,400	$3,000	10%
Bank 4	XXXX	XXXX	1/15	$50	$500	$1,000	10%

In the snowballing method, once you have organized your debt, make sure that you have a sound budget to calculate your monthly surplus (the amount of money you have left over after all of your expenses are paid).

Your budget should include within it the minimum due monthly on each piece of debt.

Using the above example, let's say that you have $200 left over after expenses as your monthly surplus. You take the $200 and apply it to the *lowest amount owed*. In this example you would pay down Bank 4 debt by an extra $200. After two months of paying an extra $200 per month to your Bank 4 debt, you will have paid down the $500 and eliminated the Bank 4 debt. Now you have an extra $50 free because the minimum due on the Bank 4 debt was $50 and your entire surplus increases by $50 to $250.

Now you need to apply the $250 to Bank 3 debt. After four months of paying $250 plus the $100 minimum to Bank 3, that debt will be eliminated. Your surplus increases by $100 (the minimum due on Bank 3), and you now have a total of $350, which can be applied to the debt owed to Bank 2. After about six months, the Bank 2 debt will be eliminated, and you now should have a $425 surplus ($350 previous surplus + $75 minimum due on Bank 2 debt). In approximately nine months, if you pay $425 extra each month toward the debt owed to Bank 1, it will be gone. If you add the minimum due on that debt to your total surplus, you will then have $475 per month to invest in other areas.

If you notice, Bank 1 has the highest interest rate, but is the last to be paid off completely. That's okay—I have found the progress that people see and feel by actually eliminating debt is worth more in motivation than the extra money being paid in interest. When people can physically see a bill eliminated, it gives them a sense of accomplishment. Now, if you feel that you would rather organize your snowball strategy and pay your debt down from the highest interest rate first, that is your call. Just be aware of that fiscal fatigue that can come into play when you are paying the same debt down for months and still have multiple bills to be paid off. Either way, just keep in mind that you are doing the best thing for your financial health.

CHAPTER EIGHT

Step Three: Energizing Your Company Retirement Plan

WHAT IS THE DIFFERENCE BETWEEN ROSS PEROT, THE MULTIBILLIONAIRE, AND YOU? More than likely, you are paying a higher tax rate than he is! That's right, even though Ross Perot is among the top 1 percent in wealth in the country (net worth, $4.2 billion according to the Forbes 2009 Top 400 Richest List), he pays less than the average man's tax rate. The average man in the United States pays more than 20 percent of his income in taxes. Mr. Perot only pays 8.5 percent of his income in taxes, which means that, yes, your tax rate is higher than a billionaire's!

How does he do it? He uses every trick available to him, such as:

- He starts companies that provide him major tax loopholes. No matter how high you might think that corporate tax rates are, there are many more tricks to decrease a corporation's tax liability than you could ever believe.
- He purchases municipal bonds, which are tax-free investments. These bonds finance roads and bridges and may give you a 4 percent return. This doesn't sound like that much, but when you consider that it is tax free, Ross Perot can easily invest $50 million into them and earn an annual income of $2 million *tax free*!
- He purchases real estate, which has many tax advantages.

- Unrealized gains in stock are not taxable until you sell it. If I record unrealized gains of $5 million in my stock portfolio, I don't have to pay a dime in taxes until I sell and "realize" my gains. My net worth increased but my tax liability didn't budge.

Now, I know what many of you might be thinking: That sounds great, but it has absolutely nothing to do with me! Well, it actually does. Ross Perot uses every tool that he has to his advantage, but you don't have to be a billionaire, a millionaire, or even a "thousandaire" to do the same thing. You may not have the capital to purchase millions of dollars of municipal bonds, but you certainly have access to many tax-deferred vehicles such as an individual retirement account, a 529 college savings plan (both to be described in later chapters), and your company retirement plan.

The Benefits of the Company Retirement Plan

Tax-Deferred Benefits

One of the major benefits of the company retirement plan is that most are tax deferred. This means that you don't have to pay taxes now on the amount that you invest in your plan and get to "defer" them until later. This allows an individual to accumulate more money over time than she would in comparable investment accounts in which earnings are taxed each year. You don't get to defer forever, however. When you make a withdrawal, Uncle Sam comes for his money. Let me give you an example.

People earning $50,000 per year are in the 25 percent tax bracket. This means that they would have to pay 25 percent of $50,000, which is $12,500, in taxes to the government. However, if they contribute 10 percent ($5,000) of their income to a 401(k) (a common company retirement plan), they would only have to pay taxes on $45,000 of their income. So let's look at their tax savings for the current year because they invested in a 401(k).

	Income	Taxable Income	Tax Bracket	Taxes Paid
No 401(k) investment	$50,000	$50,000	25%	$12,500
$5,000 401(k) investment	$50,000	$45,000	25%	$11,250
Tax Savings				$1,250

As you can see, because of the investment in the 401(k) and the ensuing tax deduction, one is able to save $1,250 for that year in taxes.

Let's take the example a step further and figure out just how much we are able to save by investing that $5,000 per year, for thirty years, at a before-tax rate of 8 percent in a tax-deferred account versus in a taxable account.

	Annual Savings	# of Years Saved	Before Tax Return	Marginal Tax Bracket	Accumulated Savings
Taxable account	$5,000	30	8%	25%	$419,008
Tax-deferred account	$5,000	30	8%	25%	$611,729

As you can see from the chart above, the ability to defer taxes has an enormous benefit. In this example, one is able to accumulate almost $200,000 more savings in the tax-deferred account than in a taxable account. However, we have not calculated the amount that Uncle Sam takes out once the individual withdraws his funds. Calculating the taxes that must be paid according to the stated tax bracket (25 percent), we reach a final figure of $458,796, which is more than we would have had in the regular account. Also, considering that many during retirement are in a much lower tax bracket, the final figure may be much more favorable when you withdraw your funds. However you look at it, you make more money in the tax-deferred account, and the earlier you start, the more of a benefit you receive.

Diversified Investment Strategy and Asset Allocation

In 1986, a study by Gary P. Brinson, L. Rudolph Hood, and Gilbert L. Beebower appeared in the *Financial Analysts Journal*. It is now known as the (first) Brinson Study. After analyzing more than ninety corporate portfolios over almost ten years, the authors concluded that over 93 percent of the variation in the portfolios ending performances could be traced to asset allocation, or the mixture of assets in the portfolios. A separate study conducted in 1991 supported the original findings, proving that asset allocation was the single most important factor in determining portfolio performance over an extended time. In short, asset allocation in establishing an efficient portfolio should not be taken lightly.

A diversified portfolio through your company retirement plan essentially means that you do not have all of your eggs in one basket. This is important when you are investing. For example, let's say that you purchase just one stock . . . Nike (more on stocks in later chapters). You follow Nike, love Nike, and feel that it is a great purchase, so you dive into the stock market. If this is the only stock that you own, you are at the whim of Nike stock. If Nike has a strike at a major factory, a bad year of sales, or poor management, you are screwed. Consider what happened to Enron. Many of the employees of this energy company had as much as 80 to 90 percent of their portfolio invested in its stock. It is estimated that when Enron went bankrupt, the loss to the Enron employees' company retirement plans was $1.2 billion. Most company retirement plans have access to mutual funds (to be described in later chapters), which offer you access to a diversified selection of stocks that you can purchase through regular deposits within your plan.

Diversifying your portfolio is wise to mitigate the risk that is inherent in all investments. However, you can't diversify away the risk of some things, such as the weather, a rise in gas prices, a Fed increase in interest rates, or the weakening of the general economy. These things are called systematic risk . . . risk that is inherent in the market. However, some risks are specific to individual stocks that you own, such as management decisions, strikes, or poor marketing strategies, and you can diversify away from those. If you own Nike and its management makes poor decisions, this will not have an impact on the other stocks in your portfolio. This is called unsystematic risk (risk that relates only to Nike stock). The most diversified portfolio is one with no unsystematic risk and only systematic risk (market risk). This portfolio is essentially the entire market (later we will discuss how you can achieve this level of diversification).

Autopilot Investing

I have talked with hundreds of thousands of people across America, and *never* have I heard someone complain about putting too much into their 401(k) plan. For those in or near retirement, it is always the same statement: "If I would have known then what I know now, I would have started earlier and invested more!"

One of the best traits about the company retirement plan is its ability to go on automatic pilot. If we had to remember to send a check or make a payment every month to the 401(k), many of us would be in trouble. I could care less how you have to trick yourself to invest monthly, as long as you are doing it!

One word of caution: Do *not* assume that just because you are putting money in every month that you have fulfilled your responsibilities. You must also make sure that you are regularly opening your statements and monitoring your portfolio. Don't just receive the mail or e-mail providing you an update and throw the letter to the side, scared to open it. In addition to reading your statements regularly, at least once per year you need to look at your 401(k) to see if you need to adjust your allocation. For example, during your yearly evaluation, ask yourself if your own risk tolerance has changed from the previous year and if the market conditions have changed tremendously from the previous year. I know many people who are in their fifties and have the same asset allocation strategy that they had when they set up the retirement plan back in their early thirties. People in their early thirties and in the beginning stages of their career definitely should have a different asset allocation strategy from someone who is nearing retirement.

Dollar-Cost-Averaging Strategy

Many people try to predict the market. The chart below is a graph of the Dow Jones Industrial Average for eleven years (January of 1999 to September of 2010). If you look at the chart below, I will demonstrate why so many people lost millions by trying to predict the market.

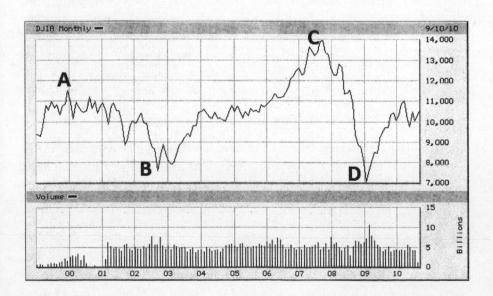

A. 2000: "The market will go up forever!"

During this period the economy had just gone through a rapid expansion. Unemployment was low and the market was on a tear that seemed to never want to end. I had friends who were day traders whose days went like this:

- 9:30 A.M.: The stock market opened and they would purchase stocks.
- 10:00 A.M.: They would leave to go play basketball and catch up with old friends.
- 3:30 P.M.: They would come home from a day of leisure and start to sell some of their stock positions.
- 4:00 P.M.: The market would close and they would have made over $10,000 for the day, if not more!

The lifestyle of easy money in the market went on for a few years. In 1999, to hear someone state that he had just made over $130,000 in a position from a penny stock was not uncommon at all. This transpired until many investors began to realize that investing in stocks because of their popularity but without doing research was not rational. Many stocks, especially Internet stocks, had never made a nickel of profit in their short lives, and should have been trading at less than $1 per share, but may have been trading at more than $100 per share (an explanation of the stock market is given in Chapter 12).

The Internet bubble burst, and on top of that the United States was attacked by terrorists on September 11, 2001. This caused a recession, and as you can see from the chart on the preceding page, the market continued to lose value until the end of 2002. All of those who had figured stocks would go up forever and purchased stocks in 2000 lost enormous sums in this recession.

B. 2002–03: "I will never buy another stock again!"

Those who got so scared from the recession began to liquidate their positions and sell everything. Everything was sold at the lowest price. Then, as you see in the graph, the market rallied from the end of 2002 through 2007, in one of the longest rallies in the history of the market.

C. 2007: "You can't lose in this market!"

The market continued to rise in 2007, and people continued to pour more and more money into stocks. Many started to believe (just as they had believed back in 2000) that no end was in sight for this rally. They played the market aggressively until the unthinkable happened—the subprime-mortgage crisis exploded, causing a tsunami within the financial markets and ushering in an extended recession considered the greatest since the Great Depression of the 1930s. Millions of people lost their entire savings.

The stock market wasn't the only thing that collapsed. When the market started to go down in 2000, the money didn't just vanish into thin air. Some kept it as cash while others started to purchase real estate and/or commodities such as gold. During the early 2000s, the real estate and gold markets were extremely hot, but the real estate market took a deep dive in 2007 as a result of the subprime-mortgage crisis.

D. 2009: "Sell everything!"

Scared that the bottom of the market would continue to depreciate into an abyss, every talking head and expert in the media was warning everyone to run for the hills in 2009. The market hit a low on March 9, 2009, and rallied over 50 percent in total value from that date. It wasn't hard to predict this rally because as a trader you learn to read public sentiment, and it becomes glaringly obvious when the public has become irrational. Warren Buffett said, "Be fearful when others are greedy, be greedy when others are fearful."

These "knee-jerk" reactions to buy at the highs of the market when we are exuberant, but sell at the lows of the market when we are scared, are the fastest way to lose money. This is why dollar-cost averaging is the best strategy and one that is automatically applied when you invest regularly within your company retirement plan.

Dollar-cost averaging is an investment strategy designed to reduce volatility in your portfolio. By purchasing securities in fixed dollar amounts over fixed intervals, regardless of what direction the market is moving, you invest regularly. For instance, if you are purchasing $200 of securities per month, when the market goes lower, you can purchase more stocks because the price is cheaper. However, when the market goes higher, the same $200 will purchase less stock because it is more expensive. Using the same chart for the Dow Jones from 1999 through 2010, those that dollar-cost averaged in their company retirement plan were able to purchase cheap stock during those years of the Great Recession, bringing down their average cost of the total amount of stock purchased.

How to Maximize Your Company Retirement Plan

Step One: Read the Package!

Too many times we get that huge, thick benefits package as we start a new job and are intimidated by its size and scope so it just collects dust in the filing cabinet. Don't sell yourself short; make sure that you read it in its entirety. No longer should we be scared of knowledge!

Step Two: Determine Your Asset Allocation

Too often I have seen people choose their asset allocation by pressing 20 percent five times in different slots by an investment that they know nothing about. Your asset allocation can be chosen by doing the following:

- **Complete an investor risk-tolerance questionnaire.** In this exercise you answer a few questions to determine how you would respond to certain market scenarios. This determines the level of risk that you are willing to take in the market. You can go to www.fincalc .com, which has a calculator to assist you in determining your risk tolerance. If you search Google for "investor risk tolerance questionnaire," you should get a few more options.
- **Analyze market conditions.** The market has a lot to do with what your risk-tolerance levels will be. I remember in 2000 when I invested most of my 401(k) in bond funds. These bond funds did really well from 2000 through 2003 as the stock market decreased in value, so I was not complaining at all.
- **Use an adviser.** Many times people fail to realize that an adviser that they independently hire can analyze their company retirement plan and help them to not only select the best investments but to choose the appropriate asset allocation. As a wealth-building principle we need to learn about the best places to spend our money. We will break down the door to spend $300 on a Play-Station during the holiday season, but we will cringe when asked to spend $300 for an adviser to have a look at a retirement plan that will determine (in many cases) the major component of our retirement.
- **Ask your company's HR benefits department for assistance.** This is tricky because the benefits department is best trained at hiring and firing people, not selecting asset allocations. However, they might

be able to provide you with some general information about which funds are the best fit for you.

- **Should you ask the fund manager?** This is a common question that many people ask. The answer is that it would be great to ask the fund manager if you could get access to the person. Many times those companies that provide your company with a retirement plan turn over the reins of control and questioning to the benefits department. While they might be able to provide you with advice, more than likely they are more concerned about quantity than quality; they are busy working to provide as many retirement plans to as many companies as possible, so to answer questions from one person when they are serving thousands or even hundreds of thousands would be quite impossible. This is all the more reason that a financial adviser would be great solution.

Step Three: Pick the Right Investments

Do not just pick any random investments. I remember a friend of mine asked me to look at her 401(k) for her. When she handed me the paperwork for her current asset allocation, I immediately saw an error. She had invested in a mutual fund that had the year (in this case 2007) in its name, which is a type of fund that automatically adjusts its investments to the age of the investor. She was only twenty-six, but she was invested in a fund that assumed she was within two years of retirement. Simple mistakes like that hinder the performance of one's retirement portfolio. I have an investment-selection strategy on page 206 for more stock/fund selection tips and strategies.

Step Four: Know the Rules

The rules for various company retirement plans vary from year to year. Make sure that you are aware of the rules within your retirement plan that pertain to you. I have listed a few below:

- **Contribution Limits.** In 2010 the total amount that an employee is eligible to contribute is $16,500 to a 401(k) or a 403(b). Employees over the age of fifty are eligible for a "catch-up" contribution. This contribution is there for those who have fallen behind and are close to retirement and feel that need to catch up in their retirement fund. This total amount of the catch-up contribution for the year 2010 is $5,500. So an employee over the age of fifty can contribute a total of $22,000 to their 401(k) or 403(b) plan. (The amount for 2011 will be announced in October 2011, which is after the publication of this book.)

- **Penalties.** Many people look at their company retirement plan as another savings account, but it is far from that. Just because your statement says $20,000, it does not mean that you have access to that amount. If you have a traditional 401(k) account, for example, you put that entire amount of funds in your account *pre*tax. This means that good ole Uncle Sam has not yet had a chance to dip into those funds. As soon as you decide that you want to take that $20,000 out of your account, you will be liable for both federal and state taxes on it. Depending upon your tax bracket, you might have to pay as much as $7,500 in taxes. Then, if you are pulling out those funds before the age of 59½, you will also have to pay a 10 percent penalty for early withdrawal.

- **Vested Funds.** I have seen people take out funds before they are fully "vested." As an incentive to stay with a company for a period of time, many companies provide a dollar-for-dollar match (up to a certain amount) of employee-contributed funds into the company retirement plan. However, many times for the employee to keep the funds that have been contributed by the employer, he or she has to stay at the firm for a certain period of time (often three to five years). If the employees leave before then, they are not considered "vested" and must return the funds. So using the above scenario, if you thought you had $20,000 in your account to withdraw, you may have taxes (federal and state) and an early-withdrawal penalty, and you may have to return company funds contributed if you are not fully vested; you may have less than $10,000 when all of the penalties are accounted for. Be sure to ask your benefits department before you decide to take funds out early. To take funds out of your account should be the absolute last option!

- **Borrow Wisely.** Many company retirement plans allow you to borrow against them, and you will often get lower interest rates than you will be able to get through a bank. However, I must remind all of you that this is a *retirement* vehicle and it was not originally intended to be leveraged. It is never wise to compromise the integrity of the vehicle, and I have seen many abuse this privilege. Also, be careful about borrowing funds if you're switching jobs; many times you will be asked to repay the loan within sixty days. Be sure that you are informed of all of the rules by your benefits department prior to making any major decisions regarding your company retirement plan.

Step Five: Don't Wait to Start

I have talked with thousands across the country who are near or in retirement, and I have never spoken to someone who stated that he or she put too much into the company retirement plan. It is always "I wish I would have put more in!" or "I wish I would have started earlier!" I have created a table below that demonstrates the power of compounding interest and the impact that waiting has on reaching your retirement goal.

The scenario below describes people who are thirty years old and have thirty years until retirement. They calculate that they can live comfortably off $1 million but haven't started investing yet. The table highlights how much they will have to invest annually (at an 8 percent rate) if they are to meet their goal. Notice the difference in the amount the longer they wait.

If You Begin Saving at Age	You Will Need to Invest This Amount Annually to Have $1 million in 30 Years at 8%
30	$11,933
33	$14,809
35	$17,195
40	$25,646
45	$40,531

As you can see, it makes a big difference to start earlier. If you have done your budget and can afford it, there is no point in waiting. Get some help, pay close attention to the rules, and start investing in your company retirement plan today!

VILLAGE VISIT

The Power of a Company Retirement Plan:
The Principal

The school is more than just a building that takes up a few square blocks in the middle of a community. The school is a place for the exchange of ideas, a farm of intellectual capital, and the cornerstone of this community. To unlock the enormous potential that lies within schools all across this country, commitment and leadership must exist within the school. The potential to bring together communities, to strengthen the bonds of families, and most important to educate our children depends upon the principal more than anyone else.

Richard Mack is my father. He is the modern-day Joe Clark as a principal—one who rules with an iron fist and a kind heart. I placed my father's story in the company retirement section because his ability to start saving early for his retirement relieved him of a lot of stress of trying to catch up in his later years. After he retired from Monnier Elementary School in Detroit, Michigan, he had more than enough in his tax shelter and 403(b) program to live comfortably. If you can ever get to the point where you are working not for the money but for the passion, I can promise you that you will be a lot less stressed and much more focused on the task at hand.

HEART BIGGER THAN A MUSTARD SEED
by Richard Mack Sr.

I was the second oldest of nine siblings. My mother worked at home and my father worked countless hours for the Chrysler Corporation. Despite his hard work, my father did not make a lot of money, so attending a major university would be totally my financial responsibility. I was set on being the first in my family to attend college, so I decided to work summers at Chrysler, as did my older brother. I utilized part of the money to help with family bills, and the remaining money was to be used to pay tuition, room, and board at Central State University.

Many students commuted to Central. However, several students, including me, paid only tuition and lived on campus as "homeless"

(continued)

students. We slept and ate when and wherever possible. We were known on campus as hannigans. It was fairly common for a student to be a hannigan for one semester until he could obtain appropriate funding for room and board. But always having to excel in everything, I finished my three and a half years at Central State University as a full-time hannigan. I held this dubious distinction with only one other Central graduate, an individual known as Wizz. (Wizz schooled me on the hardships of the hannigan lifestyle and summed it up this way: "Your heart has got to be bigger than a mustard seed." Truer words were never spoken.) On more fortunate evenings, I slept on the floor in the room of other students. On less fortunate evenings, I had to wait until all of the other students retired to their rooms and sleep in the TV room inside the dorm.

After a year of this lifestyle, I was easily recognized as being a hannigan by many people on campus, including the head dietitian in the cafeteria. On one occasion, after being banned from the cafeteria for two consecutive days, I finally managed to sneak in for breakfast. I was completely absorbed in my morning meal of sausage, eggs, corn-beef hash, sweet rolls, and any other breakfast food that the mind can think of, when suddenly, my meal tray began to slowly rise in the air. At first I attributed it to some sort of starvation-related hallucination, then I realized that someone was actually trying to take my food away. Never losing focus on my goal of satisfying my hunger, I pulled my tray back and looked straight into the eyes of the head dietitian, who was attempting some perverted game of tug-of-war with my food. My reply was a simple "No, no, no, not today!" Starvation has a way of making you take risks that you never thought possible. It's a wonder that an army of homeless people haven't marched in and taken over a Tim Hortons or the like. Anyway, she immediately called security and I was escorted to the administration building, but by then I had finished my breakfast.

This incident was reported to my mother, and we were both informed that I was never to go into the cafeteria or enter the dorms after hours. To do either would mean immediate expulsion. I interpreted this as an idle threat and assured my mother that I had a place to eat and sleep. From there it was business as usual for this hannigan. After all, I had no other choice.

(continued)

I had my obstacles though my college years, but it really seemed as if there weren't any that could prevent me from getting my college degree. Every problem had a solution. I continued my education and completed it despite all of the financial and personal odds against me and graduated from Central with a bachelor of science in elementary education. I later attended Wayne State University and received a master's in guidance and counseling and an educational specialist degree in administration. Not bad for a hannigan.

I accomplished many of my goals because, funnily enough, I never wanted to disappoint my mother. I achieved many of my objectives by often thinking of one of her favorite sayings: "Once a job has begun, never stop until it's done." I took this to heart and tried to let my life be the example, professionally and personally. And I guess it worked; my career blossomed, and I found myself constantly being called on by superintendents or assistant superintendents to help rejuvenate failing or troubled schools.

Monnier was probably my biggest challenge. Monnier was a neglected inner-city elementary school that the Detroit Board of Education had already scheduled for demolition. I entered Monnier's doors as assistant principal, a position I held for two years prior to becoming principal of the school. My initial observations of the facility left me disgusted and disbelieving. Classroom ceilings leaked water to the extent that several were in danger of collapsing. The restrooms were missing stall doors, and many of the toilets were broken. The lighting was extremely poor, and there was a severe shortage of textbooks and basic educational supplies such as paper, pencils, and chalk. To make matters even worse, a serious rodent and insect infestation posed an immediate health concern. The worst part of all, by far, was that this disease of neglect and indifference had spread so that, of course, students' academic performance was low. The school's silent mantra seemed to be "There is nothing that anyone can do to make it better, so why even try?"

When I was promoted to principal, my primary objectives were to improve the infrastructure of the school and the performance of the students. My first step was to transform the school building so that it was clean, safe, healthy, and attractive. My priority was to create an environment that promoted maximum performance by the

(continued)

students, one that all stakeholders—students, staff, parents, and the community at large—could be proud to be associated with. As the old African proverb goes, "It takes a whole village to raise a child."

I began from the inside out, first painting the interior of the building through fund-raising efforts, and purchasing uniforms for some of the school teams at Monnier. The students had been ridiculed at various sporting events and competitions by other schools for years. But I soon realized that was not enough, as one pivotal event showed me that I still had work to do before Monnier had the type of environment that everyone would be proud of.

One evening, I was waiting outside Monnier for a school bus returning with a busload of students from a chess competition. The bus included students from Monnier's newly formed chess team as well as from several other schools that had competed. I noticed my Monnier students immediately, as they were wearing their new uniforms, which included blue cardigans with a gold emblem that read MONNIER CHESS TEAM. It made me proud to see them. Then I noticed one student, named Sarah, was crying. I could only assume that she had lost her match, so I was pleasantly surprised when she assured me that she had won. But her tears were for something much bigger than a lost chess match. When the bus drove up to Monnier, the other students began to make fun of the building's poor condition, calling it a "raggedy old bootleg school"! I never wanted Sarah to feel ashamed of her school again.

Step number one was keeping Monnier's doors open. As I said earlier, the Detroit Board of Education had voted to demolish Monnier two years prior to my taking the position as assistant principal. But I proved to the board that the community obviously still needed a neighborhood school, and I got the needed funds for Monnier, which finally gave me the means to put into action the strategies that I had devised to improve the school.

I now faced the daunting challenge of changing Monnier's horrible image. To do this, I knew that I had to develop a comprehensive plan that involved everyone—students, staff, and community. I began by collaborating with the staff, who overwhelmingly voted to take the monumental step of becoming one of the first twelve Comer schools within the district. (Comer is named after James P. Comer,

(continued)

a noted educational reformer. He and his colleagues established an educational program that empowers the entire community—parents, teachers, and administrators—to become "stakeholders" and participate in developing a comprehensive plan for each school's individual goals.)

The new Monnier stakeholders met to assess the immediate needs, future goals, and the desired perception of the school. Everyone was was clearly striving for the same endgame: to educate the "whole child" in a nurturing, clean, safe haven that was productive and conducive to learning. All agreed that the immediate emphasis should be on improving the school's failing structure and visual appearance, thus improving the self-esteem of all students and staff. It seemed as though once the effort for improvements began, many others in the village were more than willing to help make these efforts a success.

Slowly but surely, we saw a positive change in the attitudes and perceptions from the community. The overall climate of the school markedly improved. Even skeptical older staff and community members were pleasantly surprised to see so many improvements taking place in such a short time.

An unexpected visitor appeared at my office door at Monnier to compliment me on the transformation of the school. He identified himself as a former student at Monnier who enjoyed driving around the school and the neighborhood whenever he was in town. The amazing difference in the appearance of the building since his last visit made him get out of his car to see the school's interior. He was so pleased that he donated $6,000 to the school and had signage placed at the front of the school that read MONNIER ELEMENTARY SCHOOL, WHERE EXCELLENCE BEGINS.

The positive changes at Monnier just continued to multiply. I had staff support, community support, and best of all the respect and support of my students. The school became so attractive and productive that Comer staff from other cities and states often toured the school as an exemplary of the Comer school project. The icing on the cake was the remarkable improvement in the students' MEAP [Michigan Education Assessment Program] scores. In one year the math scores rose 50 percent, reading rose 22 percent, and science rose

(continued)

an amazing 53 percent. This was the reality that I had imagined, that children in Monnier would have the chance to obtain the education that their parents would be proud of. They could rush home to show their report cards and, even better, carry knowledge with them that would serve them the rest of their lives.

Now that I have retired, the school sits empty, boarded up and poorly maintained, much the way it was when I came to it years ago. The best-laid plans are only as good as the actions that follow them. The fleeting but drastic transformation is all but forgotten, as many families have deserted the community, sending their children to other schools. It truly does take a whole village to raise a child, but even more, it takes many children to keep the village alive. Let us hope that we can emphasize the importance of both financial and social responsibility with our youth, so that they are able to make positive and lasting impressions in villages everywhere.

RYAN MACK'S FIVE ECONOMIC EMPOWERMENT TIPS FOR PRINCIPALS

1. As your job is already stressful, take the time to manage your personal finances responsibly. It is amazing how much stress can be added to your job when you are concerned about the unruly students that are constantly worrying Ms. Smith, the English teacher, *and* the stability of your retirement! I believe that at least a part of my father's success and ability to focus on the true needs of the school stemmed from his not having to worry about personal financial woes.

2. Bring in local community professionals to provide life-skills training for parents and staff. Organize the attorneys in the community to provide legal-rights training, the accountants to provide tax tips, financial advisers to provide personal-finance seminars, and so on. The local community will begin to see your school as a resource as well as a facility to educate young minds.

3. Teach good financial principles in your curriculum. Even at the age of six or seven, students are not too young to think about managing their money. The best way to learn something is to teach it, so create after-school programs where the older students can teach these newly learned principles to younger students. Create a school store that is run and operated by the students but

supervised by staff. Establish a partnership with a local bank that enables students to open up savings accounts. Allow the students to experience practical means of money management.

4. Learn the three D's of time management for your school, which are (1) Delegate, (2) Dump it, and (3) Do it. There are many things that you may be able to do yourself, but you are not Superman. Some things need to be dumped and some should be delegated. For instance, learning how to organize the school budget and applying for funds from the city, state, and federal governments is a full-time job that should be delegated to a qualified staff member. My father did this and was frequently able to have his assistant principal obtain funding while he dealt with unruly parents and staff.

5. Take time for yourself. Vacation days are there for a reason—use them. We know that you are passionate about your school, we know that things fall apart whenever you are away, and we know that nobody can run the school like you can. However, for the sake of your family, your school, and the village, we need you healthy to continue the good work in leading our schools.

CHAPTER NINE

Step Four: Establishing
an Emergency Fund

I TRAVELED TO DETROIT IN OCTOBER 2006, WHEN THE TEACHERS OF THE DETROIT public school system were on strike. Times were hard for them, and I offered financial-literacy courses to help them navigate through their struggles. The strike was not even a week old when many found themselves on the brink of bankruptcy, unable to support themselves without outside assistance. Their situation reminded me of an Aesop's fable, which reads:

THE ANT AND THE GRASSHOPPER

In a field one summer's day a Grasshopper was hopping about, chirping and singing to its heart's content. An Ant passed by, bearing along with great toil an ear of corn he was taking to the nest.

"Why not come and chat with me," said the Grasshopper, "instead of toiling and moiling in that way?"

"I am helping to lay up food for the winter," said the Ant, "and recommend you to do the same."

"Why bother about winter?" said the Grasshopper. "We have got plenty of food at present." But the Ant went on its way and continued its toil.

When the winter came, the Grasshopper had no food and found itself dying of hunger, while it saw the ants distributing every day corn and grain from the stores they had collected in the summer. Then the Grasshopper knew:

"It is best to prepare for the days of necessity."

Are you the grasshopper or the ant? Too many Americans don't think it's necessary to prepare for the future. I believe in making life easier, not harder. The emergency fund not only makes life a lot easier in times of economic strife, but imagine the security that people feel knowing that they have a cushion of savings in case they are laid off, their roof leaks, they are robbed, a family member becomes ill, or in case of any number of other unexpected occurrences that can cause a financial strain for them and their family.

How much of a cushion is enough? I think it is important to have six to nine months of living expenses saved. These savings should be placed in a high-yield savings account. *High yield* refers to the interest rate on the account. In a regular checking account, known to have as low as a .35 percent interest rate or 0 percent, you are losing money when you factor in inflation.

Inflation is the rise of the general level of prices in the nation related to the increase in the amount of money in circulation. The result of inflation is the loss of value of currency. Inflation is why you could buy a candy bar in the 1970s for a nickel but have to pay as much as a dollar at many stores today. Inflation is the reason that gas prices continue to increase, making it more expensive to drive. If you are keeping your money under the mattress, in a safe in the basement, or anywhere that is not earning interest, then your money is losing value as you read this. Putting your money into a high-yield savings account (more below) will ensure that your money earns interest that will outpace inflation, thereby retaining its value and even growing in real value. Good examples of high-yield savings accounts are ING Direct, Emigrant-Direct, and OneUnited Bank. However, don't take my word for it—visit www.bankrate.com for a listing of savings accounts with the highest yields.

Many of you might be thinking, "Six to nine months of living expenses?! I can barely make enough to pay the bills that I have now, much less save for six to nine months of living expenses!" If this is your mentality, you will never reach this goal. It is funny how when people want to save to purchase items such as a car, a television, that expensive necklace for a loved one for the holidays, or any other high-priced item, they seem to always find a way. One of those ways is by putting items on layaway. Why can't we force ourselves to "lay away" an emergency fund and act as if it is just as important as the flat-screen TV we have been wanting? Because it is, in fact, just as important.

MAKING MOLEHILLS FROM THE MOUNTAIN

Let's say that after you have done your budget, you have calculated your monthly living expenses to be $2,000 (use your budget to calculate exactly what your living expenses should be). This means that you should have an emergency fund of at least $12,000 in a savings account. This may seem like a huge mountain to climb because it is a lot of money, especially starting from zero dollars. We need to keep you motivated in doing this, so let's make "a molehill from your mountain."

Making a molehill from your mountain means that you might not be able to come up with $12,000 at one time, but you might be able to come up with $500. If you can just do that every month for the next two years, your emergency fund will be completed. This isn't including any tax refunds that you receive, bonuses at work, or any other unexpected windfalls that you can put toward your savings.

Quick note: If you feel that your emergency-fund amount is exorbitant, that could also be because you included too many expenses in the calculation for your emergency fund. In the example of $12,000 for six months of living expenses at $2,000 per month, you might have included expenses that you would definitely not be incurring in times of an emergency, such as eating out, shopping, luxury traveling, or biweekly visits to the spa. Your emergency fund should be for bare necessities and not those luxuries that you can afford to purchase knowing that you have a steady paycheck being deposited into your account. Most always, when you take out these excessive items, they will shave up to 20 percent or more from your calculated emergency fund.

I once watched an older gentleman who was worth over $2 million being interviewed on CNN. That might not sound amazing, but it is when you find out he had never earned more than $11 an hour in his life. He made sure to put money into a savings account monthly. He invested his money and lived beneath his means. We can learn a lot from him: Investing is not just for the rich, but for all income and age levels. The less you earn, the more important it is to be mindful of your expenditures. Less income means less financial protection to provide a cushion during financial setbacks (job loss, salary reduction, rising gas prices, or medical emergencies). Regardless of your income or financial position, it is up to you to begin saving toward financial independence today.

THE STRUCTURE OF YOUR EMERGENCY FUND

Now, you know it's important to have six to nine months of living expenses saved, but it is not so important to have it *all* in cash. Here is a breakdown of where these funds (using nine months' expenses) should be located:

One month of living expenses: These funds should be held in a checking account so that you have immediate access at all time. In the above example, you should have a minimum of $2,000 in your checking account. Once that amount is in the account, you shouldn't touch it, unless of course it's an emergency.

Five months of living expenses: These funds should be held in a high-yield savings account, and you should have access to these funds within one to three days without penalty or fee. In the above example, if your monthly living expenses are $2,000, you should have $10,000 in a high-yield savings account.

Three months of living expenses: These funds are not cash at all, but you have access to them in a line of credit through a credit card. As stated earlier, the only time that you should be using a credit card is to improve your FICO score or in the case of emergencies. So if your monthly living expenses are $2,000, you should have at least a $6,000 line of credit on a credit card in case of emergencies for when your cash reserves have been depleted.

What if you do indeed need to tap into the emergency fund? Where first to take out money from? Assuming that you have done everything possible to lower your monthly expenses, you should first tap into the cushion you have in your checking account; then tap the cash in your savings account. Only once those funds are depleted should you use your line of credit for your monthly living expenses.

SELECTING THE RIGHT EMERGENCY FUND

In a popular scene from a *Pink Panther* movie, an elderly man is sitting on a bench with a dog sitting next to him. A young man walks by and asks, "Hello, sir . . . does your dog bite?"

The elderly man states, "No . . . my dog doesn't bite."

The young man walks over to the dog, reaches out his hand to pet the dog, and the dog snarls loudly and bites the young man hard on his hand, causing it to bleed.

The young man grabs his hand in shock and yells at the elderly man, "I thought you said your dog didn't bite!"

The elderly man casually looks at the young man and says, "That's not my dog."

We always need to ask the right question, or we risk getting bit. This is true in finance and especially true when selecting an emergency fund. Below is a list of basic questions that should be asked and answered before you select a high-yield savings account for your emergency fund. (Sorry, these are just basic questions, so you will still need to read all those long, boring disclosures on the company Web site and sales literature.)

What APY will I earn in this account? APY (annual percentage yield) is the total interest you will earn on a deposit yearly. Note that online savings accounts have lower overhead than traditional banks; therefore, they will probably have higher savings rates than traditional bank accounts. Also, I am a strong advocate of joining local credit unions. Credit unions don't have to please shareholders, so they are usually able to provide higher interest rates on their savings accounts than traditional banks. Also, when you join a credit union you essentially become a part owner of this organization and reap the benefits, which include higher interest rates on savings, lower interest rates on loans that you apply for, and more effective services. Credit unions are not concerned about profits, because they are nonprofit organizations; they are only concerned about you. Check out www.bankrate.com to see which providers are offering the most competitive rates.

Is this account FDIC insured? One of the best programs that the Great Depression spurred was the Federal Deposit Insurance Corporation (FDIC). The massive number of bank failures forced the U.S. government to set up a safety net to prevent account holders from losing their money in a failed bank. So the FDIC insures deposits in banks as well as thrifts, which are depository institutions intended to encourage personal savings and home buying. The FDIC also supervises the risks associated with the banks that have its insurance and limits the negative impacts when a bank or thrift institution fails. The FDIC doesn't insure all banks and thrift institutions, so be mindful to look out for the FDIC logo before depositing any money.

At the time this book was being written, the FDIC insures up to $250,000 of the following kinds of deposits (because of the recent recession, the insurance limits were extended from $100,000 to $250,000. This extended coverage may not continue as the U.S. economy stabilizes, so keep up-to-date on the amount of coverage provided by the institution that you choose):

- Checking accounts
- Money market deposit accounts
- Savings accounts
- Certificates of deposits (CDs)
- Certain retirement accounts on deposit at a bank

Is this account protected under the NCUSIF? Credit unions also have protection that works in a similar way to the FDIC. The National Credit Union Administration (NCUA) administers the National Credit Union Share Insurance Fund (NCUSIF) to provide insurance for the deposits of credit union members of insured institutions. The NCUSIF was created in 1970 shortly after the creation of the NCUA as an independent regulator of credit unions. The beauty of the NCUSIF is that it is funded completely by participating credit unions, and taxpayers have never been called on to bail out a credit union. NCUSIF has the backing credit of the U.S. government for depositor amounts up to $250,000.

What are the fees of this account, if any? I remember reading the fine print on an account and discovering that if I didn't use these funds, or had a period of inactivity, the bank would begin to charge me a monthly maintenance fee. Ideally, you won't have *any* activity in your emergency fund because you only want to touch that account during emergencies. So make sure that you are aware of *all* the fees that are affiliated with that account. Inactivity fees, fees for dropping below a minimum level, withdrawal fees, and any other fees are required to be listed in the disclosure. Read it!

What is the minimum deposit required to open this account? Must this amount be maintained, and is there a fee if it isn't? Have you ever seen an ad for a savings account with an extremely attractive savings rate only to find out that you need to deposit $50,000 to qualify for it? Banks make money by taking your money and then investing it for a higher return. The more money they get from you, the more money they have the opportunity to earn. However, the less money you deposit, the less they earn. This is why many banks will charge a monthly fee on your account if you fall below the minimum level. Don't take it personally, it's only business. You have a right to shop around for those banks that don't have a minimum balance and don't charge a fee if you dip below a certain level. You can find out all of this information on www.bankrate.com.

Is there a maximum on the number of withdrawals allowed on this account per month? Some banks allow only so many withdrawals per month. This is important to know, but remember, we are talking about your emergency fund here, so your withdrawals should be limited. This *is not* a checking account for you; unless it is an emergency, you should act as if these funds don't exist. So just be cognizant of the number of withdrawals that are allowed. You never know what type of emergency you may have in the future, so it's good to have this information to help with your planning if/when that time comes.

Does this account provide 24-7 telephone banking services, and do I have 24-7 access to my account online? Are these services free? Because emergencies don't work with our schedule, you want to have access to your account twenty-four hours a day. If you need funds from your account because of a costly emergency, you don't want to have to wait until the morning during company hours.

Can I electronically link this savings account to my checking account for transfers? This convenience is provided by most banks and credit unions, and you want to be sure that your institution provides this. However, this blessing can also be a curse. Don't let the increased ease of access to your funds tempt you into dipping into your account for anything but an emergency. *No*, a sale at your favorite store that only lasts until midnight is *not* an emergency!

VILLAGE VISIT

The Power of the Emergency Fund:
The Corporate Professional

As much as the bigwig CEO would like to take credit for a company's success, a company is only as good as its employees. The professional worker can be found at Microsoft, on Wall Street, in the executive offices of Nike, or in the local accounting firm. Many people refer to them as the nine-to-fivers. No matter where they are found, as hard as they work is as fast as this economy grows, and we need them all.

Manyell Akinfe adds tremendous value to my company. We have

(continued)

been to prisons, with gang members, throughout the roughest neigh-borhoods of New York City, to teach the importance of financial lit-eracy, and she shows no fear. I placed Manyell's section in the emergency fund chapter because she was only able to fulfill her dream of getting into the field of finance by saving aggressively. Diligence and the sacrifice of small things to achieve great things is the path that she chose, and thousands have benefited as a result.

From Fashion to Finance
by Manyell Akinfe

I began my career in finance for selfish reasons. I was recruited right out of college to work in the buying offices at Saks Fifth Avenue, and although excited about getting my foot in the door at one of the most respected retailers, I knew I wouldn't be making enough money initially to cover my New York living expenses, pay off my student loan in a year, save money, *and* continue to feed my fashion addiction. I had to find a way to earn extra income. I could have stopped the frivolous spending, but my motto then was "If you want more, make more." As luck would have it, I met a financial services representative by chance and agreed to go to one of his meetings just on a whim, not knowing this meeting would change the direction of my life.

I considered myself a young progressive professional and hadn't learned any of the financial concepts the representative talked about in his forty-five-minute presentation. I was floored—and started asking myself tons of questions. Why hadn't anyone ever taught me this stuff? Why hadn't I learned it in high school or college? How many other people didn't have this information? By the end of the presentation I thought of more than twenty people I knew who could benefit from hearing the same. I was convinced that if people knew better, they would do better financially. These simple concepts could change someone's life. I felt this could be a perfect fit. I could learn something new, help people, and earn a substantial part-time income. It was a win, win, win.

I started small—I got together with my family and shared what

(continued)

158

I had learned. It made me more convinced that this was what I wanted to do—help people with their finances. I started conducting free seminars on what I had learned as a side gig. As I moved up the ladder at Saks, I started to think that I should put my merchandising career on hold and immerse myself in finance. I loved fashion and didn't want to throw away all the time and effort I'd spent building my reputation. And I would be trading in the safety of a salary to work on commission. For the next six months I tried to shake off the unexplainable joy I felt when helping a family get their finances in order or restoring hope in a family who thought it was impossible to reach their financial goals. What pleased me even more was the success I had with getting my peers on track. I not only understood how to keep them engaged, but I also knew how to move them to action.

Knowing God was pointing His finger toward finance but too chicken to step out on faith, I spent months praying on something to which I already knew the answer. I finally decided to leave my merchandising career and focus on spreading financial literacy and economic empowerment. My decision shocked most people. My friends felt it coming because I'd started talking about finance more than fashion. My mother, on the other hand, was a bit worried. She was from the school of "hold on to your good job and good benefits" and didn't understand why I was taking such a huge risk. My dad and brother, who are both entrepreneurs, were excited about the change and proud of me for following my heart.

Preparing to leave was not easy. The plan was to save enough money to cover my living expenses for one year. I gave myself a year and a half to make the switch. That meant no more $1,000 purses or $100 dinners. This was the first time I ever cut back my spending for the benefit of something bigger than me. It was humbling. I created a strict budget and stuck with it to meet my savings goal. I put my entire check in the bank minus my living expenses. Having no debt made it easier to save, but it was still tough. I told all my friends and family what I was doing so there would be no hard feelings when I turned down *all* invitations that required me to spend money. I continued to contribute to my 401(k) and treated myself once a month to something special. (Even in the midst of an aggressive savings

(continued)

plan I suggest treating yourself once in a while. Complete self-deprivation usually results in financial relapse, which usually leads to overspending.) I brought breakfast and lunch to work almost every day. I would go shopping over the weekend and come in on Monday to work with one or two bags of groceries to keep in the refrigerator. There was a running joke that I should start charging people to make their lunch.

Once I left Saks, I was able to hit the pavement running, spreading the financial good news. I became a serial volunteer. Making money was second to educating. I gave my all in every appointment and in every seminar. In the beginning, my clients were mainly young adults, but by the time I went full-time I was attracting a diverse clientele with a range of different needs. Because of the limited number of products my current company offered, I was turning away more people than I was comfortable with. I begin searching for a solution and discovered that if I truly had the client's best interests at heart, I needed to become a "fee only" adviser. This would give me the freedom to research which products and services fit each client best based on their income and goals.

Eventually I made it to Optimum, where I spread my wings. I organized seminar after seminar. I worked with children, convicted felons, substance-abuse victims, public-housing residents, and any other underserved demographic you can think of. These individuals could not afford my services, but that didn't mean they should have been denied access to this information. Financial literacy is deeper than stocks and bonds. Teaching these individuals how to develop a wealth mind-set and exposing the role faith plays in financial success inspired the entire community to push past its current condition.

My success with young professionals continued, and I wanted to do more. These were my peers, and no one on a national level was speaking to them. No company or organization spoke to the young urban professional; the group that were most likely first-generation investors, known for irresponsible spending and living to keep up with Joneses, were forgotten. They needed help, too, but because of the front they put up, no one knew. From the outside, this group seemed to have it all together, but in many cases they had the same level of literacy I see in public housing, prisons, and other impover-

(continued)

ished areas. Most of them were living for the now and found it hard to envision their financial future past knowing they wanted to make a lot of money. The few I came across that did have their finances in order came from families that discussed finances openly or learned by trial and error. I began pulling together all the ideas and feedback I'd collected over the years. I started analyzing my appointments with young adults and noted what moved them to action. I studied the approach of local and national financial literacy programs and read reports created by the President's Advisory Council on Financial Literacy and other agencies. After a year of research I developed the Money Movement.

The Money Movement is a social campaign designed to increase the financial literacy of young adults by embedding financial responsibility into popular culture. The objective is to create a trend of financial responsibility among adults ages twenty-one to thirty-eight. When I started the campaign, people didn't think it would work. I ignored all critics and focused on the vision God had revealed to me. The campaign now reaches thousands of people.

Individuals are able to join the Movement by signing a pledge declaring their commitment to achieving financial independence. Once the pledge is signed, they become an A-Lister. A-Listers understand the importance of financial literacy, pledge to become financially responsible, and promise to encourage others to do the same. To keep the journey of financial success exciting, the campaign partners with local and national retailers, restaurants, nightclubs, and other companies to provide incentives that are linked to how responsible A-Listers are with their money. The tagline for the campaign is "Ambassadors of Change," so in exchange for the perks of the campaign, A-Listers are responsible for hosting Mini Money Movements, which are designed to introduce the people they influence to the campaign and encourage them to get involved. I feel that we are causing a shift in how young professionals feel and think about financial literacy.

Trying to embed financial responsibility into pop culture is a tall order, and I have been selected to do it. Reflecting on my experiences, I see how everything was uniquely linked and intertwined to prepare me for this huge task. In my quest to become successful and wealthy, I almost forgot I was put here to serve. In my favorite

(continued)

book, *The Purpose Driven Life*, Rick Warren says, "What matters is not the duration of your life, but the donation of it." I thank God every day for the courage to follow the steps He lays on my spirit. My hope is that more people do the same.

Ryan Mack's Five Economic Empowerment Tips for the Professional Worker

1. Ask your boss to become a mentor. Ask him to name three problems that nobody has solved for him and show an interest by writing the responses down. This will help shield you in the days of layoffs.
2. Find a mentor outside your workplace who will help you in all aspects of your career. This is different from your best friend. Your best friend will tell you when you are right, but a mentor will also tell you when you are wrong. A best friend is comfortable with your past, but a mentor is concerned about your future.
3. Start as early as possible to save for retirement. I have *never* heard people say upon retirement that they put too much into their 401(k) plan.
4. Start to keep a weekly log that takes note of all of those extra things that you have done at your workplace to make yourself indispensable. If you do not have at least three things each week, you need to step it up.
5. Always look for the next educational or training course to improve upon your skill set. If you can't use the skills at this current job, you will have improved your résumé and might be able to use them elsewhere. If they don't offer to pay for training courses at your workplace, sign up for an occasional night course at the local community college.

CHAPTER TEN

Step Five: Establishing an Individual Retirement Account

IN COLLEGE THE TERMS *TAX-DEFERRED SAVINGS* AND *INDIVIDUAL RETIREMENT AC-count* not only seemed foreign and intimidating to me, it was like watching paint dry to read about them. I felt this way until I started to accumulate funds in my own IRA and started to personally see the benefits of tax-deferred savings. So, I know this isn't the most exciting information, but when you feel yourself drifting off, just realize that this information can help you save tens or hundreds of thousands of dollars for your retirement!

WHAT IS AN IRA?

There are many different types of IRAs, including the following:

- **Traditional IRA.** This is an individual retirement account that allows individuals to invest income, within specific annual limits, toward investments that can grow tax-deferred. If you are an individual taxpayer, you are allowed to contribute 100 percent of your income up to a specified maximum dollar amount into this account. Depending on the taxpayer's income, tax-filing status, and various other factors, the contributions to the traditional IRA may be tax deductible.

Let's say you are earning $50,000 per year in gross income. You would be in the 25 percent federal tax bracket, which means that $12,500 of your money would go to taxes. However, what if someone told you of a way that you could legally avoid paying taxes on a portion of your total income? If you put a certain amount, such as $5,000, into an IRA, which is tax-deferred, this means that your total federal tax bill would only be $11,250 ($45,000 × .25) and your tax savings for the year would be $1,250. Not only do you get to save money in taxes, but just as in the company retirement plan, the money grows in a tax-deferred account.

- **Roth IRA.** This is a modified individual retirement account that allows you to set aside *after*-tax income up to a specified amount each year. All of the earnings on the account are tax free provided that withdrawals are made after a five-year investment period *and* are made after age 59½.

- **SIMPLE IRA.** SIMPLE stands for Savings Incentive Match Plan for Employees of small employers. This retirement plan is offered by employers who do not offer any other retirement plan who have no more than one hundred employees, who earn more than $5,000 a year. This is established as a 401(k) or IRA and allows employee pretax contributions and mandatory employer matching contributions.

- **SEP IRA.** This is my favorite plan of all of the IRAs, especially for the self-employed who are the only employee. This tax-deferred retirement plan is for businesses with fewer than twenty-five employees. This is a simplified employee pension (SEP) plan that can provide a significant source of income at retirement by allowing employers to set aside money in retirement accounts for themselves and their employees.

- **Self-directed IRA.** This account offers an individual retirement arrangement allowing the owner access to a wider choice of investments. These investments could include but are not limited to stocks, bonds, mutual funds, and money market funds. Self-directed IRAs, or SDAs, may be opened at various institutions with trust powers, state FDIC-insured institutions, federal credit unions, and federally chartered savings banks or savings and loans.

The two most popular IRAs are the traditional and the Roth. Both have advantages that you should explore to decide which is the best for you. Here are the main components of each plan.

Traditional IRA Overview

- Contributions are tax deductible depending upon your income level.
- It is mandatory to begin withdrawing your funds when you turn 70½, but you can begin at age 59½.
- Uncle Sam gets its cut in taxes on whatever you withdraw from your IRA.
- You can purchase stocks, bonds, CDs, and a variety of investments with the funds that you deposit into your IRA.
- IRAs are available to everyone regardless of income, but with restrictions on who gets a tax deduction.
- All funds withdrawn (including principal contributions) before 59½ are subject to a 10 percent penalty (subject to exceptions).

Roth IRA Overview

- You cannot take tax deductions on your contributions.
- There is no mandatory age to begin distribution of funds.
- Every dime of your earnings and principal are 100 percent tax free if rules and regulations are followed.
- You can purchase stocks, bonds, CDs, and a variety of investments with the funds that you deposit into your Roth IRA.
- As of 2010, Roth IRAs are available only to single filers making up to $105,000 (to qualify for a full contribution) or married couples making a combined maximum of $167,000 (to qualify for a full contribution) annually.
- All principal contributions can be withdrawn at any time without penalty, but earnings are not eligible to be withdrawn without penalty and tax free unless those earnings meet the following rules:
  - Funds must be invested in the account for a minimum of five years.
  - Funds must be distributed on or after reaching 59½.
  - You pass away and the account is paid to your beneficiary.

- You can prove a disability.
- You are eligible for a penalty-free and tax-free withdrawal of $10,000 with a qualified "first home" purchase as long as you have invested the funds for five years.

The Roth vs. the Traditional IRA

The main difference between the traditional and Roth IRA is the way the U.S. government taxes the funds that are held within the accounts. If you earn $40,000 per year and put $2,000 in a traditional IRA, you can deduct that $2,000 from your income and will only have to pay taxes on $38,000 for that year. However, when you turn 59½ and decide to take distributions, Uncle Sam will want to get the money that he allowed you not to pay. You will have to pay ordinary income taxes on all of the principal and capital gains, interest, dividends, etc., that were earned throughout your investment of those funds.

The Roth IRA is different. If you invested the same $2,000 into a Roth IRA while earning $40,000, you would not receive a tax deduction. You can take out the $2,000 at any time; however, you will have to pay a penalty on any earnings that you take out if they're not taken out under the guidelines mentioned above. Uncle Sam didn't give you a deduction, so when you reach the age of retirement, he won't feel obligated to come after you for taxes. You will receive all of your funds in the account, regardless of the amount of appreciation, 100 percent tax free. If you are income eligible to contribute to it, the Roth IRA makes the most sense in most situations. The sense of security in knowing exactly how much you will have at retirement that the Roth IRA provides is worth its weight in gold.

Below are a few tips to adhere to in establishing your IRA.

IRA Quick Tips

1. **Start ASAP.** The faster you start, the more you will save. By waiting just five years, you could have a nest egg that is as much as 25 percent smaller when you retire and are ready to take distributions.

(continued)

2. **Follow the steps.** Don't open an IRA until you have laid the proper financial foundation.
   - By keeping adequate insurance coverage, a good credit score, up-to-date estate-planning documents, and a working budget, you will be able to mitigate financial risks that can put the security of your retirement account in jeopardy.
   - Credit cards balances should be eliminated because of the uncertainty of their interest rates.
   - The 401(k) should be a priority because many times your employer provides a match, which is free money!
   - It is important to have an emergency fund to tap into so that you won't have to tap into your IRA account, which can result in penalties and tax liabilities for early withdrawal.

3. **Forgot to make a yearly deposit?** You may make your deposit all the way up until April 15 of the following year. For instance, if it is January 15 of 2011 and you forgot to deposit your $5,000 into your IRA for 2010, you can make a 2010 deposit up until April 15 of 2011 as long as you had taxable income the year before.

4. **Select appropriate investments.** Be sure to pick the right types of investments for your IRA. For instance, you would not want to select a tax-exempt municipal bond, because your IRA account is already tax-deferred. Tax-exempt investments usually provide lower yields because of the tax advantage. However, you are already receiving a tax advantage in your IRA account, so you are essentially receiving a lower yield with no advantage.

5. **Hire a good adviser.** In Chapter 13 we discuss how to select a good adviser, and it is important here because you want to implement the best strategy for an account that might make up a substantial portion of your retirement nest egg.

6. **Diversify in and out.** It is important to diversify your investments within your account, but you should also diversify the types of accounts that you have. As indicated in the "Seven Steps to Financial Freedom," one should have an IRA, a company savings plan, *and* personal investments to ensure a well-funded retirement.

(continued)

VILLAGE VISIT

The Power of the IRA: The Teacher

Overworked, underpaid, and underappreciated . . . this is the life of a teacher. Where would you be without that one teacher who pushed you in the third grade, motivated you in middle school, or showed you enough about your future in high school that you decided to pursue higher learning, the first one to do so in your family? The teacher's salary is minimal, but the impact on our communities is immeasurable.

Ashanti Branch, a teacher in California, has made tremendous sacrifices to empower his students, from his early years when he gave up a lucrative career in construction, making over six figures, to pursue his passion to teach. Many students have a stronger foundation in financial literacy and fiscal responsibility because this teacher decided to share his knowledge in a creative way. I include Ashanti's story in the IRA section because a key moment of growth and learning for him was when he opened an IRA account.

MORE THAN A TEACHER
by Ashanti Branch

I realize today that many of the lessons about money I learned as a young boy growing up poor in Oakland were misinformed. However, my mom raised me that it was better to be poor and free than to have money and be a slave to fear. There were four of us: my mother, sister, brother, and me, the oldest child. While we did not have a lot of money, my mom was always able to create a meal that fed all of us. I remember the nights with "breakfast for dinner" or "go for what you know." Thank God we never went hungry; there was always something to eat, even if it consisted of ramen noodles, egg salad, mayonnaise sandwiches, or PB&J. For a good portion of my life I remember having to go to the local store with food stamps.

I knew early in life that I didn't like being poor. When I was in the sixth grade, I attempted to start my own business. About five blocks from my house was a store that sold penny candy.

(continued)

168

The store wasn't close to our school, but I would go from my bus stop there to buy one hundred or two hundred candies at a penny each and sell them for five cents. I was amazed how fast my money grew. My original $3 investment quickly yielded $15. I remembered seeing a movie where a man stored his money in a book, so I got a book myself and cut out a section inside to store my money. Once I earned $90, the wrinkled bills were not fitting in the book, so I began laundering them in my bathroom sink and ironing them with starch so that they would all lie flat. This experience at the age of ten told me that money could be powerful, leveraged, and that I had the power to one day be wealthy.

I graduated high schoool and arrived at college with more than $28,000 in scholarships, which allowed me to focus more on my studies instead of on getting a job. For the first three summers I worked as an intern with Pacific Gas & Electric Company. I began to earn more each summer, but my lack of financial management began to catch up with me. I quickly realized that I had learned how it feels to have or to not have money, but no one had taught me how to make my money work for me.

Only when I received my first six-month internship in the construction industry did someone teach me about money. His name was Ashok, a smart man, an engineer; he would always ask me what I was doing with my money. Discussions about money had always made me uncomfortable, since when I was growing up, we never talked about it. As the months passed, Ashok continued to inquire and give me financial information to think about. During the last month of my internship, he invited me to lunch and asked me if I knew about IRAs. I said, "Nope." He explained that it was an individual retirement account. Imagine my shock to have a conversation about retirement and I had not even graduated college yet. He showed me a graph that demonstrated what could happen to $10,000 in an IRA and compared it to a savings account, where I had all my money. I was amazed, and within a week he took me to Fidelity Investments and helped me open my first IRA. I selected the Fidelity's Magellan and Contrafund and made the maximum $1,200 contribution for the 1995 tax year.

This was the first time that I felt I was making a decision to get me on the road toward financial freedom. I was not just making money but saving it.

(continued)

When I graduated and started looking for a job, I did not know how to evaluate offers to determine a fair salary. So I asked my friend's dad, who was a bank VP whom I highly respected, to help me weigh salary offers. He asked me one of the hardest questions I have ever been asked: "How much money do you want to make?" I stuttered and mumbled and came up empty. I had no idea. He told me, "Well, Ashanti, if you don't know how much you are worth, how can someone hire you?"

Those words have remained with me until this day.

I did get a job, with an upcoming construction company. I not only liked the company's culture and philosophy, but I was also sold on their retirement plan. I began immediately contributing to my 401(k) and the company matched at the maximum level that they allowed.

After five years working in construction, however, I decided to become a teacher. It was a difficult financial decision, but an easy moral and purpose-driven decision. This would put me back in the tax bracket of the lower middle class or working poor, a subgroup I had promised myself I would never again be a part of.

I realized that teaching was exactly what I was supposed to be doing with my life. So I started a program called the Ever Forward Club. It would be a support group for boys to help them find their voice and to achieve their goals. I offered these boys lunch every Thursday in exchange for their time. I felt that if I could get them to spend one day a week talking about positive things, we could one at a time help them to change their outlook on life.

Since the school had no support in place for these at-risk kids, I paid for everything out of my pocket. As a result, all the money I had saved during those construction years quickly disappeared. If I was to be able to effectively give back to these kids every Thursday on my reduced salary, a drastic change was necessary.

In the summer of 2006, I read the book *Rich Dad Poor Dad: What the Rich Teach Their Kids About Money—That the Poor and the Middle Class Do Not!* by Robert Kiyosaki, and it has changed my life. I vowed that it would be the way I would give back to my students, my community, and myself. When school started in September, I was convinced that a powerful way to attract more students to

(continued)

my program was to talk about getting rich. They seemed to love the idea of being rich, although they had no idea of what having real wealth meant. They only knew of what MTV revealed that people with money could buy. So, with a mini-grant from Donors Choose, a program for public-school teachers, we purchased a class set of *Rich Dad Poor Dad* for teens, and the Get Rich Crew was created. Each participant received a textbook, and we began to learn the difference between income, expenses, assets, and liabilities. While I was teaching these lessons, I began to learn so much more myself.

Today the students are learning principles about money that will remain with them for the rest of their lives and can be the difference between a life of financial freedom and one of financial fear. This fear is often brought about solely through the lack of understanding, and my students are gaining this imperative understanding.

The Ever Forward Club has become a 501(c)(3) nonprofit organization that has set some huge goals to help even more students, not only by improving their financial literacy, but in setting goals in all areas of their life. We currently have chapters in three high schools, and our vision is to be in twenty schools by the year 2015.

I am currently looking for a home to purchase. I have looked at over one hundred homes and evaluated over fifty to see if the cost would be a benefit or a burden. I am on track to purchase my first home in early 2011. They say that being a teacher doesn't pay. I am glad that neither my students nor I listen to what they say.

Ryan Mack's Five Economic Empowerment Tips for Teachers

1. Spend time with your students after school teaching them about something for which you have a passion. If you do as Ashanti did and form a 501(c)(3), you can raise funds to be compensated for your time, form stronger bonds with the students, and lay a great foundation for young minds.
2. Budget well and avoid excessive consumption. On a teacher's salary every penny counts.
3. Research your 403(b) plan and other retirement options.
4. Use your summer wisely. Starting a company, writing a book, or taking additional educational classes at the local community college

are great ways to possibly make some additional money and keep your mind occupied.

5. Bring professionals into your classroom to speak to your students. The kids always love to see an outside face, and hearing from the experienced is always a great learning tool. Besides, this is a great way to give yourself a much-needed break, if only for a few minutes.

CHAPTER ELEVEN

Step Six: Eliminating Low-Risk Debt

LOW-RISK DEBT IS CALLED LOW RISK BECAUSE IT IS USUALLY BACKED BY AN ASSET; IT IS a secured debt. For instance, when you take out a loan to purchase a car, the car backs the loan and acts as collateral; if you purchase a home with a mortgage, the home acts as collateral for the loan; and if you take out a student loan, this is usually a secured debt and the lender can stake a claim to your wages if you do not repay. The interest rate on secured debt is therefore not as volatile or as high as you would find with unsecured debt such as with a credit card. If you don't pay off the loan, the lender can come after your house, your car, or your wages. This type of loan is harder to get and therefore carries more weight in determining your FICO score. Your FICO score will improve more if you pay off $5,000 of secured debt than if you pay off $5,000 of credit card debt. This is why if you take a loan to purchase a car and compile a history of paying your note on time, it will have a positive impact on your FICO score.

When asked whether I advise eliminating low-risk debt (step six) or beginning to invest in the market (step seven), I usually suggest doing both at the same time. This is because many times people like to see something tangible in savings as they pay down their debt; otherwise they are likely to suffer from fiscal fatigue, as we discussed earlier. Also, low-risk debt's interest rates are not as volatile as high-risk debt's and are not likely to be increased dramatically if you miss a payment. Many people have low interest rates on student loans or mortgages, and you may beat this rate with investments in the market (step seven) over the long run. For instance, I was working with someone who had a student loan with an astoundingly low 1.5 percent interest rate. I advised her that if she felt comfortable, she could invest in the market because over time she should be able to achieve a higher return in the market than 1.5 percent.

Another term that I like to use is *psychic income*. I define this as the mental high that you receive from paying down your debt earlier than when it is due. Even though you may be able to take more risk and achieve a higher return in the stock market or other investments, that feeling of elation that you achieve from seeing a large reduction of debt can outweigh the monetary return that you can achieve in the market. I remember when I was asked by a friend/client whether she should pay down her student-loan debt or begin to invest in the market. I found out that she had an interest rate on her student loan of only 1.5 %. Now, I would normally have told her to invest in the market because she would certainly earn more than that in the market over the long run. But when I found out that she was extremely troubled by the amount of debt that she had to pay (more than $80,000), I told her to do what she felt was right. (Many financial advisers are opposed to what I suggested because fiscally it makes more sense to get the biggest bang for the buck. However, other things in life are much more important than money, and one of those is peace of mind.)

It is important to consider expert advice along with the level of risk that you are comfortable in taking to create the best plan for you. This is why I told her that she should focus a large chunk of her surplus on paying off her student loan even though the interest rate was so low. I am quite sure that she could have made more money otherwise in the long run, but sleepless nights are not worth that. She was putting a substantial amount into her 401(k), so she was still saving for retirement, but she needed to feel at ease in knowing that her debt was being paid off before she started to focus on investing in the market. Fiscal responsibility is imperative in all of our lives, but because people are different, not all decisions will be uniform in every situation for every person. The ultimate goal for all of us should be to live a happy life, achieve financial independence, understand that many times we will have to sacrifice, but try not to sacrifice so much that we begin to feel stressed or depressed.

PAYING STUDENT LOANS EARLY

Now that you are at step six, your budget is working well, your credit cards are paid off, you are fully contributing to your IRA, and you have fulfilled all the other components of the steps to your best ability. If you are here, you are doing well because many people do not have enough funds to contribute more than what their 401(k) dictates. Now you must determine how much of your surplus you will be willing to put toward an extra payment to pay off your student loan debt, and other low-risk debt, early. The more you pay toward your debt, the less risk you have, because you have decided to use that capital to eliminate leverage (certainty) versus using that capital to invest in the market (uncertainty of return).

The table below shows the benefits of obtaining the lowest interest rate as well as paying down your debt earlier. According to a 2007–8 National Postsecondary Student Aid Study, two-thirds of college students borrow to pay for college, and their average debt load is $23,186.

Debt Balance	Interest Rate	Monthly Payment	Total # of Payments	# of Years to Pay Debt	Total Interest Paid
$23,186	7%	$200	194	16.2	$15,594
$23,186	4%	$200	147	12.3	$6,171

As you see from the table, a 4 percent interest rate makes a big difference in the total interest paid over the life of the loan . . . approximately $9,000! This is why it is so crucial for everyone to always battle for a higher FICO score. You never know when you will be given the opportunity to refinance and get a lower-rate loan.

Debt Balance	Interest Rate	Monthly Payment	Total # of Payments	# of Years to Pay Debt	Total Interest Paid
$23,186	5%	$200	159	13.3	$8,550
$23,186	5%	$250	118	9.8	$6,183
$23,186	5%	$300	94	7.8	$4,855
$23,186	5%	$350	78	6.5	$4,002

This table demonstrates the importance of squeezing out additional dollars to pay down your debt sooner. The difference between a $200-per-month payment and a $350-per-month payment is more than $4,000 in total interest paid, and you cut the total amount of time that you would be paying on the loan by more than half.

COLLEGE SAVING PROGRAMS

Student loans are among the fastest-growing low-risk debts burdening Americans. According to Sallie Mae, from 2007 through 2008 lenders provided about $17 billion in private loans, which was a 592 percent increase from a decade earlier. According to the Bureau of Labor Statistics, tuition increased by an average of 8 percent per year from 1979 through 2001. But there are a few ways to stave off these huge debts. One of the first things that you should do as soon as your child is born is to make sure that you start a college savings fund. Also, estimate that the cost of college will be three to four times current prices by the time your child is of college age. Needing this kind of money, you want to think about saving for school early on, especially since on average only about a third of total college costs are paid with gift aid from the government, the colleges and universities, and private scholarships. The other two-thirds will come from a combination of current income, savings, and loans. I do a lot of work with high school students, and it is always upsetting to see the long line of disappointed twelfth-grade students outside the counseling center in February and March because they did not receive enough financial aid for them to attend their school of first choice. When your child is in the twelfth grade is *not* when you want to start to think about saving for your child's future.

Let's put some numbers together to help you visualize what saving early can mean for your child. If you save $50 per month at a modest rate of 5 percent from when your child is born, you will have over $17,000 in your savings account by the time he or she turns eighteen. If you doubled your savings rate at 5 percent to $100 per month, you would have almost $35,000 in your savings account. A $200 monthly investment at 5 percent would net you almost $70,000. The more you save, the less you borrow, so it only makes sense to save now, because you will have to pay much more if you have to borrow those funds later while your child is in school. I hear a lot of parents say that they would rather save less because the less they save, the more financial aid they can apply for. The Federal Analysis Needs Methodology, the strategy that the government uses to calculate financial aid, does count a portion of the family's assets to determine the financial need of the family, and a family with more assets will get less need-based financial aid. However, the government does not count *all* of the assets when determining need, only a fraction. The bottom line is that a family that saves more will have money left over. It is always better to save now than borrow later, and a key wealth-building principle is to *never* depend solely upon the government for the financial prowess of your family.

COLLEGE SAVINGS VEHICLES

Many programs allow you to maximize your savings for college and consequently reduce the amount that you have to borrow to fund an education. I have listed below seven methods that individuals use.

- **Section 529 Plan.** My favorite of all of the savings plans available. This is also known as the Qualified Tuition Program (QTP). All states have plans of two types: prepaid tuition plans and college savings plans. Prepaid tuition allows you to lock in future tuition rates at in-state public colleges at current prices. College savings plans operate similarly to traditional savings plans but do not offer a guarantee the way the prepaid tuition plan does.
  I like the Section 529 plan the most because it offers:
  - Low initial investments: In many plans in various states, one is able to invest as little as $50 per month or less.
  - Low fees: If the plan is offered through the state, the fees that you will incur to invest are minimal. However, be sure to do some comparative shopping if a broker offers you a version of the 529 plan . . . it is usually more expensive.
  - Tax-deferred savings: In many plans across the country you can obtain some beneficial tax deductions of $5,000, $10,000, or even $13,000 depending upon the state. If one is earning $50,000 per year, receives a $10,000 deduction, and is only taxed on $40,000, that equals approximately a $2,500 tax savings.
  - Tax-exempt savings: This is my favorite part. If one invests $5,000 in a plan and gets the full tax deduction, he receives savings on the front end. Let's say that $5,000 doubles by the time the child goes to school to $10,000. One might think that the $5,000 capital gain is taxable; however, as long as the funds are

used for college expenses, that capital gain is available *tax free*. The college expenses that you can use these funds for are liberal and are listed below:

- Tuition
- Room and board
- Mandatory fees
- Books, computer (if required)

Great sites to check for which plans your state provides are www.savingforcollege.com and www.finaid.org.

- **Coverdell Education Savings Accounts.** These were formerly known as education IRAs. These are trusts created exclusively for the purpose of paying for the educational expenses (those that are qualified) of the designated beneficiary of the trust. The main benefit of this plan above and beyond the Section 529 plan is that you have more control over the investments that you choose for this account. However, this plan has more restrictions, some of which are:
  - Contribution amount: The maximum amount that one may contribute per beneficiary from all sources per year is $2,000 (the only exemption is when contributions come from rollover).
  - Age limit: Contributions may be made until the beneficiary is eighteen.
  - Income tax implications: Contributions are *not* deductible on federal or state income tax. This is a huge difference from the 529 savings plan, although the earnings are income-tax free as long as they are used for qualified college expenses.
- **U.S. Treasury Savings Bonds.** My mother never really had a lot of money, but she managed to purchase a few of these from time to time for our college education. These are a great way to invest capital at a low risk and at modest return for the education of your children (check treasurydirect.gov to see rates and purchase treasury bonds). These are very safe investments as they are backed by the full faith and credit of the U.S. government. So basically, as long as the government doesn't collapse, your money is safe.
- **Home Equity Line of Credit.** When you build up credit in your home, you can create an alternative to other college investment vehicles. You can tap into the equity of your home by getting a home equity line of credit. Use this as a last resort after all other options are utilized.
- **Funds from a Retirement Plan.** You may take an early, penalty-free 10 percent distribution if funds are used to pay for qualified higher-

education expenses. Note that this is *penalty* free because you are still liable to pay federal and state taxes on the funds.

You may also borrow against your 401(k) to pay for college expenses. However, I strongly advocate against this because if there is ever a choice between saving for retirement and paying for the college expenses of your children, you should choose retirement. Many parents mistakenly think that they should sacrifice anything, including their retirement, for their children's college. *Don't do it!* You do not have as long until your retirement as your children have to pay down their school loans. If you really want to help your children, make sure that your financial house is in order to put yourself in a better position to be supportive of their efforts with a solid financial foundation beneath you.

- **Variable Insurance Policies.** These are life insurance policies that build in cash value, which can be invested in a wide variety of separate accounts. Many of these policies are marketed as a college-savings vehicle because the value of the policy is sheltered from financial-aid need-analysis formulas. I would strongly advocate against using these products for college unless you have exhausted all other options because you can save for your children's college education in plenty of other more lucrative ways than by putting the full benefit of your life insurance in jeopardy should you die prematurely. The benefits of the Section 529 plan and the Coverdell ESA far outweigh the benefits of these policies for college savings. Use insurance for insurance purposes.
- **Traditional Savings.**

AUTO LOANS—BUYING VS. LEASING

A secret of most millionaires when it comes to purchasing new cars is that they value their financial independence more than they value their car. Do you really think that a millionaire would value his car more than his financial independence? Of course not! Now he can purchase any car he wants, never has to be concerned about money, and will have a legacy to pass on to the next generation.

When you lease a car, the two main charges are a depreciation charge and a finance charge. The depreciation charge is the price that the vehicle has gone down while you were using the vehicle. The finance charge reflects the interest rate that you are paying on the term of the lease. Nothing is going toward anything of real value to you. Depreciation is only an accounting expense that is the most costly in the earliest years of the vehicle, which is the time that you are leasing the vehicle.

Cars depreciate 25 percent as soon as you drive them off the lot. If you purchase a car for $20,000, as soon as you drive it off the lot, it is only worth $15,000. This is why those millionaires who really understand the value of a dollar will purchase a pre-owned vehicle (one to three years old) that has already taken its biggest hit of depreciation. This is why you will never hear of their leasing a vehicle, because they understand the value in ownership versus renting.

I am not saying that there are no benefits to leasing a vehicle. If you lease a car, you will probably have lower monthly payments, you will have little to no down payment up front, you will never owe more than what the car is worth, and if you are business owner, you may get some tax advantages if you use the car for business purposes. I get it.

However, most people who lease vehicles will for years always have a car payment and not have anything to show for it but a lower savings account. Depending upon the type of lease that you have, when your lease term is up, you either hand the keys over to the dealership and lease another vehicle, or you finance the remaining value of your car to work toward owning it and go from lease payments to loan payments. The deal you'll get if you purchase the vehicle after your lease is up is never as good as you think it will be. This is because in a lease you are paying most for the high depreciation expense and little if nothing toward the value of the vehicle.

Other disadvantages of leasing are as follows:

- Terminating the lease can be costly.
- You don't own the vehicle, so you cannot make any major changes to the car, such as painting it or adding equipment.
- Mileage restrictions can be costly if you go over the allowed limit.
- Insurers usually charge higher costs for leased vehicles (their reasoning: If you don't own the car, you are less likely to take good care of it than if you did).

Lesson: Always strive for ownership. Here are some key points to getting the most out of that ownership.

Step One: Start Saving Now

The more you can put down on a vehicle, the lower your monthly payments on your loan. Also, before you purchase the car is the best time to spend a few months acting as if you are actually pay the car note to see how much you can actually afford. If you do your budget and calculate that you can afford to pay $300 per month for a new vehicle, pay yourself $300 per month for at least three months (hopefully you can take the time to do more) in a high-yield savings account to see if that is feasible. See if your budget is stretched.

Step Two: Start Improving Your FICO Score Now

You may have seen many commercials on television that proclaim "zero percent financing available." However, you might have missed the microscopic words on the bottom of the TV screen that state that this attractive offer is not available to everyone. Your FICO score will be the major determinant of your eligibility.

Step Three: Buy a Pre-Owned Car

As stated earlier, the most costly expense in the early years of any vehicle is the depreciation. If you purchase a pre-owned vehicle that is one to three years old with low mileage, it has passed the most costly period of depreciation but you still get a car that is relatively new. Your best bet is to purchase a "certified pre-owned" car. These vehicles have been inspected and guaranteed to be better than most used cars, are less than three years old, have fewer than 50,000 miles on them, and are sold by new-car dealerships. Many independent used-car dealerships sell certified pre-owned cars, but I would use a lot of caution before buying from these dealerships because they are not sponsored by a major automaker and may not have the same standards.

Step Four: Pay Extra When Possible

No matter what loan you get, whenever you possibly can, try to pay extra toward the principal. Just because you have a four-year loan does not mean that you have to take four years to pay down your loan. As you saw in the above example, paying down your loans faster saves interest.

Step Five: Continue Paying the Note After the Loan Is Paid...to Yourself

Let's say you settled the loan after paying $300 per month for four years. Take that $300 per month and put it into a high-yield savings account for another four years. This will net you almost $15,000 after four years (at a 2 percent interest rate). Then you can take the $15,000 that you have in the bank and combine that with the trade-in value of your current car and purchase another pre-owned car *debt free*!

Now, if you continuously use this strategy to purchase another car every four years, you will own them outright and can even trade up if you want. Doesn't that sound better than being in debt or paying money to a lending company without ever owning anything?

BUYING A HOME RESPONSIBLY

I am writing this book in the middle of the hardest economic time for this country since the Great Depression. I have tried to make this book as timeless as possible, but one can learn many lessons from the "credit crisis," as it is referred to in the news. I have chosen to put this more timely portion here because, for most reading this book, purchasing a home will be the largest investment they make in their lifetime; it makes sense to learn from these times of economic hardships to prevent this travesty from repeating itself in future generations.

What happened?

The housing/financial/economic/credit crisis that started in 2007 was caused by a perfect storm of failures in our country. Failures in the government, in the corporate world, and by individuals created a disaster that caused lending and the entire economy to come to a halt.

Individuals

Too many individuals decided before they were prepared that they wanted to purchase a home. The real estate market was booming, and many had become fearful that they were going to miss the boat if they did not act quickly. These emotions of fear and impatience caused an already high demand for real estate to rapidly increase. The foreclosure rate increased to record levels and that assisted in the recession that began at the end of 2007.

Corporations

Somewhere along the line, corporations realized that interest being collected from subprime borrowers was very profitable for lenders. Subprime lenders provide loans to individuals who are not eligible to obtain prime-rate mortgages because they are considered to be a higher risk. This caused the creation of specialized mortgages (loans created specifically to target the subprime lending market), which helped to spur demand because people who had never been able to get a loan now could. Those with low FICO scores or a low/sporadic income were able to get a loan easily. The high interest rates being collected on these loans were attractive to everyone, so the local banks who originally issued these loans were able to sell them to larger institutions (such as Lehman Brothers or J. P. Morgan Chase) and absolve themselves from any risk (thereby allowing them to continue to issue subprime loans).

Below is a sample of a real advertisement that was used to entice people to purchase homes:

---

2 New Programs: Rapid Purchase or Rapid Refinancing

100% Full Doc 1–2 family homes /// 580 credit score
(Requires 18 months on-time mortgage / rent history)

100% STATED / STATED . . . 600 CREDIT SCORE
(REQUIRES 18 MONTHS ON-TIME MORTGAGE HISTORY)

MANY OTHER PROGRAMS AVAILABLE. WE HAVE NO MINIMUM CREDIT SCORE!!!

This lender is advertising two programs. The first program is a 100 percent "Full Doc" loan. This is mortgage-industry jargon for "full documentation," in which you need to present two years of income verification and seasoned assets (funds that are held in your account for longer than two months), but you only need to have a 580 FICO score (very low) to purchase a home. Such scores make the borrower "subprime"—considered a high risk to lend to and thus charged high interest rates.

The second program is even more destructive and dangerous because it is a "STATED" program. In this type of program you need little or no documentation at the time of signing. The lender simply asks you how much income you make, you "state" a number, and the lender runs with it. These are often called liar loans because all you have to do to get one is to state your income level. People get away with stating almost any income that will allow them to qualify for the loan, as long as it's within reason. It is illegal to overstate your income; however, during the real estate boom from 2000 to 2007, these loans became so popular that it became almost impossible to verify people's true income.

This ad markets loans that don't even ask you to verify your income or credit score. With these loans anyone can achieve the American Dream of owning a home, whether the person can afford it or not. (By the way, it seems as if the mortgage industry has done a great job of pushing the notion that the American Dream is to own a home. I thought that the American Dream was to achieve financial independence. . . .)

These larger institutions started to bundle these subprime loans into securities, which they then sold for profit in the secondary market. Due to the increased risk associated with these securities, these institutions had to offer insurance in case the purchaser of the property defaulted, causing the value in the security to decrease. Other hedge funds and investment managers began to see the growing market for this insurance, or derivatives. They began to purchase these products and essentially bet that the purchasers of these properties would default. An example of a derivative is a credit default swap. The credit default swap market grew from $500 million to over $60 trillion between 2000 and 2007.

So when some 10 percent defaulted on their properties, causing the value of the subprime-loan securities to fall, trillions of dollars were called to be collected by the holders of the insurance. However, the banks were so overleveraged that they never had enough money to cover these bets they were waging. Hence we saw Lehman Brothers go bankrupt, and the rest, as they say, is history.

Government

The government allowed all of this to happen with little to no oversight or regulation. The $60 trillion credit-default-swap market still has little regulation, and at the time of the writing of this book the government has a lot of work to do to restore confidence to the public that it actually has control over Wall Street greed.

Wall Street, Main Street, and the government all caused this. Hence, all must play a role in fixing it. We can picket against Wall Street greed as a solution. We can call and write letters to our local government to tell them to pass legislation to change regulations and stop the harmful practices of predatory lending. However, this book focuses on the most powerful weapon that you have control of: you! The fiscal decisions you make starting right now are what are going to empower this country more than any other campaign, call, or letter. We need you to be smart about each financial decision you make, especially as you decide to make the largest investment of your life . . . your home.

Now that you know the history and possible downsides to mortgage loans, let's walk through a few of the most important steps and necessities as you purchase your home. If there is ever again a credit crisis in this country, I want to be sure that you did your part in not contributing to it.

PURCHASING A HOME—ARE YOU TRULY READY?

This is the most important question that you need to ask yourself before making the biggest investment in your life. When I ask people who do not currently own a home if they are thinking about buying one, the usual response is yes. There is nothing wrong with this response. If you desire to own a home, then confidence and diligence are two of your most important assets (besides money).

The next question that I ask is when you would like to purchase your home. The usual response is "Within a year." Now, there is something wrong with this if you have not done the appropriate research on whether a year is feasible to achieve this. The problem with the recession of 2007 was that too many people were not willing to use another key component besides confidence and diligence . . . *patience!*

Below are a few things to think about when determining if you are ready to purchase a property.

Rent vs. Buy. There is *nothing* wrong with renting a piece of property if you are "renting with a purpose." A few advantages to renting are:

- You have less liability than when owning a home. Many are intimidated at the exorbitant mortgage that they are liable for when purchasing property.
- You can forgo the cost of work and repairs around the home. For instance, if your refrigerator breaks, the landlord must repair or replace it. Also, you are not responsible for expenditures such as property taxes.

- You aren't responsible for the upkeep of the property, such as mowing the lawn or shoveling the walkways.

However, there are downsides. A few disadvantages to renting are:

- Your monthly payments can fluctuate. If you are not in a rent-controlled or -stabilized apartment and the landlord decides to increase the rent on a new lease . . . tough luck!
- You have limited property control and usually have to request permission to do even minor things such as painting the walls or changing the carpet.
- You have poor investment maximization because your payments are not going toward anything that you own and aren't building equity, but are helping someone else pay off his or her mortgage.

Overall, nothing is wrong with renting. However, if you are saving money by renting as opposed to buying, something is wrong if you are not using that money saved to put toward owning your own home, a business idea, retirement, or another long-term goal. For instance, if your rent is $1,000 per month, and to own that same home would cost you $1,200 per month, you should be proactive and put that $200 into savings every month. There is no point to saving money if you are going to waste the savings!

Below is a chart for making your own rent vs. buy analysis:

RENT VS. BUY ANALYSIS
A. Total Cost to Rent
a. Annual renting costs (12×monthly rent of $_____)
b. Renter's insurance _____
Total Annual Rent Cost = A.a. + A.b. = _____
B. Total Cost to Buy
a. Annual mortgage payments (12×monthly mortgage of $_____)
b. Property taxes (_____% of price of home)
c. Homeowner's insurance (_____% of price of home)
(continued)

d. Maintenance (_____% of price of home)
e. After-tax cost of interest on down payment and closing costs ($_____ × _____% after-tax rate of return)
f. **Total Cost (Add Lines B.a. Through B.e.)** = _____
Minus:
g. Principal reduction in loan balance
h. Total savings in taxes due to property-tax deductions (Line B.b. × tax rate of _____%)
i. Total savings due to interest deductions (Interest portion of mortgage payments $_____ × tax rate of _____%)
j. **Total Deductions (Sum of Lines B.g. Through B.i.)** = _____
k. Annual after-tax cost of homeownership (Line B.f. minus B.j.)
l. Estimated annual price appreciation of home (_____% of price of home)
Total Cost to Buy (B.k. − B.l.) = _____

If this is too complicated, you can simply go to www.fincalc.com and utilize the "Rent vs. Buy" calculator. You can also simply do an Internet search for a "rent vs. buy" calculator and find plenty of additional calculators to choose from on many different sites.

Self-Reflection Time. Outside of the numbers, you need to do some serious self-reflection before you purchase a home. You should ask yourself:

- Is your income steady enough to afford a monthly mortgage?
- Have you been in and out of work for the past few years?
- Do you expect any major life changes in the next few years that will significantly change your income (children, going back to school, a career change, retirement, etc.)?
- Do you have a lot of outstanding loans that are troubling you now?
- Do you have enough for a down payment or would you have to get a "specialty" loan to be able to purchase?

- Are you responsible in paying your bills on time?
- If you calculate the mortgage plus all of the additional costs, can you really afford it (maintenance, insurance, gas, electricity, etc.)?
- Is your FICO score above 750?

HOW MUCH CAN YOU AFFORD?

The rule of thumb for purchasing a home is, the property shouldn't be more than two or three times your income level. Assuming that you have a $50,000-per-year income, you should be looking at homes around the $150,000 range. This is assuming that you have the 20 percent down payment and only an average amount of long-term debts such as school loans, car loans, and credit card bills. If you have no debt, you might be able to afford a home that is as much as four to five times your income.

Another rule of thumb: Your monthly mortgage payment shouldn't be more than 30 percent of your monthly gross income. To make sure you are purchasing a home that is within this limit, follow this three-step process.

Step One: Determine Monthly Net Income or Estimate

In the following example I used a $75,000-per-year salary to determine an estimated monthly income. The estimated monthly net pay for this level of income is $4,026.78. For figuring out your own monthly net income, you can use PaycheckCity.com or refer to your tax returns, a recent W2, or recent pay stubs.

SALARY PAYCHECK CALCULATOR (PROVIDED BY PAYCHECKCITY.COM)

Your Paycheck Results		Calculation Based On	
Monthly gross pay	$6,250.00	Tax year	2009
Federal withholding	$1,178.84	Gross pay	$75,000.00
Social Security	$387.50	Pay frequency	Monthly
Medicare	$90.63	Federal filing status	Single
New York State tax	$355.23	# of federal exemptions	0
			(continued)

Your Paycheck Results		Calculation Based On	
NY SDI	$2.60	Additional federal W/H	$0.00
City tax	$208.42	State	New York
		Filing status	Single
Net pay	$4,026.78	Allowances	0
		Additional state W/H	$0.00
		NY SDI	Yes
		NYC allowances	0
		City tax	NYC resident

Other Web sites that you can use are www.fincalc.com, www.1040.com, www.yourmoneypage.com, or www.bankrate.com.

Step Two: Determine Maximum Mortgage Payment

Take your calculated monthly net pay and multiply by 30 percent. In this example, that equals $1,208.03, which means the estimated maximum mortgage that an earner of $75,000 could afford is $1,208.03 per month.

Step Three: Determine Mortgage Amount

To determine the mortgage amount, I used a financial calculator, which you can find online. I calculated mortgage amounts using two different scenarios. I did two to show how different FICO scores can affect your interest rate. You'll notice that a 100 FICO score difference can result in as much as a 2 percent increase of the interest rate. So what does that teach us? To improve your FICO score as much as possible before trying to buy a home. Also, ask the lender what FICO score they consider to be a prime-rate borrower. Let's say a lender's eligibility minimum is 701 and your score is 698. This knowledge can save you a lot of money, as I have advised that individuals wait to improve their score those last three points before applying for the loan.

- **Scenario One: Good FICO Score of 750**
  - Income = $75,000
  - Interest rate (estimate) = 5.5%

- 30-year fixed loan
- Monthly payment = $1,208.03
- Mortgage = $212,765.65
- ($212,765.65 loan value)/($75,000 income) = 2.8 × income
- **Scenario Two: Bad FICO Score of 650**
  - Income = $75,000
  - Interest rate (estimate) = 7.5%
  - 30-year fixed loan
  - Monthly payment = $1,208.03
  - Mortgage = $172,769.58
  - ($172,769.58 loan value)/($75,000 income) = 2.3 × income

With a good FICO score of 750 and a $75,000 salary, a good estimate of a home that you can afford is $212,765. With a lower FICO score of 650 and a salary of $75,000, a good estimate of a home that you can afford is $172,769. Those two percentage points in interest (7.5 versus 5.5 percent) equates to $40,000 in home-value difference just for paying your bills on time! I hope you now see the importance of doing so.

Once you figure out what you can afford, begin saving for your new home. If you calculated under scenario one that you can afford a $212,765 home, simply multiply that by 20 percent and add closing costs, which can range between 1 and 8 percent of the purchase price on a home (though more typically 2 to 3 percent). Your savings goal on your home should equal approximately 22 to 23 percent of its purchase price. In this example you should save approximately $48,936 ($212,765 × 23%).

Now that you have all of your numbers together, the best way to see if you are able to afford a house is to pretend you bought it. If your rent is $800 per month but your calculated mortgage on your dream home is $1,200, start putting the $400 difference into a high-yield savings account every month. If you have to call the plumber to fix a leaky pipe and the landlord picks up the bill, act as if you had to pay the bill yourself and put the billed amount into your savings account. When the end of the year comes and the landlord has to pay property taxes, act as if you have to pay property taxes and deposit the amount of the property taxes into your savings account as well. Every time your landlord makes a payment toward your apartment, take the same amount and deposit it in your account without fail for six to twelve months, or until you have the 23 percent down payment that you will need for your imaginary home. If you find that you can make these payments and still live comfortably without overextending your budget, then you are on your way to having that new house.

THE IMPORTANCE OF PUTTING 20 PERCENT DOWN

It is entirely possible to purchase a home without putting 20 percent down on it. However, our society has become so driven by debt and impatience that we frequently use debt as a substitute for financial planning. You may be allowed to put only 15, 10, or even 0 percent of the total property value down to purchase it. However, actually saving 20 percent down on a home is a great opportunity to decrease the amount of leverage that you take upon yourself when purchasing a home, you develop the great habit of saving and paying your bills on time, and you can avoid having to pay PMI—private mortgage insurance. This insurance protects the mortgage lender from financial loss if the borrower can't or won't make the mortgage payments any longer. You can avoid this amount if you make a 20 percent down payment on the home. If you don't have 20 percent down, you should figure out how much you will have to pay for PMI. For the first year, multiply your mortgage by .006. This will be your first-year payment (up front). If your mortgage is $100,000, then your PMI for the first year will be $600. If your mortgage is $400,000, then your PMI for the first year will be $2,400. This payment does not end after the first year of owning the property. Each month, in addition to your mortgage payments, you are required to make a PMI payment. This additional payment is calculated by dividing your total initial PMI payment by twelve. So for the $100,000 mortgage, you would have to pay $600 up front, and $50 per month. For the $400,000 loan, you are required to pay $2,400 up front and $200 per month (again, this is in addition to your regular expected mortgage payment).

You are only required to pay PMI until you have established 20 percent equity. But many people don't realize that the PMI payments will continue even after you hit this benchmark. It is *your* responsibility to call your lender and have them stop your PMI bills. Make sure that you have paid down your mortgage to 80 percent of its value based upon the lesser of the original appraised value or purchase price before you give the lender a call. Before you sign any mortgage papers, have the lender put in writing that they will cancel the PMI payments when you reach the 20 percent equity mark. Even if the lender agrees to this in writing, make sure to call and remind them to cancel your PMI payments. When you call, they might require a current appraisal to protect against declining home value. Upon canceling, you will have the initial, first-year PMI payment returned to you. Don't forget to ask for this money back.

Be careful of those banks that claim not to charge PMI. Many times banks will load PMI charges into the original rate of the loan. For instance, a bank will say that they will charge you 7.5 percent interest, and you don't have to pay PMI no matter how much you initially put down. However, they fail to tell you that they have added another 0.5 percent to the loan rate to compensate for the lack of PMI payments (they make a 7 percent loan into a 7.5 percent loan). Essentially, you have been locked into paying PMI for the duration of the loan, instead of up until you have reached the 20 percent equity mark. If you have a thirty-year loan, you'll be paying this higher amount for thirty years, not just the one to two years that it would normally take to get up to 20 percent equity.

DOWN PAYMENT OPTIONS

Considering that it is often difficult to come up with the 20 percent down, below is a list of places where you might want to consider looking for additional funds to purchase your home above and beyond savings.

- **Gifts from Relatives or Friends.** Gifts of over $13,000 (as of 2009) within a calendar year may incur taxes from the IRS.
- **Private Loans.** Be careful about taking these from family or friends because these can hinder a relationship.
- **Equity from Previous Home.**
- **Stock Sales.** Make sure that you talk with an accountant to see your tax liability.
- **Life Insurance.** Talk with your insurance agent to get a thorough explanation.
- **Personal Item Sales.** Do you really need that jewelry, boat, or extra car?
- **IRA.** You can withdraw $10,000 in a lifetime from your IRA penalty-free; however, you are still liable for taxes. The funds must be used within 120 days of the date they are received, and you must be a first-time homebuyer. (If a couple is withdrawing from their IRA, they must *both* be first-time homebuyers.) Go to www.irs.gov to peruse all of the rules that apply to you.
- **401(k).** You may borrow against your 401(k), and the conditions under which you may do so are set by your employer. Make sure that you are fully aware of what happens to the loan if you leave your employer—sometimes it becomes immediately due. I must cau-

tion against this alternative because the 401(k) was not intended to be used as a leverage vehicle, but as a retirement plan.

SHOPPING FOR A LENDER

Before you apply for a loan you must first shop for lenders. If you are pre-approved for a loan through a lender, meaning a lender approves you to purchase a home up to a certain amount, home shopping becomes that much easier. Within three to four weeks you should compare the loans and their fees of at least six lenders. This might save you thousands of dollars.

Be sure to choose a lender that is accommodating. When you go in to discuss their loan programs, they should make you feel comfortable to ask questions and to ask for explanations of those things that you don't understand. Having a company that can approve your loan locally could be a plus, because local lenders are familiar with the home values and conditions within your state. Lastly, ask for recommendations. Many of your friends who own homes in the area may have had a great experience and can give you a good referral. If you get a recommendation from your real estate agent, be sure to ask if the lender has paid the broker a fee for referrals—any opinion that you get should be free from a conflict of interest.

APPLYING FOR A LOAN

Below is a list of all of the paperwork that you should have with you when applying for a loan.

- Addresses in the past two years
- List of debts and assets
- Divorce papers
- Child-support agreements
- Paperwork proving extra income
- Foreclosure and bankruptcy status
- Social Security number
- Gift letters from all of those giving you money
- Tax returns, check stubs, income and employment records

CHOOSING THE RIGHT LOAN

Choosing the right loan is critical in purchasing your home. The mortgage industry has evolved, and created many different types of loans to encourage homeownership. However, as we saw from the recession of 2007, which was brought about by a record number of foreclosures, most of those who were given a loan that was eventually foreclosed upon were unable to afford the loan when they originally signed up for it. Also, as many loan rates began to adjust upward according to preset terms, costs began to rise faster than many borrowers could afford.

Here are some basic questions you need to have addressed when discerning what type of loan is right for you:

- Is your financial situation going to be changing in the near or long term?
- How long do you think you will be living in this new residence?
- How comfortable are you in dealing with fluctuating interest rates?
- What are your long-term financial goals and desires?
- How much do you have in down payment savings?

SAMPLE LOAN TYPES

Loan Type	Description/Comments
Traditional fixed loan—30-year	• Conventional • Not government issued or guaranteed • Usually allows LTV (loan to value) ratio of 80% • Designed to last 30 years and is predictable
Traditional fixed loan—15-year	• Conventional • Not government issued or guaranteed • Usually allows LTV (loan to value) ratio of 80% • Designed to last 15 years and is predictable • Monthly payment increases 30 to 40% above that for a 30-year loan • Less total interest paid than with a 30-year loan
Adjustable-rate mortgage	• Interest rates change during the life of the loan based on a variety of indices • Adjustable rates transfer interest rate risk from lender

(continued)

Loan Type	Description/Comments
Balloon mortgage	• Borrower pays a fixed amount originally and agrees that after a certain time (usually 3 to 7 years) he or she will pay off the remaining debt or apply for another loan • Uncertain financial future of the refinancing option • Do you have the funds to cover the entire loan and will your score be good enough to refinance?
Interest-only loan	• Borrower is responsible for payment of only interest on the loan for an initial period, making mortgage payments much cheaper than payments of interest plus principal in traditional loans • In time, principal becomes due and payment requirement increases dramatically

It is important that you learn as much as possible about the loan that you are considering. Many Americans were duped into purchasing loans such as interest-only mortgages. Under these mortgages the borrower is only obligated to pay the interest portion of the loan as opposed to the interest plus the principal. This, obviously, makes the loan more inexpensive for a time. However, because many borrowers throughout America were not properly educated about these loans, they were unaware that this introductory period would soon expire. After this period expires, the borrower is obligated to begin repayment of principal of the loan, making the mortgage payments increase, over 500 percent in many cases. It was not uncommon to see a mortgage increase from $500 a month (which the borrower could afford) to $2,500 a month (which was unaffordable for the borrower). A few hours of research by borrowers could have avoided the millions of foreclosures that we are seeing across this nation.

AVOIDING PREDATORY LOANS

Before you sign on the dotted line on any loan, however, I also want you to get three outside opinions to be sure that you are making the best decision on the mortgage.

- **Opinion One:** A mortgage professional. Get an opinion from a mortgage lender whom you are comfortable with who seems to be trustworthy. Ideally you would want to find one whom you are not working with and who has no interest but to assist you; however, the information from the mortgage broker you are using has value even though he may want to earn a commission . . . just make sure that you solicit the two additional opinions below.
- **Opinion Two:** An unbiased party (knowledgeable friend/financial adviser). Get an opinion from an unbiased party who does not have a conflict of interest. While it is good to have a professional opinion from a qualified mortgage lender, these professionals often have a conflict of interest in earning a commission. The larger the loan you take out, the larger the commission they earn.
- **Opinion Three:** You. The days of going to the financial professional without researching the various products for ourselves is over. If I steal a car, and I know that I will be arrested if caught, does that mean that I could be my own lawyer? No. It does mean that I have the basic knowledge of the law that keeps me out of trouble. This same applies to our finances.

To educate yourself and find programs that can assist you in purchasing your home, you can go to the following Web sites:

The Federal Housing Administration—www.fha.com
The U.S. Department of Housing and Urban Development—www.hud
 .gov
HSH Associates Financial Publishers—www.hsh.com
Bankrate.com—www.bankrate.com
Fannie Mae—www.fanniemae.com
Freddie Mac—www.freddiemac.com
Mortgage Bankers Association—www.mbaa.org

Paying Your Loan Early

Many people have asked about the possibilities of paying off their mortgage early. I have always been a huge fan of early mortgage payments. You should consider two things before doing this, however. One, don't start paying down your mortgage until you have established an adequate emergency fund—you should always have access to cash in case of unexpected

13 Tips to Avoiding Predatory Lending

1. Read everything carefully before you sign.
2. Hire a qualified real estate attorney to help you understand the documents that you sign.
3. Do not sign any blank documents.
4. Hire a qualified financial adviser to help you calculate how much you can afford.
5. Do not purchase property for another party.
6. Be honest about your employment status.
7. Do not exaggerate your assets.
8. Report all of your debts.
9. Do not alter your tax returns.
10. Tell the truth about all gifts and financial help.
11. Be truthful about credit difficulties.
12. Do not provide any false documentation.
13. Do not mislead.

life events. Second, your contributions for your tax-deferred assets such as your IRA and your 401(k) should come first, and you should be deducting the maximum amount from your paycheck. I have also heard that paying extra principal contributes to extra equity in your home that isn't readily accessible. There is also the argument that if you have a low-interest mortgage, and an opportunity arises to invest the principal payment in an investment with a higher return than the tax-effective rate of your mortgage interest, you should probably do that. However, for many reasons, I still prefer that you pay your mortgage early, provided that your emergency fund and tax-deferred assets are in order.

If you have invested in your retirement—IRA and/or 401(k)—you have an emergency fund, you have eliminated your high-risk debt, and you have some excess cash, you could be in a great position to begin paying down your mortgage early. It is a misconception that early-mortgage payments have "disappeared" in your home's equity value and you have wasted your money. Here are four advantages of paying down your mortgage early:

1. **Building Equity.** Equity is the amount of your home that you own that has been built up through payments and appreciation. Your home is an investment, and just like a stock, that equity has the potential to generate you a return.

2. **Medicaid Eligibility.** If you are older, many states consider your home an exempt asset when it comes to qualifying for Medicaid, regardless of how much equity you have in it.

3. **Home-Equity Line Access.** You can always apply for an equity line of credit if you are ever in a bind and need some cash (preferably while you are still working and have an income). If you should use this option, make sure that you get a line of credit where you can write a check against it only if you need it. This way you will have access to the cash, but aren't paying interest on it until you actually use it. Chances are, payments for this line of credit will be less than your mortgage payments would have been.

4. **Psychic Income.** It is an empowering feeling if you are retired and don't have to worry about a mortgage expense. Arguably, you may have gotten a higher return in the market than in your home, but nothing beats the feeling of being debt free to relieve your mind!

There is no guarantee that you will receive a return in the stock market that's higher than the rate of interest on your mortgage. To some, paying off that mortgage early might not make sense these days. However, I rate peace of mind higher than any other economic rational out there. If we can all strive for that day when we are debt free, we can then work to put full attention toward our savings. So why not opt for that fifteen-year mortgage instead of that thirty-year that is so popular? Or get a thirty-year and treat it like a fifteen-year mortgage by finding out from your financial planner the amount that you should increase your monthly payment to cut the length of your mortgage in half. Many people prepay the next month's principal in addition to their regular monthly payment (be sure to ask the lender if there is a prepayment penalty). Imagine how much more modest your living costs will be without any debts or house payments.

We all want to live the dream of owning our own home. To come home to something that we own is a magical feeling. This comes at a hefty price, however. Take the time to make this decision wisely. Cross every *t,* dot every *i.* In the end it will be worth the time invested.

HAVING PROBLEMS WITH MORTGAGE PAYMENTS?

Do you already own a home but for whatever reason are finding it more and more difficult to pay the mortgage? Sometimes life can throw us a curveball that we didn't expect. The first thing *not* to do is to panic. Understand that although it might seem like a rough situation, there are ways to get you through this successfully. Here are a few things that can assist you in finding a way out of your financial hole if you feel that you are in danger of becoming a foreclosure statistic.

Step One: Assemble a Plan

Many people try to contact the lender before they have a plan themselves. Put yourself in the seat of the lender whose capital is at risk. Would you work with someone who doesn't seem to have a plan of action to repay your funds? Write out a budget, articulate your goals on paper, and have a plan for yourself before you talk to the lender.

Step Two: Act Quickly

Your job is to contact them before they have to contact you. If you see yourself in a financial bind and might miss a payment, *before* you miss your first payment, you should arrange a meeting with your lender to discuss your situation. It is costly for them to go through with a foreclosure, and in this environment lenders do not want extra leverage on their balance sheets that they are accountable for.

Step Three: Know Your Options

- *Were you a victim of predatory lending?* A good mortgage attorney will help you to pursue your rights.
- *Loan workout*: You can negotiate the best type of plan that fits your needs.
  - **Loan Modification.** You might be able to modify the rate, the balance of the loan, the fees owed for being delinquent, or even the term of the loan. This is purely at the discretion of the lender. Many people never even check if their lender would be willing to modify the loan. It never hurts to ask.
  - **Repayment Plan.** Don't forget, the lender has an interest in your paying off the loan because your interest is how they earn

income. If you present the lender with a plan that you think you can follow according to your budget, they might be willing to work with you.

- Short sale: This should be the last resort. In a short sale you sell a home for less than what you owe on it, which may result in a liability to the bank that you still have to pay.
- Forbearance plan: This is the most frequently used plan and delays or reduces the number of payments for a short time.

- **Preforeclosure Sale.** Many people cannot repay their loan even if their payments are lowered. A program offered by the Department of Housing and Urban Development allows the mortgagor in default to sell his or her home and use the net sale proceeds to satisfy the mortgage debt even if those are less than the amount owed. The difference between this and a short sale is that a preforeclosure sale assumes that the borrower has been delinquent. To learn more about this program and to see if you are eligible, visit www.hud.gov.
- **Deed in Lieu of Foreclosure.** This is not as bad as a foreclosure but does require that you relinquish your property. This instrument conveys all interest in a property to the lender to satisfy the loan and to avoid foreclosure proceedings.

CHAPTER TWELVE

Step Seven: Adopting a Diversified Investment Strategy

Pop quiz!

Which of the six below is the best place to invest your money?

a. Stocks
b. Bonds
c. Real estate
d. Business
e. Gold
f. Oil

Think about it before you continue. Which has had the best returns or will have the best returns? While you ponder, let's analyze the history of the markets since the 1970s.

In the 1970s . . .

Gold was hot. It rose almost 300 percent in ten years. Since the fall of the market in 2000, it has been considered a safe haven for investment dollars and has flourished tremendously, providing an annual return of almost 17 percent between 1999 and 2006.

In the 1980s . . .

Oil was hot. The second oil crisis had just concluded in 1980. In 1979 a new regime that took control in Iran attempted to resume oil exports, but at an inconsistent and lower volume, causing oil prices to soar. This continued as Iraq invaded Iran in 1980 and both Iran's and Iraq's production of oil was severely cut. Oil prices declined for six years after 1980, but we have seen returns similar to this in 2003 when the United States invaded Iraq.

In the 1990s . . .

Stocks were hot. The S&P posted gains of as much as 220 percent and annual returns in excess of 20 percent. You could pick stocks by throwing a dart at a board and make great returns!

In the 2000s . . .

Real estate was hot. U.S. real estate prices increased more than 56 percent from the beginning of 1999 to the end of 2004. They continued to provide stellar returns until they peaked in 2007.

Okay . . . I will ask again. Now, which one of the six below do you think is the best place to invest your money?

a. Stocks
b. Bonds
c. Real estate
d. Business
e. Gold
f. Oil

Let me give you some additional information. Let's compare stocks to real estate between the years of 1980 and 2004:

- Real estate return, 1980–2004: 247%
- S&P 500 return, 1980–2004: 1,000%

I know many people say that real estate is better than stocks. Does seeing this comparison change your mind about stocks . . . are stocks better than real estate? Are you confused yet as to the best place to invest your funds?

The answer is simple: The *best* place to invest your funds is in all of them! Not to say that you should run out now and invest within every asset class, because we all have different risk-tolerance levels. Some of you may never invest in a business, some may prefer bonds to stocks because you are in or near retirement, and some may prefer stocks because you are young and ready to take on lots of risk. However, what I am saying is there is no singular "best" investment but only the mixture of investments that is most appropriate for you.

It amazes me the number of advertisements that I see on television and from people in various professions that attempt to prove their investment vehicles are better than others. A mortgage broker or a real estate agent might try to convince you that real estate is the *best* way to accumulate wealth. A stock trader might try to convince you that stocks are the easiest way to become independently wealthy. You turn on the television or the radio and you might hear how gold is simply "a gift from God" when it comes to investments because of its great historical returns. In reality, one investment of the six has consistently given the greatest returns: business investment. Starting your own company has historically been the place where you can get returns that are not even measurable. What sort of return did Bill Gates get from starting Microsoft with minimal investment in his garage? I don't think that they have a calculator that can hold all of those numbers! However, starting a business also has the most risk attached to it, so you need to be sure that you are well prepared to start a business venture. So we need to be smart with our investments and apply two simple rules that state that we are never to put all of our eggs in one basket . . . diversification and asset allocation.

STOCKS

What Is Stock and How Do I Buy It?

Stock is:

a. The outstanding capital of a company or corporation.
b. The shares of a particular company or corporation.
c. The certificate of ownership of such stock: stock certificate.*

---

* stock. (n.d.). *Dictionary.com Unabridged* (v 1.0.1). Retrieved November 15, 2006, from Dictionary.com, http://dictionary.reference.com/browse/stock.

Simply put, stock is a piece of ownership of a company. You can go to Starbucks and purchase coffee to be a customer. However, you can purchase stock in Starbucks and become an owner of the company. As an owner, you have a stake in every coffee that is purchased. The more shares you purchase, the larger your stake becomes.

Stocks are traded on "exchanges." An *exchange* is "an association of stockbrokers who meet to buy and sell stocks and bonds according to fixed regulations."* There are many exchanges in which to buy and sell stocks. Starbucks trades on the National Association of Securities Dealers Automated Quotations exchange (NASDAQ). A *stockbroker* is a broker or an individual "employed by a member firm of a stock exchange, who buys and sells stocks and other securities for customers." If you want to own a share of Starbucks by purchasing stock, here is the process:

1. You go to a stockbroker, who works for a hypothetical company called ACME Inc. He places an order for one hundred shares of Starbucks.

2. The broker quotes you the last trading price of $38.48 for each single share of Starbucks stock (you will spend approximately $3,848 plus the commission that the broker charges you).

3. He writes a ticket for the order, enters the order into a computer, and sends the order up to the "stock trader" to execute the order. The stock trader's sole job is to buy and sell stock for ACME Inc.

4. The stock trader, who is on the exchange (in this case NASDAQ), either sells you one hundred shares of Starbucks stock himself or finds another trader on the NASDAQ who is willing to sell you one hundred shares of Starbucks.

5. Upon finding another person who is willing to sell you the stock, the trader sends your order to him for execution.

6. He gets a price, which is normally pretty close to the quoted price (in this case, $38.48), and he sends the report back to the broker.

7. The broker tells you the price at which you purchased the stock, and you now own one hundred shares of Starbucks for the total cost of $3,848 plus commission.

History has proven that over time, stocks generally go up in value.

* stock exchange. (n.d.). *The American Heritage Dictionary of the English Language,* 4th ed. Retrieved November 15, 2006, from Dictionary.com, http://dictionary.reference.com/browse/stock exchange.

However, a great deal of risk is involved in purchasing stock, as there is never any guarantee that your stock will increase in price. From 1997 through 2000 many people got rich when the stock market appeared to have such a great run that it would go up forever. However, most people lost more than the fortunes they gained when the stock market seemed to go straight down in value through 2003. Then the market returned to its strength through 2007, until the collapse of the real estate market and the ensuing credit crunch. Since the market bottomed out in 2009 we have seen a modest recovery and a lot of volatility through 2010.

So "playing" the stock market can be a somewhat volatile way of investing, but some tricks will help you keep risk at bay. The best way to manage the risk in owning stocks is to diversify your holdings. Before we analyze how to purchase stocks, we must analyze the types of risks that are inherent in the market. Two types of risk are involved in purchasing stocks: (1) unsystematic risk and (2) systematic risk. *Unsystematic risk* is the risk that is specific to an industry or firm. For example, if Starbucks has a strike, this represents risk that is specific to Starbucks. *Systematic risk* is the risk inherent to the entire market or entire market segment. If the federal government announces a rise in interest rates to slow the growth of the economy, all stocks will be affected . . . including Starbucks. If you only own Starbucks, then you have both unsystematic risk and systematic risk in your portfolio, which is a lot of risk. However, if you purchase different stocks from varying segments of the economy, then the specific risk of each individual stock begins to weaken. One stock may have a strike, but the odds of their all having a strike are low. The more different stocks you own, or the more diversification you have in your portfolio, the less unsystematic risk you have.

An ideal portfolio has no unsystematic risk and minimal systematic risk (this can't be completely eliminated). Many portfolio managers limit each individual stock's value to 5 percent of their total portfolio value. For instance, if a portfolio manager owned $1 million of stock, he or she would not own more than $50,000 in Starbucks stock. The percentage that you hold in each investment is your *asset allocation*. This is the allocation of your assets, or division of your assets, among various categories such as bonds, stock, cash, business, and real estate. Its major purpose is to reduce risk by diversifying the portfolio.

Many say that asset allocation is the single most important aspect of any portfolio and, as we discussed in the company-retirement-plan chapter, can account for as much as 90 percent of portfolio return. Each person will have a different asset allocation, and it is based primarily on the risk tolerance of the investor. A younger individual might have an asset allocation of 70 percent stocks and 30 percent bonds. Stocks are more volatile than bonds but tend to have a greater return over time. A younger investor has time to recover from any major market fluctuations. In contrast, an older investor near or in retirement might have an asset allocation of 20 percent stocks and 80 percent bonds. One who is thinking of retirement should primarily be concerned with conserving capital, not with investment appreciation. Each asset allocation should remain until the investor decides to change it. As the market goes up and down, so will the asset allocation. It is up to the investor to rebalance the portfolio periodically to assure that the asset allocation remains as he wishes it to be.

How to Research a Stock

A man sits in front of his computer and checks his e-mail, seeing this message:

> WXLYQ IS TRADING AT .001 AND IS COMING OUT WITH BIG NEWS TODAY! IT SHOULD GO TO .02 BY THE END OF THE TRADING DAY! GET IN NOW WHILE YOU STILL CAN!

The man reads this message, thinks for a second, and grabs his calculator. He thinks aloud, "If I put in $100 at .001, then I can buy 100,000 shares! If it goes to .02, I will have $2,000! Wait a minute, if I put in $1,000, I can buy 1 million shares. If it only goes to .01, half of what they predict, I will have $10,000! This is a no-brainer! *Where do I sign?!*"

What he doesn't know is that he has just been scammed by one of the oldest tricks in the book . . . the pump-and-dump trick. He doesn't realize that the person who sent that message already owns the stock WXLYQ and has sent that same message out to thousands (sometimes millions) of people. If just a small fraction of them take the bait, then he will create a small volume fluctuation. Many traders have their alerts set to these volume fluctuations and will purchase the stock just because they see a spike in volume. The end of this chain reaction is that the original sender of the message will sell all of his stock at .01 and leave all of the other buyers holding a piece of crap! The stock goes back to .001 because nobody is left to purchase the stock, and it remains at that price level until it is taken off the market (delisted). All you can expect is a write-off on your taxes for your losses (you can write off up to $3,000 per year for tax losses).

Is this unethical and illegal? Yes, it is. However, there isn't much you can do, because it happens frequently. "An ounce of prevention is worth a pound of cure," and the best way you can prevent this is to do your homework on every stock you purchase.

The first question you should ask is "Does this stock earn money?" Earnings are a major measure of value in the stock market. Four times a year, each stock trading on an exchange is required to report earnings. These are the most watched numbers on Wall Street. Beginning each quarter, analysts give their estimate of how they feel a company will do for that quarter. The estimates are averaged, and that average becomes the consensus estimate. If the company does worse than this estimate, its stock price almost certainly falls in the following trading sessions.

Earnings estimates are an example of *fundamental analysis*.

Fundamental analysis is the analysis of security values grounded in basic factors such as earnings, balance-sheet variables, and management quality. Fundamental analysis attempts to determine the true value of a security. If the market price of a stock deviates from this value, one can take advantage of the difference by acquiring or selling the stock. Fundamental analysis may involve investigating a firm's financial statements, visiting its managers, or examining how a particular industry is affected by changes in the economy.

There are many ways of running a fundamental analysis on a stock—some of the basic methods are described below. Keep in mind that the ratios below mean nothing by themselves. To use them effectively, they must each be compared against the average for the industry to which the company being analyzed belongs.

Price-to-Earnings Ratio (P/E) = (market value per share)/(earnings per share). This ratio compares the current price with earnings to see if a stock is over- or undervalued. If the Starbucks P/E ratio is 54.71, and the Specialty Eateries industry (the industry in which Starbucks is grouped) has a P/E ratio of 30.4, this could signal that Starbucks is overvalued and should be sold.

Return on Equity (ROE) = (net income)/(shareholders' equity). This ratio measures the level of return a company management gets on the owners' investment. On the day this chapter was written, Starbucks had an ROE of

23.88 percent. The Specialty Eateries industry had a ratio of 21.7 percent. This means that for the time period measured, the management of Starbucks got a better return on shareholders' investment than the industry as a whole.

You can learn more about fundamental analysis at www.investopedia.com.

You can also do a *technical analysis* on a stock. This was my primary weapon of choice when I was a stock trader. This method analyzes patterns and statistics created through market activity such as past prices and volume. In no way do we attempt to measure a stock's intrinsic value, as is done through fundamental analysis, but instead we use charts to identify patterns that might suggest future activity.

Technical analysis only takes historical performance into account. For example, take a stock that is trading at $6 per share; one year later it has appreciated to $10 per share; then one year later it goes back to $6. One who uses technical analysis might purchase the stock thinking that because of past performance it has formed a trend and will hit $10 the following year.

Once you research a stock and decide to purchase it, you must then commit to a regular investment strategy, such as dollar-cost averaging. You could purchase many shares at one time, but below you will read why it is more beneficial to spread your purchases over regular intervals.

Dollar-Cost Averaging. Investment of a fixed amount of money at regular intervals, usually each month. This results in the purchase of extra shares during market downturns and fewer shares during market upturns. Dollar-cost averaging is based on the belief that a particular stock will rise in price over the long term and that it is not worthwhile (or even possible) to identify intermediate highs and lows.

If you do the research on your stocks, you will be able to conduct dollar-cost averaging with high-quality stocks. You do this automatically if you invest by being enrolled through your company retirement plan at your job. If you have a brokerage account, you can do this by regularly depositing funds and purchasing stocks through your account.

Make It Easy on Yourself

For most people, researching individual stocks is complex and requires time and knowledge of the market. Many earn a living by doing market research, but they, too, have difficulty selecting the best stocks for themselves or prospective clients. Most American households have only limited time to conduct market research and, more important, only limited finds to invest, so it is difficult to establish and maintain a properly allocated and diversified portfolio. It is easy for portfolio managers with $500 million in capital to set rules to limit the total value of each stock to 5 to 10 percent of the total value of the portfolio. However, what about the individual investor who has only $1,000 to $5,000 in cash to invest? After paying commissions to an investment firm, one might be able to buy only four to five shares of each stock. Well, there is an easier way, and that way is through the purchase of a *mutual fund*.

Mutual Fund. A fund that gives small investors access to a well-diversified portfolio of equities, bonds, and other securities. Each shareholder participates in the gain or loss of the fund. Shares are issued and can be redeemed as needed.

Each mutual fund is managed by a qualified portfolio manager, ideally, whose sole job is to get those who invest in his mutual fund a solid return. The thousands of mutual funds have thousands of managers whose styles and strategies are extremely different. Your job as an investor is to make sure that you select the mutual fund that is most appropriate for your needs and preferences. However, with such a wide variety of mutual funds, how do you select the best one for you? Many things distinguish one mutual fund from another, and the following will touch upon a few key areas of focus when selecting one.

No-Load Mutual Funds. Sold directly to customers at net asset value without a sales commission.

Commissions can erode the long-term return of a portfolio. Hence I select *no-load* mutual funds in the portfolios for my clients. Many investment advisers will suggest that you select *loaded* mutual funds, or funds that when bought and sold generate a commission. I promise you that for every one loaded fund, you can find five no-load mutual funds that can give you an equivalent or better performance.

To display the impact of commissions on your investment portfolio, I have outlined a scenario below. Both scenarios reflect an investment of $500 per month, at a 10 percent yield, for forty years. One scenario assumes monthly commission charges of $50.

	Monthly Investment	Yield	Account Value After 40 Years
Without Commission	$500	10%	$3,162,039.79
With Commission (Average $50/month)	$500	10%	$2,845,835.81
Cost of Commissions			$316,203.98

As you can see, commissions can significantly erode the long-term portfolio value.

Management Tenure. It is important for the manager of the mutual fund to have significant experience in directing the investments of the fund. You want to determine the success a particular manager has had with managing the mutual fund. If you see that a mutual fund has a five-year average return of 20 percent per year, see if that performance was generated by a previous manager or the current manager. It is usually best to ensure that the current management has directed the mutual fund for at least five years.

Morningstar Rating. Morningstar is a well-known and respected analyst service. It rates funds based upon performance against the rest of their peers—one star being the lowest rating and five the highest. Generally speaking, it is best to select funds with a minimum of four stars.

Risk Rating. For you to be able to sleep at night, select funds that don't have excessive risk. Selection of high-risk funds means that the manager's investment strategy or the investments that he selects are often volatile. I usually suggest that the risk rating of a fund be from low to average compared to its peers.

Performance Measurement. Performance measurement is the calculation of return a money manager is able to achieve over a stated interval. As one year is not a sufficient time, it is common to measure the return over the past three, five, *and* ten years of the life of the fund. It is common to assess the return by comparing it to a benchmark over the same interval. One commonly used benchmark is the S&P 500. If a mutual fund has outperformed the benchmark during *all three* intervals (under the same manager), this is a good indication of a quality investing strategy, in which you may want to invest. Here is a hypothetical example:

VWXYZ, a mutual fund, has achieved a return of:

- 36 percent for the past three years versus an S&P 500 return of 34 percent for the past three years.
- 25 percent for the past five years versus an S&P return of 21 percent for the past five years.
- 90 percent for the past ten years versus an S&P return of 88 percent for the past ten years.

In the above example, mutual fund VWXYZ has outperformed the S&P 500 in each time interval.

Exchange-Traded Funds. To achieve ultimate diversification, one would have to purchase a share of every stock in the market. This sounds far-fetched, but it isn't entirely impossible. Some funds are designed to trade according to how an entire index trades, just as if you had purchased every stock in the stated index. If you are just starting out and don't have much money to invest, it may be wise for you to simplify your portfolio even further beyond mutual funds. One of the best portfolios to select for beginning investors is composed of exchange-traded funds, or ETFs.

An ETF is a security that tracks an index and represents a basket of stocks like an index fund, but trades like a stock on an exchange, thus experiencing price changes throughout the day as it is bought and sold.*

The advantages of owning an ETF over a mutual fund or a stock are:

- You receive the diversification of an entire index.
- Since the trades are computer-generated, the expense ratios are lower than those of the average mutual fund.

For the investor looking to start a portfolio from scratch, I have assembled a basic portfolio composed of exchange-traded funds. These are an easy way to obtain broad diversification with low expenses. The following

---

* ETF. (n.d.). *Investopedia.com*. Retrieved November 16, 2006, from Dictionary.com, http://dictionary.reference.com/browse/ETF.

table doesn't take the place of advice from a qualified adviser but shows you a sample of what a portfolio could look like if you followed the principles that we have been discussing.

A Hypothetical Portfolio for Beginners

Fund	Ticker Symbol	Investor Age	Hypothetical Allocation of Assets	Investment Stage
SPDRS	SPY	25	55%	Accumulation (most risk)
iShares MSCI Emerging Markets Index	EEM	25	15%	
Vanguard Total Bond Market Fund	BND	25	20%	
SPDR Gold Shares	GLD	25	10%	
SPDRS	SPY	45	30%	Conservation (average risk)
iShares MSCI Emerging Markets Index	EEM	45	10%	
Vanguard Total Bond Market Fund	BND	45	50%	
SPDR Gold Shares	GLD	45	10%	
SPDRS	SPY	65	15%	Distribution (least risk)
iShares MSCI Emerging Markets Index	EEM	65	5%	
Vanguard Total Bond Market Fund	BND	65	75%	
SPDR Gold Shares	GLD	65	5%	

The investment stages in the final column represent the various stages that one goes through in life.

The *accumulation stage* is when someone has just started working, is roughly between the ages of twenty-one and thirty-eight, and has many years before contemplating retirement. At this stage you can take the most risk because you have more time to recover from a downturn in the market. This hypothetical portfolio has an 80 percent investment in stocks and precious metals.

The *conservation stage* occurs roughly between the ages of thirty-nine and fifty. During this stage, ideally you have accumulated a nice-size nest egg from your earlier years, have just started thinking about retirement, still have more than ten years until you actually retire, but are now a lot more concerned about the loss of capital than you once were. In the hypothetical portfolio you have 50 percent in bonds and only 50 percent in stock and precious-metal investments.

The *distribution stage* occurs roughly between the ages of fifty-one and retirement. During this stage the person's ultimate goal is the conservation of capital and outpacing inflation. The hypothetical example has a 75 percent bond investment. This is important because when you are in the distribution stage, you don't have that much time to recover from downturns in the economy. I can't tell you how many calls I have received that go like this: "I am fifty-five years old. I just lost eighty percent of my portfolio value, and I am wondering, what should I do to save my retirement?"

I ask, "What is your current asset allocation?"

"I have eighty percent of my portfolio in stocks."

Now, I wish I could be Superman, fly backward around the earth to reverse time, and make sure that these people had the *proper* asset allocation in their portfolio, which wouldn't consist of 80 percent stocks. However, as much as I would like to be able to reach into a magic bags of tricks to provide a fancy and insightful response, it comes down to only the following:

1. Work longer years/delay retirement.
2. Save more money.
3. Do both.

I am hoping that those reading this book can avert this disaster and make sure that they have the proper asset allocation in their portfolio.

VILLAGE VISIT

The Power of Investing: Community Youth

Prison industries forecast the number of prisons that will be needed based upon third- and fourth-grade reading levels, for those who cannot read as well as their peers at this age have a much higher chance of becoming incarcerated. If you want to forecast the success of the village, you need to measure the success of the youth in the village. The future of our country depends upon our ability to teach our children, the ability of our children to learn, and most important, their ability to implement what they have learned for the sake of themselves and their community.

Akil King is one of the star pupils in my youth financial-literacy group, All About Business. Through committed community service that began when he was young, he has created many financial-literacy workshops for all ages, teaching those principles that he worked hard to learn as a teen. By further implementing his learned skills, he created a successful company while still in school, which provided educational programming that enhanced the lives of college students with life-skills training. He is paying his own way through school, helping others, making money, and positioning himself to be a viable economic powerhouse in his community. At eighteen, Akil put together his first diversified stock portfolio (full of exchange-traded funds) in his Roth IRA, using many of the principles outlined in this chapter.

THE LUCKY ORPHAN
by Akil King

Here I was, barely twenty-one years old, participating in a candid one-hour conversation in the office of a vice president of one of the most profitable Fortune 100 companies in the world. That I was in the presence of someone so successful, influential, and driven was mind-boggling. We talked about life, school, and growing up in New York City, all while communicating effortlessly. I didn't know

(*continued*)

what decisions, right or wrong, ultimately resulted in my being in this position, but I knew that I was grateful that I made them.

I was born in Brooklyn, New York, in April 1988. Brooklyn has a storied history for being the heart of New York City, but also for its notoriously rough neighborhoods. I was too young to remember the crime rates that had spiked in the eighties and early nineties, but I definitely remember the happenings of my neighborhood. Like many young kids who grew up there, I was part of a single-parent home in which my mother struggled to make ends meet for my older brother and me. She worked long hours and weekends to ensure that we had food on the table. Because of this, at the age of five, I took the bus to and from school, navigating my way home from the bus stop, letting myself into my building and apartment. I would sometimes prepare my food. During the summer of 1995 my mother passed away due to kidney failure brought on by HIV/AIDS. At the age of seven, much of my personal connection to this world was ripped away from me, and I was thrust into the cold reality of life.

While my aunt and other family members all contributed to my upbringing, I used basketball as therapy. It was a chance for me to take my mind off my problems and be myself. My outgoing and competitive spirit came out on the court, and I gained many friends through basketball. When I thought about my future, I knew I wanted to be somebody. My friends and I idolized professional players such as Michael Jordan and Allen Iverson, and who could blame us? We never saw any black CEOs, entrepreneurs, or presidents. The only successful black people we knew were rappers, singers, and sports stars. None of us could rap or sing, so we put our hopes in basketball.

In the weeks prior to my senior year in high school, my basketball dreams were shattered when I tore tendons in both my ankles. As I sat in the doctor's office barely able to walk, I could not stop crying. Not because of the pain that was piercing my body, but because I was thinking, "How will I get a scholarship to play in college?" After weeks of frustration and distress, the realization hit me. I knew I wanted to be successful and wealthy, but with my basketball dreams looking less and less likely, I know that I would need to find success through an alternate route.

(continued)

School had always been easy for me and I put forth little effort. With one year left before I graduated, I knew it was time for me to get serious. To my surprise, getting A's was relatively easy when I buckled down. I now began focusing on building my grades to get into a commendable institution of higher learning. I still didn't know what I wanted to do with my life, until one day my friends and I were on our way out of school and ran into our vice principal. "Hey, you guys, can you do me a huge favor?" he said. We looked at each other with hesitation. "Uh, yeah, what is it?" my friend Steve said. The vice principal then explained that he had a company president coming to start an educational series after school teaching about investments, and he needed some students to go for a bit, even if was only fifteen minutes. After some hesitation, we agreed. We figured we weren't doing anything but hanging out after school and we could leave when we saw fit, so why not? Little did we know that we would immediately be captivated in that tiny classroom as the young, energetic business owner named Ryan Mack told us that he quit his job trading securities in which he was making six figures to open his own financial-planning and investment firm. "Quitting a job that paid six figures?" I thought. "Well, whatever he was doing must be worth it. I want to know more."

We began meeting every Tuesday to learn about strategic investments and their importance in wealth management. We learned about call and put options, ETFs, 401(k)s, IRAs, budgeting, and all the ways to make your money work for you. This form of wealth building was so interesting that we started researching on our own and eventually, as high school seniors, began teaching the information we learned throughout the community. We taught at junior high schools, elementary schools, churches, workshops, and even to adults at colleges. Empowering the community with our newfound knowledge was the most exciting and vivifying feeling. I was always excited to go to different places, meet different people, and relay information that many times changed people's lives. As eager as I was to teach this information, I was even more excited to finally have the chance to use it. I would gain the chance sooner than I thought.

I had gotten into college, and my first couple weeks at Hampton University were invigorating. To see intelligent and driven young

(continued)

African-Americans from all over the country embarking on a journey to achieve an education for life was inspiring. Learning about the various cultures found in different regions across the United States was interesting and eye-opening. Then, out of nowhere, everything began getting extremely routine and boring. Every event, every party, and every outing seemed to be exactly the same. At first, I thought it was just me. I was from New York City; maybe my vision of fun was unrealistic and I just needed to adapt to the atmosphere. But then I started asking around, and an overwhelming number of students felt the same way. Our campus was in desperate need of a spark; a jolt of life and excitement. So I got a couple of friends together and came up with an idea. Why couldn't we change the way events were produced and parties were thrown at Hampton?

So that freshman year, we started a company whose sole purpose was to enhance student life. Cash Advance Entertainment LLC would cater to the two main reasons we believed students go away to college: academic achievement and social life fulfillment. Our company was a hit. At the first event there were two hundred people; at the next, three hundred; then, four hundred. At the conclusion of our freshman year, we figured we should start trying to capitalize on the influence that we had on campus. We began turning this service into revenue. By the time we were juniors, some of our events were yielding over 200 percent profits.

Between my company, part-time job, and investments such as a high-interest savings account, annuity, and Roth IRA, I gained enough money to pay for school and living expenses and attend a study-abroad program at Middlesex University in London, England. Using the foundation laid in that high school classroom every Tuesday after school, I had begun my own wealth initiative. The ability not only to learn about investments, but also to implement what I learned in building revenue, practicing entrepreneurship, and becoming financially stable, has molded me personally and professionally. In the summer of 2009, I landed an internship in marketing with Apple Inc., which has been declared the best marketing company in the world. The truly amazing thing was that I was the only undergraduate student to intern with Apple marketing. Here I was, a kid who'd just turned twenty-one a month before, in a roundtable with Harvard

(continued)

MBAs, Stanford grad students, and the best from Carnegie Mellon. All the interns were extremely intelligent, articulate, and personable. I sat there feeling a bit intimated and thought, "Why am I even in the same position as these people?" I was much younger, had much less work experience, and they went to the best schools. Then I thought, "Maybe it's because I started my own company, maybe because of my international experience, maybe because I am the only one at the table who was profiled in *Black Enterprise* magazine, or maybe even because I am doing my undergraduate degree and MBA in five years." Maybe it wasn't because of any of those reasons. Maybe it was just luck. Well, if so, maybe the luck of an orphan from Brooklyn, New York, changed unbeknownst to him at the exact moment he decided to pursue success by means of financial literacy.

RYAN MACK'S FIVE ECONOMIC EMPOWERMENT TIPS FOR YOUTH

1. Find your passion. Volunteer and do community service in your neighborhood. Network with other volunteers and take note of when you had the most fun. Those things that you are willing to do for free could be your passion. If you have fun doing something for free, how much fun will you have doing it while receiving a paycheck?
2. Read one book per month outside of your schoolwork on financial literacy, leadership, entrepreneurship, and books that provide you exposure to a wide variety of careers.
3. Become a teacher and motivator of youth. If you are in college, take trips to local high schools to discuss how you became a college student. If you are in high school, visit local middle schools in your area. If you are in middle school, work with your teachers to organize supervised field teaching trips for elementary schools in your area. Youth listen more attentively to their peers, and you not only have the opportunity to make a large impact, you can develop leadership skills while enhancing your résumé.
4. Travel as much as you can. If you can't afford to travel, research other countries at your local library or on the Internet. The world is much larger than your block.
5. Start a company. Think of an idea that you feel can make money; put together a team for you to manage; enlist a few mentors that

you can obtain guidance from; write a business plan; create and implement a marketing strategy; and go as hard as you can to make your business successful. If you fail, you have a great story to tell at your next interview.

BONDS

A bond is a certificate of ownership of a specified portion of debt scheduled to be paid by a government or corporation to an individual holder and usually bearing a fixed rate of interest.

Both governments and corporations need to raise capital to operate. Salaries, supplies, and facilities are all examples of expenses that an employer incurs. Welfare, Social Security, Medicaid, public schools, and the Iraq war are all examples of programs and events that require significant funding from the government. One of the ways to pay for expenses and programming is to borrow from individuals by issuing bonds. If you purchase a bond, you are lending that entity money, and it promises to return the funds borrowed *plus* interest.

If I approached you and asked to borrow money, and you were contemplating more profitable uses of your funds than to let me use them, you would not allow me to borrow them. So for me to entice you to let me borrow the money, I would have to make it worth your while by giving you a rate of return. This is why bonds always have an interest rate.

If I asked to borrow money to start a company, and you knew that I was irresponsible, always goofing around, and not a good businessperson, you would not be particularly willing to let me borrow the money because you might never see it again. However, if I said that I would give you a high interest rate on the funds that you lent to me, you would be more likely to let me borrow the money because you would be compensated for risk. If, however, I possessed the same amount of money and business experience as Bill Gates and asked to borrow some money from you, the scenario would be a little different. You would know that I was experienced and had a lot of collateral to back up the loan, and the chances of your getting the money back would be high. Therefore, I would not have to give you as high an interest rate on the loan because you are more certain of getting your money back and less risk is attached to the loan. However, you still need to be compensated for the opportunity cost of letting me use your money. Risk is part of what determines the amount of interest a bond will be paying for the loan. The risk that is attached to the entity, the time at which you are lending the funds, and market conditions all play a role in the amount of interest you will receive for a bond investment.

Bonds should be an integral part of every portfolio. However, the amount of bonds that you have in your portfolio is determined by your age and the risk that you are able to bear. The older you are, the more likely you are to increase the percentage of bonds in your portfolio.

GOLD AND OTHER PRECIOUS METALS

Gold and other precious metals are great hedges for investors. These investments are often negatively correlated with the stock market because they are considered safe havens when the market has problems. When the market goes down, people look for places to put their money that are not as heavily influenced by systematic risk as are investments within the market, so they often choose gold or other precious metals. They are also hedges against inflation if people are concerned about the strength of the U.S. dollar. Gold is a great investment, but should never be held as a primary investment . . . only a defensive investment. A few ways to invest in gold are highlighted below:

1. **Direct Ownership.** Our currency, the dollar, is nothing more than an IOU or a promissory note that is not backed up with any tangible value. It is called *fiat* money but it only has value because the government has declared it to have value. If the dollar falls in value, those holding tangible goods such as resources and precious metals will benefit. Gold cannot be changed or controlled by the government or the Fed chairman, who decides what to do with interest rates or the number of dollars in circulation. Only the natural laws of supply and demand come into effect with gold. However, a direct purchase can be risky because you purchase gold at retail and sell at wholesale. A big jump in price will be needed just to break even, making a long-term perspective even more important. The easiest way to purchase gold is through minted coins, such as American Eagles or Canadian Maple Leafs.

2. **Exchange-Traded Funds.** In the hypothetical portfolio on page 212 composed of ETFs, the symbol GLD represents SPDR Gold Shares. This fund and other gold ETFs trade on a stock exchange like an ordinary stock. The portfolio of all these ETFs is fixed

and does not change. GLD holds gold bullion as their one and only asset. This is a more practical way of investing in gold as opposed to direct ownership.

3. **Gold Mutual Funds.** These funds hold companies that might mine for gold. The one problem about this investment strategy is that the price also depends upon management, administration, and the profit of the company. You want to research these funds the same way that you do any other fund as outlined in the section on mutual funds.

4. **Gold Options and Futures.** Many commercials play up the advantages of options and futures trading. If you are not willing to commit the time to become a full-time professional trader, then I would highly caution you against this option because the risk and volatility in this market is extremely high. It's really only for the experienced investor who wants to speculate on the price of gold.

REAL ESTATE INVESTMENTS

Real estate is land plus anything permanently fixed to it, including buildings and other items attached to the structure.

One of my favorite authors is *Rich Dad Poor Dad*'s Robert Kiyosaki. I feel that he is a perfect example of someone who is "living in the village" in the right way. Not only has he put in the hard work to make himself millions through investments, but he is now taking his knowledge and teaching others how to do what he has done. He represents the principles of this book better than most. However, I do not want to see another person claiming to be a real estate expert after reading that one book who then maxed out handfuls of credit cards using "other people's money," purchasing property in an irresponsible manner.

As much as I loved that book, one should never think that one book makes one an expert. I am sure that Mr. Kiyosaki would agree with me that it takes much more effort. What those people don't realize is that he spent years researching, learning, and perfecting his craft as a real estate investor.

Real estate is a proven profitable investment strategy that can generate millions or even billions of dollars in wealth *if* done properly. The perks can be tremendous, the wealth accumulation astounding, and the revenue streams are almost endless, but you must be properly prepared. I want to give you some important tips to make sure that you are not among the hundreds of people who go broke trying to play this game the wrong way.

Step One: What You Don't Know Can Bankrupt You!

If you are thinking about entering this market, you must do more than read one book and have a positive attitude.

- Read as many books as possible to make sure that you are getting different perspectives of how to invest in real estate.
- Look for any real estate classes that are offered through your local church, nonprofit, or community center.
- Tap your network for anyone who might practice real estate investing to see if he or she would be willing to become your mentor.
- Lastly, getting a mortgage broker's or real estate agent's license will give you a tremendous amount of knowledge about the ins and outs of the industry.

Step Two: What Is Your Plan?

Once you have obtained the knowledge, now you must lay out a plan/strategy for investing in real estate. The plan that you lay out should include the following:

- The type of properties that you are going to invest in
- The geographic area that will be your focus
- The best strategy to invest in that property type and area

Step Three: Take Your Time; Don't Overload Yourself

I understand the anxiety of trying to get your first deal done, but your first property acquisition especially should be as unrushed and methodical as possible. You should only be doing one deal at a time if this is your first investment property.

Step Four: Plan for the Worst but Expect the Best

You should have more than one exit strategy and be prepared for all worst-case scenarios.

- What if the renter in your property moves out? Do you have enough to pay at least six months of the mortgage?
- What happens if it is a renter's market and you can't get enough to cover your entire mortgage? Do you have enough money to cover the difference indefinitely?
- What would you do if there was a fire on the property? Do you have enough to pay for homeowner's insurance?

Step Five: Be Wise!

Make sure that you are being as prudent as possible when you purchase real estate. Three don'ts to remember are:

1. Don't become that investor that puts 100 percent of his or her capital into real estate. You should always consider other investments that we have discussed here. I spoke to many people in 2007 when the market turned down who were overleveraged with too many properties in their portfolio.
2. Don't forget that the best deals usually don't have any competition, so don't be afraid to be unique and do plenty of research.
3. Don't chase the market! Many people are guilty of looking for the hottest markets and thinking those are the best places to invest. "Buy low, sell high" applies in the stock market and also in the real estate market. If you were going shopping and saw a shirt that was marked *up* 200 percent, would you buy it? Of course you wouldn't; you would rather it be marked *down* 50 percent because it is cheaper. So if you wouldn't want to purchase a shirt that is marked up, why would you want to make a multi-thousand- or -million-dollar investment that is marked up? If you ever hear someone say, "Why would you ever want to invest in property there?" this is your cue to start looking for a good piece of property in that area to buy.

VILLAGE VISIT

The Power of Investing in Real Estate:
The Real Estate Developer

The real estate developer determines what your neighborhood will look like and can have a heavy influence on who can live there. Whether it is a stadium being built in the community, a new school, a condo unit, or a new home on the corner, it requires a lot of knowledge of the real estate market and learning how to navigate the funding "minefield" to make it in this industry. Those who are good at this game become multibillionaires, but those who are not careful end up homeless themselves.

At age thirty-three, Amin Irving is young in the game of real estate development, but he has hit the ground running. He became the owner of a $7.7 million, 175-unit housing complex in 2005; he built thirty single-family homes in Ohio in 2006; closed on a $5 million, 76-unit apartment building in Detroit in 2007; and successfully navigated through arguably the toughest real estate economy of all time with the skill of a thirty-year veteran of the trade. We can easily talk about all the many awards he has received for his achievements in such a short time, but I would rather discuss how he empowers his tenants. He is always calling me and other organizations that can educate his tenants about various life skills. He treats his tenants like an extension of his family, and I am sure has received a lot of flak for investing in improvements that were not even necessary to pass inspection. He just wanted his tenants to feel a sense of pride in where they live. I want you to hear from a pro about not only how to invest in real estate, but how to do it in a way that empowers others as well as makes money for yourself.

LOST THE BATTLE . . . WON THE WAR
by Amin Irving

It all started in 1989, when I was twelve years old and my mother was too weak to go to the store to buy groceries. In a single-parent

(continued)

household with no brothers or sisters, I was at an early age forced to do more than what I thought I could do. Mom explained to me how to drive a stick-shift car at twelve, and at age thirteen I received a minor's restricted license and took care of most of the family operations. When I was in high school, my mom was diagnosed with cancer, and two months after my high school graduation she passed away. So there I was, my entire world overturned: no mother, bad grades, and my closest friends leaving for college. I was left with the house in which I grew up, a job working as a movie cashier, and bills that I couldn't afford to pay.

I didn't realize it at the time, but I started to get rid of the things that I knew would eventually ruin me, most important, my mother's house and a lack of quality education. I couldn't afford the house, so I found a real estate agent. He suggested selling the house for $20,000 less than I thought someone would pay for it. It's not as if I analyzed the market and knew what the prices were in the area, but I'd lived in this house for seven years and felt that he was lowballing the price. So I suggested that the house be put on the market for $20,000 higher. Within two weeks it sold at my price (in retrospect, the price should have been even higher). That's when I thought to myself, "This real estate stuff is easy."

I enrolled at Lansing Community College (LCC). I knew that if I earned good grades my freshman year, I could transfer to any school I wanted. I decided to take advantage of everything LCC had to offer, and the best thing was that all of their services were free. I ended my freshman year with a 3.64 GPA and was accepted at the University of Michigan. I will forever be grateful to LCC because that institution gave me a second chance at success.

Ever since I can remember, I've always had a passion for business. I used to draw pictures of semitrailers with IRVING ENTERPRISES on the trailers. In elementary school, a buddy and I used to collect cans at Michigan State University home football games and return them to the local store for ten cents a can (we went to Space Camp on that money), so when I started attending the University of Michigan, I knew I wanted to major in business.

At the time, the business school was a two-year college and you had to apply your sophomore year. Well, just my luck, the U of M

(continued)

business school was ranked number one in the country the same year I wanted to apply, making my likelihood of being accepted even lower. I studied my butt off that sophomore year and was accepted to the business school. During my junior year at the business school, I landed an internship with Citigroup in its real estate division. The job, in real estate equity placement, offered me a big-picture view of the real estate industry. There was only one problem. After all the anticipation of landing a good job with great pay, I didn't like it much. I was doing all of the stuff I had dreamed—taking limousine rides home from work, going to all the hot Broadway shows and to *Letterman* and *Conan O'Brien*—but I realized I was not happy. I had built up in my mind that a high-paying job with all the perks would be the greatest thing ever, but it wasn't buying me happiness. Senior year, Citigroup offered me a full-time position, complete with moving expenses and a preapproved mortgage for a new home. At first I accepted the offer, but as the start date got closer and closer, the more miserable and depressed I became. I knew, deep down, that I was getting into something that I didn't want to do. One morning during the summer before I was to start full-time at Citigroup, I was reading the Bible and realized that one of God's names is I AM. That means HE IS; He is my source for everything: happiness, joy, peace, contentment, health, job, and financial prosperity. At that moment I received the boldness to fax Citigroup my resignation letter.

I had no job and was squatting at a friend's apartment on his couch. I started calling business school alumni living in the Lansing, Michigan, area. I was not asking them for a job, but asking them for wisdom on how they had succeeded in an area I wanted to work in. I was looking to build relationships more than I wanted a job, even though I was secretly hoping that someone would offer me a job through a relationship. It worked and I was offered a job as a financial analyst at a Medicaid HMO.

I had a job, but I felt my life was lacking a purpose. I knew that I wasn't put on this earth to help facilitate the production and sustainability of my current employer. I was not put on this planet to make this Medicaid HMO rich. The more I thought about it, the angrier I became. I asked myself, "If I could take my mind, will,

(continued)

226

emotions, and physical ability, package it all up, and sell it, what would that be worth?" Suddenly I realized that this annual figure was *way more* than what my current employer was paying me; I was getting cheated, and I wasn't going to put up with it anymore!

Therefore, I decided to cancel my cable subscription and put away my television until I figured out what my true passion in life was. It took six months for me to understand my purpose, passion, mission, life commitment, and plan to accomplish them all. Once this occurred, it opened up a whole new realm of behavior. I stopped doing the things that didn't have anything to do with my purpose, and I started doing things that did. As a result, I found that my short-term goals were accomplished at a much faster pace and opportunities appeared more often. I knew that owning my own successful business was a major component in carrying out my purpose, and real estate was something I enjoyed.

I met an affordable-housing veteran at a Christian business owners' meeting at the church I belonged to. John had been redeveloping multiple-family buildings for years, and his partners were considering retirement. We went to breakfast every Saturday morning at the local Big Boy for two years. During that time we developed a strong mentor-mentee relationship through which he taught me the ins and outs of affordable-housing real estate development. One day he offered me the opportunity to purchase a 175-unit apartment complex in Battle Creek, Michigan. The opportunity came when I was prepared to embrace it. I became so intimately involved with the opportunity that I was able to sell the idea to a bank, which gave me the necessary financing to commence the transaction. In the summer of 2005, I closed a $7.7 million real estate transaction in which I was the owner.

After closing my first deal I hadn't left my job, but it was getting difficult to juggle both. In 2006, I built thirty new single-family homes in Ohio and rented them out to economically challenged people. That was the year that I decided to go full-time with my own company. In 2007, I closed on a seventy-six-unit apartment building in Detroit totaling $5 million. In late 2007, I knew the market was about to go south fast, and debt and equity providers began to tell me that they were starting to have discussions about tightening the

(continued)

money supply. Despite the gloomy economic outlook, I knew (through reading the Bible) that many successful people made most of their money in times of economic famine. During 2008 and 2009, I took the money my company made from the previous deals and began to obtain site control over many apartment complexes at discounted prices.

What makes this most rewarding is that I am providing housing to families in situations similar to mine as a child. Ginosko Development Company provides substantial rehabilitation efforts whereby families receive virtually new apartments (or new homes) without any extra costs to them. Within my developments, families receive homeownership counseling, new appliances, freshly painted walls, new cabinets, countertops, carpet, light fixtures, and bathroom amenities—all while, typically, decreasing their rent from 5 percent to 70 percent (yes, 70 percent) for qualified tenants. It doesn't get any more rewarding than to see a family cry tears of joy after they enter their new apartment or home while you are being told that you are an answer to their prayer. I try to do this every day by doing the very thing I am most passionate about, and you can do the same. If you want to know how, I can teach you.

RYAN MACK'S FIVE ECONOMIC EMPOWERMENT TIPS FOR REAL ESTATE DEVELOPERS

1. Find a mentor. Before he jumped in, Amin first met a veteran who showed him the ropes to the game. Amin made sure to take his knowledge from the classes at University of Michigan, the knowledge from working in the industry over the summer, and the knowledge from his mentor to make the most educated decisions.
2. Don't be afraid of risk, but take calculated risk. Amin knew that New York was not for him, so he took a job locally to save up enough to do what he really wanted to do. Proper planning makes all risk much less dangerous.
3. Plan for disasters. Amin was able to navigate through such a terrible recession because he took risk, but never so much that it left him totally exposed. As a result, when the market turned down, he not only was able to survive but he had extra capital to purchase property cheaply and average down his costs.

4. Treat your tenants with respect; empower them, even if it might not seem as cost-effective. Not all returns can be measured in dollars, and the level of psychic income that you create when you invest in people is immeasurable.

5. Don't allow your past struggles to bring you down; use them to motivate you and shape your future. The struggles that Amin had growing up are reflected in the way that he treats his tenants. He might have had many mishaps in his life, but those only served to motivate him to do bigger and better things.

ENTREPRENEURSHIP

Entrepreneurship is the organization and management of a business or enterprise, usually implying an assumption of risk and a new opportunity.

I had the privilege of meeting Ted Sorensen, President John F. Kennedy's special counsel and adviser, legendary speechwriter, and ghostwriter of Kennedy's Pulitzer Prize–winning book, *Profiles in Courage*. I had so many questions to ask him but was at a total loss for words. He was JFK's right-hand man for almost ten years. What do you say to the man who is partly responsible for writing some of the greatest speeches in the history of the world?

After I came around, we began talking about JFK, the Obama campaign, health-care reform, and a few other political issues. Then Mr. Sorensen gave me something that resonated with me, a poem that he had given to JFK.

Mr. Sorensen said, "I gave this poem to JFK to give in a speech. I know that you give speeches, so I will give you the same poem. 'Bullfight critics row on row. Fill the enormous plaza full. But only one man is in the know. And he is the one who is fighting the bull.'"

That poem speaks to entrepreneurs because whenever it comes to reviving an economy, the business owner represents the bullfighter, who is really in the know. Small businesses represent over 95 percent of all employer firms, they employ over half of all private sector employees, and they have generated between 60 and 80 percent of net new jobs over the last decade. So if you are going to start a business, you must put your passion into action. We need you!

Did you know that over half of all of the S&P 500 companies, five hundred of the most successful companies in America today, were formed during times of a recession? This is because hunger breeds creativity. My most creative moments in my business came when I had the most severe financial struggles. The next idea that could turn this economy around could be locked inside your head waiting on you to let it out. A quick look at history will clearly demonstrate this point to you.

The recession of the early 1980s lasted for thirty months because of the Iranian revolution, the ensuing increase in the price of oil, and the Fed implementing a tight monetary policy to control inflation. However, out of this recession the following companies were formed:

- 1980—Applebee's, Fuddruckers, and Ben & Jerry's
- 1981—Buffalo Wild Wings; also, IBM sold the first personal computer
- 1982—Olive Garden and Dave & Buster's
- 1983—The first Hooters was opened in Clearwater, Florida

The recession of the early 1990s, caused by a decrease in industrial production and manufacturing-trade sales, lasted for ten months. However, the following companies were formed during these hard times:

- 1990—Jamba Juice, Caribou Coffee, Zaxby's, and Baja Fresh
- 1991—The five hundredth Tim Hortons opens
- 1992—Starbucks and Cheesecake Factory both go public

The 2000 recession was caused by the collapse of the dot-com bubble and accounting scandals. This lasted for eighteen months, but the following companies obviously didn't get the memo that they shouldn't dare to be a success in the midst of a recession:

- 2000—Bonefish Grill and Cheeseburger in Paradise
- 2001—Wikipedia Foundation was established
- 2001—The first Apple store opened
- 2000 through 2001—Google, PayPal, and Salesforce.com thrived

The following companies were all formed during times of recession:

- Burger King—1954
- CNN—1980
- Facebook—2004
- GE—1876
- Microsoft—1975

True entrepreneurs can be a success when they have the right mentality. They understand that they are not victims of their circumstances, such as a rough economy, but can create life and success in any situation. They do this by not focusing on the obstacles, but by focusing on the opportunities that they can create.

I remember when I was starting my company. Twelve months after I left Wall Street I ran out of savings. I didn't have enough to pay for my lights . . . I just got some candles and kept moving forward. I couldn't afford to pay my heat bill . . . I got some extra blankets and kept moving forward. On those few days when I couldn't afford to get a meal . . . I declared a fast and kept moving forward. It is vital that entrepreneurs understand that they are larger than the problems they are faced with; therefore, instead of trying to find reasons why they are not going to be a success, they are relentless in their faith and self-confidence and honestly believe that failure is not an option.

The essence of this book is that if we plan properly and have that unwavering confidence, this will dramatically increase the odds of our success. With new successful companies come employment opportunities for others. This is why all of our successes in a community are linked. The more successful you are, the easier the path you create for someone else. However, you must take the right steps and prepare yourself to become a successful entrepreneur, because the better you prepare, the stronger role model you can be, and the more empowerment you can provide to others. Below are a few questions that you should ask yourself to be certain that you are ready to invest in your new business.

Is the Business You Are Starting Really Your Passion?

I know that new multilevel-marketing venture that your best friend pitched you sounds great even though he is broke. However, think twice to be sure that you can give each new business venture you want to start a 100 percent effort. You are more likely to be able to give this level of effort if you are passionate about the idea. Do you think that I would have been able to endure days of not eating much and my lights/heat getting turned off if I was not working at something I loved? Absolutely not!

ACTION STEP. A good way to find your passion is to volunteer your time. If you are willing to do something for free, then you would definitely do it for a paycheck. If you want to start a restaurant, volunteer your time to work at a soup kitchen. If you want to start a construction company, volunteer your time to work at Habitat for Humanity. If you want to start a day care, volunteer to work at a local orphanage. These are ways that you can learn your craft for free while giving back to the community.

Can You See Yourself in This Industry for Ten Years, Twenty Years, or for the Rest of Your Life?

There is definitely a difference between a job and a career. A job is what you do just to pay the bills and is usually just a stepping-stone to help you get to where you want to go (retirement, paying for your children's college, another job, etc.). However, when you start your business in a career that is truly your passion, then you have reached your destination. I can honestly say that I want to be doing just what I am doing now until I go to meet my maker. Of course I am going to improve upon it and things might eventually change, but for now I am 100 percent content where I am.

ACTION STEP. When you think of your vision, create an intricate budget of what you will be making and spending monthly. This helps to make your vision real and subconsciously gives you tangible income goals for your vision.

Are You Building Your Network as Aggressively as You Should?

You are only one person away from a success. People think that because I am on TV that I am somehow different from them. I am no different than anybody reading this book and have done nothing that anyone reading this right now cannot do.

ACTION STEP. Start making a purposeful effort to build your network. Collect cards and information and insert this information into your database. (Card scanners can assist you to do this.) Create social networking pages—on Facebook, MySpace, LinkedIn—that are specific to your company. If you are starting an accounting firm, create a social networking page and newsletter where you give regular tax tips. For those starting new law firms, create pages and send out newsletters that teach your network the importance of knowing their rights. Your network will grow because you are giving valuable information away, they will respect your intellect, and when they need services, they will gravitate toward you first because you have proven your knowledge in the area.

Can You Consider Yourself an Expert in Your Business?

For me to successfully start my own firm, I took some time off to educate myself about the financial services industry. I took a class that taught me how to start a wealth-management company; I interviewed with other companies so I could collect marketing material to get ideas to implement in my company; I read three to four financial literacy books per month plus instructional books on how to start a financial-planning company, I created and taught personal financial literacy courses at local colleges in the community; I volunteered to teach weekly financial literacy courses to youth at the local high school; and I volunteered with Crown.org to help educate people on the need to budget and improve their credit scores. The best way to learn something is to teach it, and when you teach it enough, you become that expert that people will want to utilize for services.

ACTION STEP. Read at least one book per month about how to start your business and profit from your passion. The best way to learn something is to teach it, so before you start your company, develop an eight- or sixteen-week curriculum and go to the local community college and become an adjunct professor; or you can go to the local high school and teach an after-school program in your area of expertise. Create informative newsletters about what you are reading about and send them to your network; this will reinforce your learning of the information that you are talking about. Start giving free seminars in your local churches, community centers, stores, and other establishments about your area of expertise. You will notice that your grasp of the information is becoming second to none after you have had regular practice.

Do You Have a Business Plan?

Writing my business plan was the best thing that I could ever have done. I had read five books on how to start a financial planning company, but putting together that business plan showed me exactly what I was missing and the areas where I was weak. It forced me to become organized.

ACTION STEP. Go to www.Score.org or www.SBA.gov and use their free business-plan templates/tutorials to write up your own business plan.

Are You Truly Ready to Start Your Business?

- Have your checked your credit in case you need to procure financing? Go through the steps mentioned in the earlier chapters to make sure that your credit is sound.

- Have you prepared the basics of your company?
  - Select the proper business structure for your business in Appendix F, and go to a Web site such as www.inc-it-now.com to file for the appropriate business entity.
  - Go to www.IRS.gov and file for your EIN (Employer Identification Number).
  - Once you get your EIN, go to the local bank that you trust and open a separate account for your business.
  - List your business address on local search engines such as www.google.com, www.yahoo.com, or www.yellowpages.com.
  - Make sure that you have all of the necessary licenses, permits, insurances, and registrations necessary to operate your business.
  - Create a domain name and a Web page on a site such as www.yahoo.com for less than $15. Or you can pay approximately $30 and $12 per month to create a more elaborate page, but make sure that you take your time to make the page look professional (this is if you don't have the $3,000 to have a professional site created for you). A free option for a decent start-up Web site for your company can be found at www.wix.com.
  - Go to LogoMaid.com and get a professionally designed logo for around $100 and put the logo and site address on a set of professionally made business cards. (Although www.vista.com makes cards for next to nothing, the cards are not of great quality, and to have the Vista logo on the back of your card lets people know that you cut corners. I am all for cutting corners, but there's no need to broadcast it to everybody. Nothing's worse than getting a flimsy card with a Vista logo on the back.)
- Have you established your business credit (three steps)?
  - **Step One:** Establish a Profile with Dun & Bradstreet
    - They are the largest tracker of business credit and can be found at www.dnb.com.
    - It normally takes approximately thirty days upon filling out the information.
    - You can establish credit immediately by selecting the paid-for credit-builder services. While I prefer that you save your money and wait the thirty days, if you decide on this route, be aware that any mark that you write on your credit report is there permanently.
  - **Step Two:** Apply for Business Credit

- Some companies, such as Office Depot, Staples, FedEx/Kinko's, Dell Computers, and OfficeMax, do not require a personal guarantee, and you should apply for a line of credit from them.
- **Step Three:** Pay *Before* Time
  - Business credit is different from personal credit in that the sooner you pay, the more it benefits your credit score.
  - Business scores range from 0 to 100.
  - A Paydex score of 80 is good, based upon a history with at least six vendors.

If You Have an Established Business, Do You Have a Succession/Estate Plan in Place?

The success of your company is important to this economy, and I want it to last longer than you live for the sake of future generations.

ACTION STEP. You should be talking with a trusted estate planner to be sure that you are keeping your documents in order and updated and avoiding mishaps, such as making insurance payable to your estate, making the proceeds taxable.

Do You Have a Proper Insurance Plan in Place for Your Company?

Do you know the type of insurance that you have, and are all the key members of your company covered? Just because you can afford to pay for whole life insurance as key-person insurance, ask yourself if it is more cost-efficient to pay for term life and increase cash flow. Does it make sense to pay for insurance with a higher deductible and lower premiums to increase cash flow?

ACTION STEP. These are some basic questions that you should be discussing with your insurance agent. Remember, just as with personal insurance, it is important to be educated before you see the agent to be sure that you actually need what you are purchasing.

Are You Able to Perform an Objective Performance Review at Any Time?

Established companies should prepare themselves as if they have a banker review coming up even if they don't. Many companies cannot produce what they paid on their phone bills for the past six months. Ill-prepared financials are an easy way for a company to mismanage funds, causing an unexpected shortfall when they need the money most.

ACTION STEP. Purchase the software that is easiest for you to use and will assist you in creating reports that can help you analyze your company. All established companies should create a board of directors and make their banker a member of the board. If you are a small business, you should definitely have a board of directors, which can be composed of close friends and colleagues who are willing to provide objective advice and guidance.

Are You Using Your Debt Wisely?

Businesses are using their debt far too irresponsibly. The economy shut down in part because when the credit crunch occurred, companies could not pay their employees when they could not get loans. Companies across America made a consistent practice of borrowing money to pay employees, anticipating paying back the loan with the next month's earnings. I understand the power of leverage and how it allows your business to grow; however, whenever you borrow today for what you think you will earn tomorrow, you are putting yourself in a dangerous situation. Business owners, I am speaking directly to you—we need you to be responsible because you drive the employment market.

ACTION STEP. Examine each purchase that requires taking on additional debt and ask, "Does this item pay for itself over time?" If it doesn't, perhaps you don't need it. It might look cool to invest in a big screen for all of your office computers, but don't the smaller screens get the job done just as well, and is it really worth going into debt over it? You will also need to look at your short-term versus long-term debt structure and figure out how to begin to pay your debt down. Lastly, you must be careful when you borrow against "life savings" accounts such as a 401(k), your home, your insurance policy, or an IRA. These accounts were meant to help you establish financial security for your retirement and enable you to pass a financial legacy to future generations, not to use as a leverage tool. I understand that many times we get into binds where it feels we need to use these accounts, but try as best you can to find alternative ways, and let's try to prevent the fire by being proactive.

Are You Minding Your Family?

As driven as you are, when you have the full support of your family behind you, nothing can stop you! However, you need to be consistently investing love and time in your family to let them know that they are your priority and are as important as your company.

ACTION STEP. Involve your family in your company and allow them to express interest in what you do, but don't let it consume all of your conversations. Set aside time every week to sit down and have long conversations that allow you to catch up on what happened over the week. When I went to teach in South Africa, the family that I stayed with talked with each other for the entire day every Sunday. When they told me about this practice, I thought that they were planning to torture me by forcing me to talk from noon through 9:00 P.M. However, I found it pleasant and time flew by faster than ever. We needed no TV, radio, or Internet...all we needed was each other and some conversation. That taught me that talking and spending time with family is the best investment that one can make. Try it!

How Is Your Faith Holding Up?

As a business owner you will go through a roller coaster of emotions that will inevitably try your faith and test if you have the fortitude to stick it out. As stated in earlier chapters, faith is half believing and half acting on that belief. It all starts in the mind, so make sure that you are doing what it takes to keep your confidence high!

ACTION STEP. Find activities that keep your spirits high. I love to attend church, read motivational books, talk with other business owners to share war stories, spend time giving back in my community to those who are less fortunate, and spend time with family doing something that requires no brainpower! You need to find your release.

Action Steps:

1. Review your progress regularly.
2. Check your progress against goals.
3. Make necessary adjustments.
4. Plan for new projects and expanding your business or offerings.
5. Execute with confidence and assertiveness.

Owning and operating your own business has proven to provide the highest return of all investment vehicles. However, this investment also has the highest risk. The risk is worth it because you are investing in your own ideas. With the right preparation, you can be a part of the clique of entrepreneurs who drive this economy!

Village Visit

The Power of the Business: The Entrepreneur

The entrepreneur is the backbone of the U.S. economy. This country will rise and fall according to the ideas generated in the heads of its citizens, their ability to create plans for these ideas, and how well they execute their product or service. If you have any thoughts about starting your own business . . . hurry up, we need you! No idea or business is too small; over half of all people in the United States are employed by small businesses. That mom-and-pop store on the corner or that business that you started from your home are the drivers of this economy. I urge you, no more paralysis of analysis; let's put that idea on paper and make it real!

Many business coaches claim to know a lot about starting a multimillion-dollar business, but few have actually done it. Andrew Morrison was not on Oprah because of his winning smile, but because he was a millionaire at age thirty-one, having started a multimillion-dollar direct-marketing company. He has traveled from Hawaii to Nigeria teaching thousands upon thousands how to start businesses, and he is still going strong. I haven't heard anybody more clearly articulate the why and how of starting your own business than Andrew.

The Business Inside You
by Andrew Morrison

If you can read this article, then you already have all that it takes to start your own business with little money.

If you can read this, that tells me that you're smarter than a third-grader, and you only have to be smarter than a third-grader to

(continued)

become an entrepreneur. By fourth grade you can read. If you can read, then you can process new information, and if you can process new information, then you can change and grow. In addition, you can communicate new thoughts and ideas. Communication is the starting point of any enterprise. You are already overqualified to begin the entrepreneurial journey.

These tough economic times won't last, but the tough need to get going. Whether you work in a hospital or you own a construction company, this article will enable you to become more expansive in your thinking. People often say to think outside the box; well, I want to suggest to you that there's money inside the box. There are opportunities right there in your industry; opportunities for you to shine, grow, and make more money as well.

Here are the three fundamental steps to growing a business: Number one, awareness. What are you doing to increase customer awareness? Once people are aware of your product, of your service, of your brand, of your position in the company, the second step is trial. Get somebody to try you out. Get someone to read your book. Get someone to test this new product. Step number three is to repeat. Once someone has tried your product, how can you get them to use it over and over and over? The fastest way to build awareness is by writing and speaking.

Owning a business is one of the best ways to share your gifts with the world. I want to give you permission to talk about your gifts. Too many people are in hiding. I'd like you to stop hiding! Come out, come out, wherever you are. Become bold when talking about your gifts. Just begin to make room for your gifts.

I know why you're not talking about your gifts. You are afraid. You're afraid that people will call you arrogant. That people will call you uppity.

Who does she think she is? She thinks she's cute. You can't do that, you better sit down, nobody will believe in you. No one will visit your store, and no one will buy your product, blah, blah, blah, blah, blah.

You can't let these naysayers defeat you.

During my first few years out of college I tried to do everything. I tried to have a travel agency. I tried to fix computers. I tried to sell

(continued)

computers. I was writing computer software. I was selling fax machines for a while there. I was trying to publish a magazine. I was doing data entry. I was working with the Black Expos going around helping Jerry Roebuck to build a database of people who attended Black Expos.

I was a jack-of-all-trades and master of none. I learned the hard way the importance of staying focused and staying committed to one thing. You need to pick one thing; you need to focus on one thing in your business. I know the pain of being all over the place and trying to be global, trying to be diversified, and working out of your mama's basement. That doesn't work. I once asked Jerry Roebuck, "Listen, out of all these things I'm doing, which one should I really focus on?" The one idea he liked of mine was the African-American value-pack concept. He helped me realize that many small-business owners could not afford the cost of doing their own direct-mail campaign. So I decided to develop this first-ever pack of discount cards mailed to ten thousand African-American households.

Back in the late eighties, many people were saying that African-Americans were not responsive to direct-mail, and I proved the opposite to be the case. This was a demonstration of the concept the "power of you," declaring your expertise in a particular niche.

I called my direct-mail concept Nia's Coupons for Savings. It all started by my mailing to ten thousand households, at which time I was only making a few thousand dollars. However, once I proved that my business model could work on a small scale, I was able to mail to nearly 10 million households. As a result, my favorite advice to give my clients is to start small, start slow, and for God's sake start now. Don't wait, you can all start something small. Never despise humble beginnings. From an acorn grows a forest, not simply a mighty oak tree, but an entire forest starts with an acorn.

People who are new to money say it takes money to make money, but people who have had money for quite some time say it doesn't take money to make money; it takes wisdom to make money. You already have what I call underperforming assets. You already have some past experience, some past results. You already have some resources that you can begin to turn into cash. Don't allow the lack of money to prevent you from starting your business, from growing your nonprofit.

(continued)

If you attend a house of worship, they have a space for you to start your mentoring program for young girls. By using somebody else's space in their nonprofit, and by writing for a grant for a nonprofit, you can make money with no money.

I want to be clear about something. You never really start with nothing because faith is the substance of things hoped for and the evidence of things unseen. As you began this journey toward building your business or nonprofit, you already have evidence; the evidence is your mental blueprint; it's in your mind. The evidence is a proposal, your past relationships. It really starts with faith, something that's practical, something that's tangible.

This book that you're holding right now is actually faith in motion. It's a manifestation of Ryan's faith, of his publisher's faith. It's a manifestation of the bookstore's faith. It's also a manifestation of your spending your hard-earned dollars to purchase this book. Faith is a process, it's not static.

You may be wondering, how did I decide or what made me decide to give my life to serving other business owners and other individuals? At no point did I make that decision. My calling is to inspire, to motivate, and to support others. My calling is not dependent upon my career or upon a job. Some of you think you need to leave a job. Some of you feel you need to go start a business for you to exercise your calling. That is not so. If you step into your calling, wherever you are can be a manifestation of that calling. That can only happen when you begin to release your brilliance. I want you to stop hiding. I want you to begin to shine because you were not given a spirit of doubt, a spirit of fear, a spirit of timidity; you have a spirit of power. Use it.

Here's a story that illustrates one of the most important things you have to begin to do if you want to deal with obstacles and release your greatness:

Once, my wife and I decided to go for a scuba-diving lesson. In the class, the instructor said, "Okay, let's get in the boat and launch into the deep." You're reading this book because you're about to launch into the deep. You're about to go ahead and do something wonderful. You're about to go ahead and do something powerful. I want you to hear clearly what this instructor said to me when I was

(continued)

about to go scuba diving. We were in the boat, with all this equipment on, with several people, and he said to everybody, "Okay, before you go out and jump into this unfamiliar territory, here's the one thing I want you to do."

My wife is an emergency-room physician and she knows what can go wrong when it comes to scuba diving. I was super receptive to my instructor's advice. I want you to listen carefully to this advice as well. He said to the entire group, "I've trained you on how to use your equipment. I trained you on different pressure gauges. I trained you on various hand signals to communicate with me and others. I trained you on how to pull on the rope if you feel you're in danger. But whatever happens, I want you to remember this one thing." And I want this one thing to be what you remember as you launch into the deep, as you begin to build your nonprofit and serve people. He said, "Whatever happens down there, remember to *breathe*. Remember to *breathe*." Stop waiting to exhale. Stop anticipating inhalation. I'd like you to simply remember to breathe, and by remembering to simply breathe, and remembering to be at peace, then you can be like the lilies of the valley and watch how they grow. Breathing is natural. Next time somebody challenges you, remember to breathe. The next time you feel overwhelmed, remember to breathe. So keep on reading, keep on learning, and keep on breathing.

Ryan Mack's Five Economic Empowerment Tips for Entrepreneurs

1. Surround yourself with positive people. When you're starting or growing a business, there is no room for negative thinking. Negative people can bring you down and cause you to have doubt when you should be overflowing with confidence in your ability to be successful.

2. Find and stick to your passion. Many people start multilevel marketing companies, and over 90 percent fail. Why? They are thinking about the money but couldn't give a darn about the product or service they are selling. On those lonely nights when you have no friends but a computer screen, you are hungry, debts are high, and funds are low . . . are you really going to stick it out to continue selling vacuum covers? Of course not. However, what if you knew that what you were selling was improving the quality

of life for those in your community? I remember those nights, and it was my passion and known impact that kept me going.

3. Invest your own money initially. I understand that leverage and equity can help you grow faster, but nothing is more motivating than having your own skin in the game.

4. Don't be greedy with people that work for you. If you feel that someone working for you is adding tremendous value, give the person a percentage of ownership in your company. Employees tend to work more productively if they feel that they have ownership in the business.

5. You will never be perfect, so don't doubt yourself because you have made mistakes. Conversely, always strive for perfection. If you are new to the industry, other, larger companies are ready to eat you alive, so make sure that you are always striving to improve your systems, financial statements and record upkeep, marketing strategies, and everything that makes your company tick.

CHAPTER THIRTEEN

Selecting the Right Adviser and Building Your Financial Team

DURING THE HOLIDAY SEASON OF 2007, THE YEAR OF THE WORST RECESSION SINCE THE Great Depression, I remember watching the news about Black Friday, the day after Thanksgiving. A person was trampled to death by shoppers who were too excited to get into the store to find the biggest deal. What have we come to in this country when we kill someone because of a sale? What if we were just as excited about purchasing things that would actually improve our lives as opposed to adding no value, decreasing our savings, and increasing our debt? What if we were that excited about getting a financial adviser that we can trust who will help us to figure out a path to financial freedom, early retirement, fully funded college savings, a new home, the new business, and eliminating all of our debt?

The rich understand the importance of making investments in things that add value. This is why 5 percent of the country owns 95 percent of the wealth—they do the things necessary to retain wealth and not squander it. A good financial adviser can help you do this, too. The best way for you to prepare for retirement, how to properly plan for your estate, how to discern the right amount of insurance to protect your family, planning to start a business, and reaching those important financial goals in your life are all things that should be covered by a good adviser. If you are not familiar with how to navigate through many of the tough financial obstacles that plague you, or if you are financially savvy but like most of us don't have the time to put together and monitor a comprehensive financial plan, it is a wise move to ask for assistance. The hardest part is selecting the best adviser for your needs. Below are a few questions to ask the financial adviser to make sure that he or she is a good match for you.

Do You Have a CFP?

To be a certified financial planner one must take an exam that is equivalent to the CPA exam for accountants. He or she is required to complete a series of requirements that include education, experience, ethics, and the exam. Passing this exam proves that he or she actually knows the curriculum of financial planning. Suze Orman, my idol and mentor even though I have never met her, is a CFP. Some great advisers do not have a CFP, but your job is to lessen the odds of choosing an adviser who is not qualified . . . so select a CFP.

Can I See a Copy of Your ADV?

Every registered investment adviser must register with the state security agency or the SEC on an ADV. This will tell you how the adviser is compensated, incentives that he or she is entitled to, educational and business background, and investment strategy. If the person cannot produce an ADV, then walk away.

If the firm gets paid by selecting investments on commission, which you can find out on the ADV, then I suggest you not use it and find a *fee-only* adviser. This sort of adviser has no conflict of interest when suggesting which securities you should invest in, or if you should be investing at all. I remember talking to an adviser and asking him why his firm didn't sell any no-load mutual funds. He responded simply, "How are we supposed to get paid?" I have met many individuals who were pressured into purchasing investments even though they had over $10,000 in credit card debt at 18 percent interest. Does it make sense to put money in the stock market to *hopefully* earn an 18 percent return when you have a certain 18 percent yield in credit card debt? Absolutely not! You want an adviser who can see that and not have you purchase stocks just so he or she can earn a commission.

Can I Obtain at Least Three Referrals from Clients That You Have Worked With?

This is important because nobody will have a greater feel for the type of work that this adviser will do than people who have actually worked with the adviser. Be sure to call the referrals and take good notes.

What Is Your Area of Expertise?

Many advisers may be good at selecting investments, but maybe you just want someone who can help you get out of debt, improve your credit, and budget responsibly. Make sure that you list and prioritize your financial goals and needs—college planning, cash-flow management, insurance planning, retirement, investment, etc.

How Long Have You Been Practicing in This Area?

An adviser that has set up shop for five years or more will by now have established either a good or a bad reputation.

What Sort of Clients Do You Serve?

It is good to have a planner that deals with clients with similar needs and income levels as yours.

What Is Your Investment Philosophy?

Every adviser has an investment philosophy, whether it is aggressive, conservative, or mixed. If you feel that a particular adviser is a wild cowboy trader and you are looking for someone who is conservative, you probably shouldn't pursue it any further.

Do You Practice Community Outreach?

If you want to know if an adviser is in it for the money or for the cause of empowering people with the important principles of fiscal responsibility, get an overview of his or her community outreach. If advisers are willing to teach people this information for free, they are more likely to be in it because they have the heart to empower people than because they just want to make a quick dollar.

Many companies are run like a multilevel marketing company. Your adviser should not also be in the business of trying to make you an adviser in his "down line" so he can make a percentage of your sales. Imagine if a lawyer defended you in court, then after the case was concluded gave you a six-week course to obtain your JD so you could practice under him and he could get a percentage of all your cases tried. This sounds ridiculous because it is. Lawyers, doctors, accountants, and financial planners all need to have a proper education and training to be qualified.

Other Important Members of Your Advisory Team

Other important members of an advisory team that you should consider are:

1. **Bookkeeper.** This person handles all of your monthly bank statements and reconciles your account. If you don't have a business, then you can do this for yourself. However, if you do have a business and it is in your budget to pay someone to do this for you, it is definitely worth the expense. The stress of keeping track of your receipts and summarizing your accounts is something I am sure that you can live without if you can afford it.

2. **Accountant.** Whether you own a business or not, you need a good accountant. Many people think that they can go to the "cookie-cutter" accounting agencies, which can be okay for those with simple tax returns; but I always prefer to go to someone who can give me a little more individual attention. If you have a business, you need to find someone who can advise you of all the deductions that you are allowed under law. Below are a few tips on how to find a good accountant.
   - Get referrals.
   - Find a CPA (a good resource for this is to search online at the American Institute of Certified Public Accountants at www.aicpa .org).
   - Conduct an interview—some questions to ask are:
     - How long have you been a CPA and how long have you practiced?
     - What school did you graduate from?
     - Have you ever worked with the IRS?

- Can you assist me in an audit?
- What software do you use to do my taxes, and do you back up your work in case your computer crashes?
- How much do you charge?
- Are you the primary person who will be doing my taxes? If so, will I be able to get in contact with you during the busy season . . . do you have some help?

3. **Personal Banker.** If you don't have a business, you probably don't need a personal banker; however, if you do have a business, you should use this service to discuss lines of credit and various tools that you can use for your business. Personal bankers can help you set up your account, establish a business line of credit, and may want to assist you in opening an investment account. (I would leave the investing to your financial planner, who will more likely give you individualized attention.)

4. **Attorney.** Everybody needs a good attorney on speed dial just in case.
   - **Estate Planner.** An easy way to find an estate planner is through referrals. If you don't have anybody who can give you a good referral, I like using the National Association of Estate Planners and Councils. Your estate planner should be an accredited estate planner (AEP) and/or an estate planning law specialist (EPLS) if your estate is more complex (over $2 million in assets) and might need more than a simple will.
   - **Corporate.** If you have a business, you should have a good corporate attorney. Be sure to get a few referrals, then have a meeting with the attorney and ask about his or her educational background.
   - **Criminal.** You never know what sort of trouble lies ahead. I have had friends who were falsely accused of things give me a call because they knew that I know good attorneys willing to help.

5. **Real Estate Agent.** A good real estate agent can be valuable when you decide to purchase a home. Below is a checklist of those things that you should look for in a good agent.
   A good agent will:
   - Help you focus and analyze your market.
   - Set up appointments for you to view prospective homes.
   - Accompany you on your visit.
   - Coordinate certain aspects of the transaction.

A good agent is:

- Working full-time as an agent.
- Experienced in the types of services you require.
- Full of integrity.
- A local resident.
- Able to communicate effectively.
- Always accessible and reliable.
- Sensitive to your needs.
- Able to produce a multiple-listing service of the area.

You must always:

- Interview your agent.
- Ask for references.

CHAPTER FOURTEEN

The Unofficial Step Eight:
Investing in the Community

ONE AREA OF INVESTMENT IS NOT FREQUENTLY EXPLORED BUT HAS TREMENDOUS potential and an almost unlimited upside. Doubling and tripling your investment in this area would be an enormous underexpansion. What is it?

I will give you a clue . . . you wake up and go to sleep in it every day. You eat in it, you take your children to school in it, you attend block parties in it, and many of your family members and friends may also live in it. If you haven't guessed by now, I am referring to the community. That's right . . . an investment in your community is the greatest investment you can make. By investing in the community, what are the returns for me, you ask? How does one invest in a community? You can invest in your community in many ways, and not all of them involve money. You can also invest time. Let me explain.

COMMUNITY BUSINESSES

Your community has many businesses. These businesses, if successful, will bring respectable traffic to your community. Restaurants, bakeries, schools, libraries, and more are all a reflection of the upkeep and character of the community. Outsiders often get a sense of the community by the quality of service, experience, and ambience within its restaurants and other institutions. The upkeep of the schools and libraries is noticed by drive-through visitors. Frequent investment is crucial to property values and quality of life. Time and money that flow through these community institutions will always be reflected in the property values and ultimately the quality of life for the community's residents. So take time to eat in your community restaurants, donate books to your local libraries and schools, and frequent the stores and shops in your community.

ENTREPRENEURSHIP

How large of a return did Bill Gates, Russell Simmons, or Oprah Winfrey get on their original dollars of investment? The number is far too large for any ordinary calculator to hold. Let's look at each person and what he or she accomplished through his or her endeavors.

- **Bill Gates.** Most people will measure the success of Bill Gates by his wealth, and at over $50 billion, his net worth is tremendous. However, I would rather look at the impact that he is creating through his entrepreneurship. Microsoft, the company that he formed, started as just an idea in his garage. Today that idea is the reason that almost sixty thousand people around the world are gainfully employed and can put food on their table and help support their family. In addition to employing all those people, Bill Gates was able to take some of the earnings of this idea and invest in the Bill and Melinda Gates Foundation, which today is the largest transparently operated private foundation in the world, with an endowment of over $33 billion as of 2009, giving over $800 million yearly to promote global health, and contributing millions every year for global development.

- **Russell Simmons.** Many people focus on how Russell Simmons is the fourth-richest figure in hip-hop, with a net worth estimated at over $330 million. However, I personally have been impacted by his work in hip-hop, a culture that I grew up in and that shaped much of my childhood. His Hip-Hop Summit Action Network educates thousands every year in the hip-hop community about voting, pursuing education, financial literacy (my favorite), AIDS awareness, and poverty. His multiple companies, which have employed hundreds of people over time, his *Def Poetry Jam* show, which exposed millions to the art of poetry, and much more are examples of the work that he has been able to do because of the funds that he generated from his ideas and entrepreneurship. Sure, I call him out for his promotion of a financial predator, the RushCard, but that doesn't take away from my respect for his work to empower millions in communities around the world.

- **Oprah Winfrey.** Oprah is a brand. She is a billionaire, probably a few times over, but she, like Gates, is also a big philanthropist. Her media companies and magazines employ hundreds of people, her Angel Network has raised more than $51 million for charitable programs (including a school in South Africa and relief support for the victims of Hurricane Katrina), and politically savvy as she is, she even proposed a law that created a nationwide database of convicted child abusers that was signed into law by President Clinton in 1994.

Successful entrepreneurship has always given one of the largest returns on an investment, and I feel that we can measure return in much more than monetary terms. In this book I prefer to measure return in terms of benefit to the community. Each of those people above has clearly had a major impact on the community.

I understand that when you see the big names above, you may feel that what they have accomplished is out of your reach. However, I want you to see the common thread in all three of them, each personal testimony in this book, and yourself . . . all have ideas! You are still breathing for a reason, and that idea that you have in your head right now is there for a reason. Can you imagine if those three didn't take the effort to capitalize on their ideas? Sure, you might not ever become a billionaire, or even a millionaire, but I place just as much value on your ideas as I do on theirs because they all serve to help empower and uplift the entire community. That Laundromat that you are hesitating to open that will employ three people and help keep our clothes clean is just as valuable to the community as Microsoft, which employs sixty thousand, because each one adds to the progress of the community. The barbershop that you have always wanted that will employ several barbers and provide a central place for men to gather and discuss sports, women, lie about previous accomplishments, as well as get a good haircut, is just as important as Oprah's platform. So your idea will not only fill your pockets, it may help to solve the country's high unemployment rate, or create capital for another idea that you would like to fulfill, or provide a means for you to send your child to school, or inspire someone who had a similar idea to work harder by seeing your success. All of these things are possible and even probable . . . but none are possible if you don't act on that idea.

YOUTH

Investing in the youth of our communities will not only yield enormous returns, but returns that are often the most immediate and most fulfilling. The youth of our communities are crying out for our assistance and support. Within my firm we started a youth financial-literacy organization called All About Business (AAB). I have been volunteering my time for at least four days per month for more than six years teaching youth financial literacy within the local school system. The program has grown and expanded into something that I had never imagined.

I met once a week with these students, and after a while they began to grasp the information so well that I felt that they were ready to teach this information all around the community . . . even to adults. It was amazing to see a fifteen-year-old teach a group of adults about complex financial principles. Not only did this group of youth conduct their own seminars, they began to embody the principles that they were learning. Many began to research and win scholarships to school. Many received internships. Various types of businesses even popped up—an event-planning company, a car service, a construction service company, and a clothing line, to name a few. We must raise the level of expectations for our youth in every way.

Seeing a smile on a youngster's face—a smile that you helped to create—is one of the most rewarding experiences one can have. How many young Bob Johnsons, Warren Buffetts, or Bill Clintons will never reach their potential because we didn't take the time to invest in them? I urge all to take time to volunteer at their local school and talk to the children. Career days, tutor programs, after-school programs, and more are all opportunities to stop by and spend some time with the children of your neighborhood. They are our future, and investment in their lives is also an investment in yours.

COMMUNITY BANKS AND CREDIT UNIONS

An important part of building your community is also to utilize its businesses, and this includes your community banks and credit unions. Using your local community banks and credit unions as opposed to larger, national banks has many advantages. Here are four reasons to consider moving to a smaller bank or a credit union:

1. The irresponsible investment strategies and excessive risk-taking that caused the recession of 2007 was primarily done by the larger national banks.
2. Smaller community banks are generally much more attached to the community, develop relationships to local businesses, and are more apt to provide funding to local businesses, especially in a tough economic climate when credit is tight.
3. Credit unions don't have the problems of having to please shareholders and pay profits as dividends (they are nonprofits). Therefore they are usually able to provide higher interest rates on savings accounts and lower interest rates on loans.
4. Joining a credit union essentially means that you become an owner of this organization.

As long as the community bank is FDIC-insured, or the credit union is a part of the National Credit Union Share Insurance Fund (as mentioned in Chapter 9), your money is insured up to $250,000 and is secure. To research the quality of community banks in your area, go to Institutional Risk Analytics (www.irabankratings.com) or find a local bank at the Independent Community Bankers of America (www.icba.org). To research a local credit union, go to the National Credit Union Administration (www.ncua.gov) or find a local credit union at America's Credit Unions (www.creditunion.coop). You can also find information about the ratings of local banks and credit unions at BankRate.com (www.bankrate.com). This is an easy way to place your money into the pipeline of the community. Putting your capital in those institutions that have the largest and most direct stake in the success of your local community is a great way to create your own stimulus for your community.

So I urge you to think about how you are contributing to your own communities. If you are not active, then how can you get active? Many people look to the politicians to create change and often fail to realize that they can create positive change and movement right in their own communities. How much time are you putting into the care and upkeep of your community? Do you throw cigarette butts, chicken bones, and other trash on the streets, in yards, or on subway tracks? Participate in your community, donate to your community (time and money), invest in your youth, patronize your community businesses, start a community business, and most of all, *respect* your community. It will go a long way for you, me, and American society as a whole.

VILLAGE VISIT

The Power of Community Investment:
The Community Activist

A community activist is the person who gives a voice and action to those in need within the neighborhood. When the village needs someone to help fight poverty, drug usage, unequal rights, hunger, or STDs, the community activist steps up to the plate. Most of the time, they are fighting for little or no money—many times not even a thank-you. What keeps them going is when they see someone get that job, get an education, stay out of prison, or move into a new home because of something that they did. For them, this is payment enough.

Nakia Smith is one of these community activists. She has given so much to her community to make a better way for so many. One of the primary reasons that she is able to help so many with so little is because she possesses an uncanny ability to manage her finances. I can't think of another person that I know personally who invests so much into her community.

MY LIFE BEFORE AND AFTER
MY BLESSING
by Nakia Smith

I was born and raised on the North Side of Philadelphia. By the time my mother was twenty-eight she was a single parent with two children (she later had another child). As a little girl of five, I was fortunate to have formed a strong bond with my grandmother. She would always speak to me in a soft tone as if she were whispering and what she said was for my ears alone. I was twelve when my grandmother passed away, and I immediately felt the huge loss. I was angry, hurt,

(continued)

confused, and saddest of all, even though I had my immediate family around me, I felt very much alone.

I thought I could make that feeling of loneliness subside by joining the army, and after high school I was stationed at Fort Jackson in South Carolina. Fortunately, the military helped me in more ways than one. It gave me confidence, a feeling of being included, helping me to rely on others and grow as a woman. I also learned financial discipline, which helped me to budget. I styled women's hair to earn money, which I would spend on personal items, but I would put my military checks into savings. People would call me cheap because I preferred to save money rather than spend it.

After Fort Jackson, I accepted a job at First Union Bank. There I implemented the financial budgeting skills I perfected while in the military. I started my 401(k) and placed $150 from every paycheck into it. I was always thinking that the more money you save for a rainy day, the more you will be financially comfortable later. As a result of my financial mind-set, I was able to buy my first house in May of 2001 with the use of savings and a good credit score, the same year I had my son, Dymere; I was only twenty-two.

My son was only a month old when he was diagnosed as not growing at a rate the doctors thought he should and as blind in his left eye. Doctors performed many tests, but they still couldn't find the source of my son's debilitating illness. All over again, I begin to feel like the helpless, lonely little girl I used to be. But I just continued praying, asking for strength, and told the Lord that if He let me have my son in good health, anybody that needed me I would not turn away. I vowed to always help in any way I could, financially or by simply giving strangers a place to lay their head.

Two years later, Dymere and I added a new member to our family. His name was Milford, but we call him BJ. BJ's biological mother, my cousin, was unable to take care of him financially, mentally, and physically, so I took him in. BJ was a drug-addicted baby and suffered from the symptoms of drug withdrawal. Many times I felt I had taken on too much by allowing BJ to live with my son and me, but ultimately I knew that I could give him a good home.

The moment I felt I had a handle on both Dymere's illness and the new arrival of BJ, I was laid off from First Union Bank. Fortu-

(continued)

nately, I had become accustomed to saving money and I was thankful I had enough savings to pay my bills. Even being unemployed, I was not going to worry. I remembered the promise I once made to God, that if He helped me, I would continue to help others in any capacity. My next experience certainly tested my ability to help others, this time a complete stranger.

It was a Friday, the sun was shining and bright; I was coming from a friend's house, and on the bus, in the back, a young girl was crying her eyes out. I kindly asked, "Are you okay?" in a whispering tone, the way my grandma used to talk to me. As I handed her some tissue, she looked up at me, but never replied. My stop was getting near, so I wrote my phone number and name on a piece of tissue and told her to call me if she needed to talk. Around nine that night I received a phone call; it was the girl from the bus. I asked her how she was doing, even though I knew she wasn't well. I wanted her to know that I was concerned and that I cared, so I asked, "What is your name?" She replied, "Jennifer," then asked if she could call from time to time. I told her, "Sure, no problem, whenever you are ready to talk, I will listen."

Never in a million years did I imagine Jennifer would ever call me back, but she did. It was the next morning around seven. "Hello, Ms. Kia," she said, crying hysterically. I couldn't understand anything she was saying, so I simply told her I was going to take her to breakfast.

When I arrived at McDonald's, I could see that Jennifer was still crying, and whatever was bothering her was starting to bother me as well. I was determined to find out what was wrong so I could assist her. I broke the silence by showing her a picture of my son and letting her know that I would do anything for him. In my mind I knew she was scared and grasping at her last straw. I know this because she was sitting there with me, desperate for help from a complete stranger. I was frightened, too, because I didn't know what I was walking into.

After we got acquainted, Jennifer opened up and informed me that she was being sexually abused by her stepfather and living from house to house, trying to stay away from the abuse. Immediately my hands started to sweat, then she revealed she was six months pregnant. Tears, as if on cue, fell from both of our faces. As I listened to Jennifer's problems, my heart went out to her. I then revealed to her that I was also sexually abused as a child by a close friend of the

(continued)

family's and also never told my mother about it. Feeling a strong sense of empathy for her, I offered her a place to stay where no one could harm her anymore.

She stayed at my house for two weeks. Once she moved in, I start getting paranoid thinking someone was going to find out that I was harboring a minor. I had received money from a car accident two months earlier, so instead of purchasing a new car I helped move Jennifer into an efficiency apartment. Helping out someone else that was in need meant more to me than buying a new car; a person's life was at stake. Jennifer eventually had the baby and named it Brianna Nakia Jamison. Jennifer is currently working at Macy's department store and attends college, majoring in child psychology. She has a 3.5 GPA. I also decided to go back to school. My major is business management and I have a 4.0 GPA, and I started a nonprofit organization called H.O.P.I.N., which stands for Helping Other People In Need. H.O.P.I.N.'s mission is to provide professional assistance in developing and implementing programs designed to meet the physical, emotional, intellectual, and social needs of at-risk children and their families in the Philadelphia community. I currently have over forty children active in the program, and most of them affectionately call me Mother. It's my third year of running this program full-time, and I obtain 100 percent of the funds necessary from the fund-raising initiatives that I created and administer in my community. It is a blessing to say that the community that I am supporting is also supporting me!

I'm going to leave everyone with this quote: "It's not where you live, it's how you live. If you live a destructive life, it will be filled with negativity, but if you live a positive life and keep the faith, you will be at peace at all times." I live a peaceful life; when times get hard and someone else is worse off than me, helping these people out financially or just comforting them in their time of need just seems to be the right solution.

RYAN MACK'S FIVE ECONOMIC EMPOWERMENT TIPS FOR COMMUNITY ACTIVISTS

1. I wish I had a dollar for every community activist that has dropped out of existence because of financial woes. Granted, it is hard to be in the streets fighting for jobs, education, and training for

people when you are getting evicted. This field does not pay a lot, so what money you do have you must make work. You are no good to the community if you are too broke to feed yourself, so don't overcommitt yourself.

2. Develop an expertise, create a curriculum out of it, and provide workshops for the community. Eventually you can start to charge a fee or become a hired public speaker.

3. Get to know people in your community. Don't limit the size of your community to your block or even your city. Nakia is able to support herself because the entire city and suburbs of Philadelphia are her stomping grounds. Use social-networking platforms, join groups in your neighborhood, attend town-hall meetings, and get involved.

4. Give something that people can use but not spend. Nakia could have given Jennifer money, but she paid for housing. It is great to be giving, but one must teach a person how to fish so the person asking doesn't have to depend upon you. Nakia did this, and now the young lady has a 3.5 GPA, a roof over her head, and a healthy baby girl.

5. Take time for yourself and don't worry. As a community activist myself, I know how consuming it can be. You wake up with the community on your mind, you go to sleep with it on your mind, and you even eat thinking about what you can do to make the community better. But remember, you are not a superhero, and as bad as I know you want to, you can't fix every problem overnight. All you can do is your best, and nothing more.

CHAPTER FIFTEEN

The Five Points of Economic Prosperity

WHAT IS PROSPERITY?

Many people feel that to be prosperous you must have a house that can be viewed on *MTV Cribs,* drive four cars, and have more than seven zeros after the first number in your net worth (assets minus liabilities). This is the furthest thing from the truth. I have met many people who live in public housing, prison, and even on a subsidized income who can be considered prosperous. "How?" you ask. Prosperity doesn't necessarily have a monetary value; prosperity means that one has achieved a desired level in life. This level can be monetary, but most of the time it isn't; however, every level of prosperity has an impact not only on your life but on the lives of those around you.

THE FIVE POINTS OF PROSPERITY

1. Physical prosperity
2. Social prosperity
3. Spiritual prosperity
4. Mental prosperity
5. Financial prosperity

1. Physical Prosperity

At the time of the writing this book, Congress has just passed the largest health reform in the history of this country. It seems as if the country is split down the middle for and against this reform. However, regardless of how you feel about this legislation, physical prosperity doesn't start with legislation . . . it starts with you!

Check out these statistics of how we are living in the United States, pulled from the Centers for Disease Control and Prevention Web site (www .cdc.gov).

Cholesterol

- Percent of adults age 20 years and over with high serum cholesterol: 16% (2003–6)
- Mean serum cholesterol level for adults age 20 years and over: 200 mg/dl (2003–6)

Diabetes

- Percent of noninstitutionalized adults 20 years and older with diabetes (diagnosed or undiagnosed): 10% (2003–6)

Heart Disease

- Number of noninstitutionalized adults with diagnosed heart disease: 26.6 million
- Percent of noninstitutionalized adults with diagnosed heart disease: 12%

Hypertension

- Percent of noninstitutionalized adults ages 20 and over with hypertension: 32% (2003–6)

Obesity and Overweight

- Percent of noninstitutionalized adults age 20 years and over who are overweight or obese: 67% (2005–6)
- Percent of noninstitutionalized adults age 20 years and over who are obese: 34% (2005–6)

If you don't think that these stats are bad or impact your pocketbook, in 2007 over 60 percent of all bankruptcies were caused by medical bills, and most of these individuals (nearly 80 percent) had health insurance. No matter how you feel about health reform, the most important reform to change the horrific stats above should start with you. Below are a few tips that can help lead you to physical prosperity.

Exercise!

We should be working out at least three days per week. If you are filled with excuses as to why you can't join the gym, then try to develop a work-out regimen at home. Jog/run with the dog, chase the kids around the house, join a salsa class with your spouse, or just do something that makes you move!

Cut the Crap!

I can't lie . . . nothing is more tasty to me than a Double Whopper with cheese and a couple of slabs of bacon, fries on the side, and a strawberry shake! However, years ago I had to cut that out because I felt as if I had to order a side of angioplasty to go with it, it was so heavy. I am not saying that you can't have fried foods, burgers, and other fatty meats (e.g., pork, ham, ribs, sausage, etc.), but for the sake of our kids, who want us to be here for many more years, and our pocketbooks, we must eat them only in moderation. Dairy products . . . try to eat them in the low-fat or fat-free versions. To all of my bacon-, bratwurst-, and smothered-steak-loving brothers and sisters in America . . . I know, someone played a cruel trick on us because with the deliverance of fat was the flavor. Just as we learned to like them, we can learn to like the healthier meals!

Chill Out!

Stress has consumed our society and it only gets worse with the twenty-four-hour media cycles that continuously tell us how bad things are. Turn off the television and pick up a good book from time to time. Every single day you should spend at least thirty to sixty minutes doing something that you love to do. It doesn't have to be the same thing every day, but each day you should do something, such as playing at the park with your dog, reading a great book, watching a movie or television show, getting a massage, or walking along the beach.

Just Say No!

Are you still one of the few who smoke? Why? This has got to be one of the stupidest habits ever created. It is mostly psychological, and most smokers admit that it doesn't even give them a buzz as it did when they first started. So you are essentially killing yourself because you have gotten accustomed to the feeling of tar going into your lungs, shortening your life span. If you really need to have something in your hands, how about grabbing a Tootsie Pop instead?

Another slow-death drug is excessive drinking. One glass (two glasses for men) of red wine per day can help to prevent heart disease (notice they didn't say an entire bottle). More than that and the damage that you are doing to your liver and kidneys can be irreparable.

Don't Worry . . . Be Happy!

Optimism is a crucial component to every person's health plan. Try to see the good in every person and situation. It is hard for you to feel down if you are smiling, singing a happy song, or eating a tasty ice cream cone. So grab a cone on the way home from a long day at work to make you feel better!

2. Social Prosperity

One of our many programs focuses on teaching financial literacy to those who were formerly incarcerated, to fight recidivism. Recidivism is when someone comes out of prison, then for whatever reason ends up going back. Of the more than 2 million people incarcerated in this country, 650,000 will be released in the year. Of the 650,000 released, over 60 percent will be back in prison in three years. Why do I care about this so much? As long as people are committing crimes in the streets, there will be victims of crimes. High crime rates in the community impact housing prices, business traffic, and the entire economic foundation of the community.

I don't want to live in a community with criminals and crooks who feel that they have to rob and steal to survive. They might just decide to steal from someone in my family or even worse. So my solution is to teach financial literacy to those who were formerly incarcerated to expose them to alternatives of living legitimately and to help them on the road to becoming viable contributors to the community.

Many social issues impact communities all across America. They include but are certainly not limited to:

- Poverty
- Hunger
- Illiteracy
- Financial illiteracy
- STDs
- Poor health
- Domestic abuse
- Breast cancer

The list can go on forever. Your job as a contributor to this village and one who is striving for social prosperity is to choose a cause that you feel passionately about and fight for it. Form a social-networking group on a social-networking site, have regular meetings, host events in your community, and do what is necessary to bring light to this cause and how it impacts the community in hopes of getting others to join and have an impact. You would be surprised at how many multimillion-dollar-a-year nonprofits were formed because someone believed in a cause and wanted to fight for it. What do you want to fight for? Once you pick your fight, be sure to let me know what it is and I will support you in any way I can.

3. Spiritual Prosperity

In a world with many different faiths, religions, and creeds, one will find many different definitions of spiritual prosperity. I believe that it is a wonderful thing to live in such a melting pot because this diversity lends itself to some tremendous personal growth. However, I have found a common link among believers in a higher power, and one religion that everyone of all faiths can follow—obey God.

No matter what your definition is or how you choose to follow God, spiritual prosperity is all about making sure that you are striving to follow as closely as possible those principles that mean the most to you. The way I choose to achieve spiritual prosperity is by following the principles in the Bible because I am Christian. Your principles may be found through the Koran if you are Muslim, the Torah if you are Jewish, the Tripitaka if you are Buddhist, the Bhagavad Gita if you are Hindu, or you may not have a book at all but a set of core values that you believe the creator wants you to live by. Even if you are an atheist, you probably have a set of principles that you believe is best to live life in accordance with . . . you just call it morality or humanism rather than spiritual principles.

No matter what you call it, you should be trying to guide your decisions by it every day. These most certainly have an economic impact on our lives. Just look at the recession of 2007, which was driven by greed. Greed of corporations who wanted to take advantage of those who didn't know any better; greed of government, which was receiving too much funding from corporations to regulate the greed of corporations; and greed of people who were so enticed by the thought of owning a home that they didn't take their time and allowed the corporations to take advantage of them.

Did we really act according to the Golden Rule in the recession of 2007, "Do unto others as you would have them do unto you"? Did we really act according to the principle of "I am my brother's or sister's keeper"? If we are truthful with ourselves, the prospect of earning more money and building fast wealth caused us to lose all sense of prudence, diligence, and accountability for each other. We must get back to these basic principles of life if we are going to move forward economically.

4. Mental Prosperity

I learned a poem while I was pledging my fraternity that has always stuck in my mind that I feel best fits this section on mental prosperity.

"THE MAN WHO THINKS HE CAN"
by Walter D. Wintle

If you think you are beaten, you are;
If you think you dare not, you don't.
If you'd like to win, but think you can't
It's almost a cinch you won't.
If you think you'll lose, you've lost,
For out in the world we find
Success being with a fellow's will;
It's all in the state of mind.

If you think you're outclassed, you are:
You've got to think high to rise.
You've got to be sure of yourself before
You can ever win a prize.

Life's battles don't always go
To the stronger or faster man,
But soon or late the man who wins
Is the one who thinks he can.

I always recite this poem to myself whenever I doubt myself or even come close to feeling that obstacles are too great for me to overcome. We discussed the power of the mind earlier, but it is such an important element that it bears repeating. The moment that you start to believe that you don't have it in you to be successful, you are destined not to be a success. If you think that you are forever going to be broke, then you will forever be broke.

The power of the mind will help you differentiate between the facts and the truth of life. There is a need for this because they are very different. I remember a friend of mine was diagnosed with cancer and was given six months to live. The facts showed that she had cancer. The facts showed that she was doomed to share the terminal fate of those who'd shared the diagnosis. There was no disputing the tests that were administered time and time again.

However, while the doctors and even many of her family members were focusing on the facts, she was focusing on the truth. She believed that she would be healed. She believed with all of her mind and spirit that she had many more years left to enjoy. As much as the doctors tried to show her the facts, she chose to believe the truth. I am happy to tell you the diagnosis was over five years ago, and she is not only still with us, but she has been given a clean bill of health. The doctors and the facts had written her off, but her mind chose to believe the truth!

Many of you reading this now might be living check to check or have bank accounts that are dangerously close to zero after you've paid your bills. I would like to remind you of the facts versus the truth. The facts show that your bank account is light, but I want you to believe, with your entire mind and spirit, the truth. The truth is you have it in you to change your situation. The truth is that you don't have to ask for anything from anybody; everything that you need to be successful you already have. Your family may not be as supportive as you would like them to be, your church may have failed you, the government may have let you down, but that is okay; the truth is that you can overcome all of the obstacles that have come your way. That is what I believe about you, but you need to believe that about yourself.

Your mind controls your thoughts and what you believe. If you believe it, you will begin to speak it. Once you speak it, you will begin to act out what you speak. When you begin to act out what you speak, you begin those actions that become your habits. Those habits that you have created will begin to form your character. Your character will determine your destiny. See how it all fits together? If you want to change your destiny, just change the way that you think! This is the secret to becoming mentally prosperous.

5. Financial Prosperity

This is my area of specialty, and the primary focus of this book. However, I hope that I have conveyed the point that financial prosperity is not about making millions of dollars. The testimonies that you have read in this book show you that you don't have to be a millionaire to change your community. It helps a lot, but if you are wise with your funds, you can prepare yourself to create change.

But it is hard to empower the community if your house is about to be foreclosed on or creditors are calling. We must do the basic things such as to stop borrowing from tomorrow for material items that we want today. If you take away anything from this book, take these four simple rules that will help you on the road to financial prosperity.

1. **Spend less than you earn.** This sounds simple, but as stated in previous chapters, most people in America don't accomplish this.
2. **Minimize your debt.** Many people complain that they can't pay their bills, when the simplest solution would be to just stop making bills! How many items are in your garage right now collecting dust, are no longer useful to you, but you are still paying the bill?
3. **Purchase more things that add to net worth, and fewer that subtract from it.** You should be putting yourself in a position to purchase more investments and things that add to your net worth, such as stocks, bonds, real estate, and savings accounts, where interest works for you, while purchasing fewer things that depreciate, such as cars, clothes, material things, and debt, where the excessive interest works against you.
4. **Minimize your taxes.** Starting a company, buying a house, or maximizing tax-deferred savings accounts can provide you enormous tax advantages.

VILLAGE VISIT

The Power of Prosperity: The Professional Athlete

When chaos erupts—layoffs at your job, the wife reminding you about your ever-growing "Honey-Do" list, and the mother-in-law staying with you for the week—everything seems to get a little better if the home team is winning. Something about sports allows you to cheer and cry tears of joy for a moment in the midst of life's turmoil. Sports have brought out the best in cities, states, and entire nations. There is power in sports, and I will be the first to say that I had not a problem in the world when "my" Detroit Pistons won the NBA championship. I say "my" because people take ownership of their teams, and they respect the athletes that play the sports.

Dhani Jones, of the Cincinnati Bengals, is one of the most humble people that you could ever meet. Sometimes I think that the NFL is a hobby to Dhani because he is always doing so much more. Speaking out against global warming, spending time with young students, exposing communities to other cultures, starting businesses, and bringing his friends together to help them start businesses are just a few things that Dhani does regularly. Many people idolize those athletes who play professional sports and have visions of living the life of a professional athlete. Dhani Jones is a perfect example of an athlete whom you can be just like, but you will never have to touch a football in your life or play a professional sport. All you have to do is to live a well-rounded life, treat your finances with respect, and give back to your community, and you can be just like Dhani. Dhani is a prime example of all five points of prosperity.

THE RENAISSANCE LINEBACKER
by Dhani Jones

I have always been a person ruled by passion. I need it to face my day. I call on it whenever I am faced with a challenge. It's what drives and motivates me. From my day job with the Cincinnati Ben-

(continued)

gals to my off-season gig tackling international sports and culture, passion remains the driving force. With my love of both football and travel, I, thankfully, find myself in an enviable position, for which I am continually grateful. I have been afforded many opportunities and blessings, but it hasn't been easy, nor a walk in the park. It took plenty of personal fuel, drive, and hard work to make my dreams a reality.

I am a poet, and we poets like metaphors. I can't separate the power of sports from the power of things that impact our world. To me, they go hand in hand. There's always a lesson in the competition, in the battle, and I feel that everything we deal with or face can, directly or indirectly, be explained through the game of life. I have gained three key principles from sports that have enhanced my life's achievements. First, I was able to curb a nasty adolescent temper through the outlet of football. Second, I mastered the invaluable skills of discipline and hard work. And last, I embraced the powerful network of teamwork. I believe a fusion of these three beliefs can have an immense impact on one's life, especially since they continue to have an impact on mine.

I am a firm believer that we must channel our energies, so that what we put in, we also put out. I am constantly learning new and exciting things about myself. At times, we all lose sight of who we are and neglect to hear the slight whispers speaking from within. Life tends to bog us down with its demands and we falter from our course. I combat this by continually finding new methods of channeling my energy. Yes, it takes some effort to find what's lurking deep inside you, but when you do take hold and don't look back.

A natural magnifying glass comes with being in the NFL. People are always sizing you up, analyzing your game, observing how you conduct yourself on and off the field. I have never balked at this; in fact, I welcome it. I believe if I continue to follow my dreams and interests, then I will serve as a true example to others on not setting limitations in life. For me, wearing bow ties was more than a signature look, so I steadily charted a course to start my first business, Five Star Ties. Becoming an entrepreneur was always a dream of mine, whether I was in the NFL or not. However, I lived pretty

(continued)

frugally until I got my contract with the Eagles in 2004, and then I seized the moment to launch my business. Even after the increase in my salary, my first four thrifty years in the league had become a set practice and truly prepared me for the challenges of being a business owner. Additionally, it left room for me to set something aside, day by day, so that even my most outlandish aspirations could one day be real. Today, Five Star Ties is still going strong, with a new direction in the works.

Then the environment became a serious talking point and I felt quite ignorant and helpless. I knew that I wanted to learn more ways to curb global warming, conserve energy, and reduce pollution, but I didn't know how. I saw *An Inconvenient Truth* and it utterly changed me. Consequently, I was invigorated and motivated to do my part. I started riding my bike to work, recycled regularly, and even used a canvas bag when grocery shopping. Then, pure chance, through connections from people sensing my passion on the issue, I met Al Gore. Amazingly enough, it led to me to attend a three-day seminar, ultimately becoming one of Gore's nationwide lecturers spreading the word on how everyday people can make a difference in our world. I had no idea at first that any of that would transpire, but I had an internal spark and it led to something incredible.

As I was a sixth-round draft pick in 2000, many skeptics would probably have dismissed my chances of becoming a ten-year pro in the NFL. For me to have lasted this long in spite of the many challenges, setbacks, and hurdles was sheer, pure work. This notion applies to everything, not just football. What you put in is what you get out. Getting to the next level or building something from scratch, even reconstructing from past failures, takes unfiltered effort. It's never easy to grind and hustle, but when the rewards began to trickle in, then it becomes slightly addictive. Athletes understand this. We like to win. There's no better feeling than coming home with a solid, hard-fought win. We live for it and work for it. We also know that sometimes the odds are against us, things go wrong, and losses occur. But every athlete who is worth his or her salt will work even harder. The same applies to life. One must become addicted to wins, success, and it doesn't have to be over-the-top achievements, because most

(continued)

times it's the small feats that truly motivate and move individuals to great pursuits.

When I received the dual deal of working for the Bengals and the Travel Channel, I knew it wasn't going to be easy. However, the demanding toil pales in comparison to the impact my global experiences may have on the mind of a young person who may never have left his or her own state. I aspire through my experiences for people to feel comfortable in exploring. It doesn't have to be on international level, but that would be even better. If everyone could have a passport, then I would be happy. I hope that people see through me that the world is, indeed, their playground, a place of tremendous discovery and promise. It goes back to setting something aside, a little money every month or whatever it takes to get out and see the world, landscapes, cultures, and people, in their entire splendor.

Finally, one must not underestimate the power of teamwork. Whether it's through mentoring, networking, or supporters, a personal team is crucial to fulfilling dreams. I am a creative person, through and through, and at times my ideas get the best of me. I learned early on that I need to have people on my side who will tell me the truth and not always what I want to hear. Those who can take my idea and determine if it's viable, significant, or worthwhile. I am notorious for assembling the "perfect" team to ensure success not only for me, but for all those involved. Seeking an edge is vital to one's success, and having the right team is essential. Finding the appropriate people who fill voids and provide solutions can take any endeavor to the next level and beyond. It's important to have people who understand your direction, complement your personality, and even counterbalance your shortcomings.

Most important, dreamers need encouragers. Passion is a spark, but true, genuine support can sustain even the dimmest flicker. Nothing thrills me more than motivational speaking, whether I am on the sideline yelling at my teammates or in a classroom coloring with second-graders. I enjoy sharing my story because I enjoy hearing others' stories. There's nothing like hearing people share their story, revealing the keys and pitfalls to their drive and success. It's all a part of the human experience, the universal language of true teamwork.

(continued)

271

I'll never forget when I first heard Ben Carson, the first black pediatric neurosurgeon, in college. I was so moved and inspired by him that I decided I, too, would become a pediatric neurosurgeon. He was a man of action, intelligence, faith, inner peace, and inspiring ambition. He became a personal mentor and the perfect role model. At the time, I was so impressed that he took time out of his busy schedule to connect with a bunch of scatterbrained college kids that I never forgot him or his story. I didn't know where my life would take me, but Ben Carson definitely had a large role in my journey. He once said, "An individual must believe in himself and his abilities. To do his best, one needs a confidence that says, 'I can do anything, and if I can't do it, I know how to get help.'" That embodies the genuine cycle of authentic teamwork. I didn't hesitate to fully involve myself and "help" within the community, especially when I began playing for the NFL. I believe we must all take each other's stories, learn from one another, and freely discuss and share mistakes and triumphs. I appreciate the moments when I am able to give, but I truly cherish the moments when there's an exchange. All of our lives are connected lessons for each of us to grow and uplift one another.

We are all striving for our personal and professional best. We aim to succeed in this game of life. And I wholeheartedly believe that if people honor their "calling," work like mad to make it happen, and carve out a circle of authentic support, then they'll find victory. Life is about choices, challenges, and chances. Friends, create your choices, embrace your challenges, and seize every chance you get.

RYAN MACK'S FIVE ECONOMIC EMPOWERMENT TIPS FOR THE PROFESSIONAL ATHLETE

1. I know that you are just so excited to live the life of a millionaire now that you have your first million, but wait! Live life as if you were only taking home $100,000 per year after taxes and save the rest. In many sports, if you are lucky, you career will last five years. However, let's say that you are *really* lucky and it lasts ten. If you are twenty-one when you start, you will be thirty-one when you finish. You still have an entire life ahead of you that you will need to plan for. Live as if you were a "thousandaire," but invest like like millionaire.

2. Build your financial team with people you can trust, and conduct many interviews. The first person that you should hire is a good attorney. As you hire your financial adviser, accountant, and others, have your attorney look over their documents and give his or her opinion. Please use Chapter 13 for how to build your team of professionals and whom to put on it.

3. Limit extravagant gifts to your parents or guardians. If they live in a bad neighborhood, move them into a better neighborhood, but don't purchase a huge home yet. Purchase a starter home for your parents, move them in, build *your* foundation and make sure that it is steady, then after a few years you can upgrade. Don't give the rest of your family and friends any money, but help them within limits to afford things that will help them move forward (e.g., college tuition, a consultant to help build a business, food and clothes if they are poor and don't have much, etc.). Don't purchase any items that are a *want* and not a *need*.

4. Start to involve yourself in hobbies that can develop into a long-term career. Create a nonprofit organization that helps people in your community around a cause that you are passionate about. This is a great way to give back, and it will give you a sense of how to run a business. It will definitely help you transition into your next longer-term career, uplift your community, require little initial investment, and you are more prone than most to get private funding (especially from banks) because you have a name.

5. Stay grounded. For most professional athletes in sports such as football, baseball, or basketball, their first check as a pro is the largest they have ever seen. Don't lose your head.

CHAPTER SIXTEEN

Next Steps

I KNOW THAT FOR SOME OF YOU, MANY OF THE CONCEPTS AND PRINCIPLES HERE were complex and perhaps difficult to understand. If you did not understand something in this reading, reread it. Purchase another book about financial literacy to obtain a different perspective. When I first learned about tax-deferred accounts, I was perplexed as well, but that was not my cue to be frustrated and give up. That was my cue to pick up another book, ask someone else, or read another article that helped to explain the concept.

Also, I know many people who have read many books on financial literacy but have yet to progress because they are stuck in the information-gathering stage. How many people in America are going to live and die at the drawing board because they do not have the faith and fortitude to take the necessary action to implement the plan? No more paralysis of analysis. Knowledge is not enough! With no action you have no plan, so I urge you to take action today. Gather your friends and family to form support groups that discuss financial literacy regularly. This is a new language for many, and I do not expect anyone to learn it overnight. However, we must do all that is necessary to make sure that we are walking that path toward economic empowerment and financial independence.

My grandmother used to tell me a story of a horse being ridden by his master into a dark tunnel. When the horse stops and refuses to go into the pitch-black tunnel, the master takes out his handkerchief, blindfolds the horse, and they ride into the tunnel. Suddenly the master sees a huge hole. Going at such a fast speed, the master knows it is impossible to stop the horse. Thinking quickly, the master jumps off just in time to safety, but the horse falls to the bottom of the hole to his death. Whose fault is it that the horse died? The horse's fault!

Without the basic knowledge of how to control our finances, without being equipped or supplied with an ability to think for ourselves, we are no better off than that horse being led into a dark tunnel blindfolded. Let's make sure that we can see a clearer financial future for ourselves . . . more important, for our communities across this country.

Most of you reading this book are not millionaires, but all of you have the ability to become millionaires if that is your desire. However, if had my way, I would wish you to take two things away from this book. The first thing is, we should not be pursuing money, we should be pursuing passion. If you never become a millionaire, that is quite all right. Money does not equate to happiness, but living a life of purpose and passion should equate to a life of true fulfillment. The principles outlined in this book will not make you rich. Your passion will make you rich. The principles in this book are simply designed to remove money as an obstacle and liability to your success.

The second thing is, your net worth or how much money you have should not determine your efforts to become fiscally responsible, and it does not dictate your ability to make a change in this world. We have heard stories of people from all walks of life who are not even close to being considered rich by society's standards but are still managing their money well *and* making the world a better place. You can do the same in your life, and you should start with at least one person at a time. If you are married, see what you can do to empower your mate. If you are a parent, read segments of this book with your child and have a discussion afterward. If you are single, become a mentor to a child in need. If you are a business owner, give back to the community that has helped your company to thrive and treat the community with integrity. I don't believe that your success is just possible . . . I believe that your success in life is also probable. This book was designed to help alleviate financial obstacles in your life that can inhibit your greatness. There are not a lot of guarantees in life, but I can guarantee that you—the person who is reading this right now—have something inside you that is designed to make this world a better place. Your success in allowing your light to shine bright is in all of our best interests. So I hope that the tips presented in this book have made your path to greatness that much easier. I want to see a better world, and that can come through a better you. Let's start now!

Appendix A: Four Steps to Success

Where there is no vision, the people perish.
—*Proverbs 29:18*

What Is Your Passion?
Write five talents, skills, hobbies, or things you always find yourself talking about in the lines below.

1. _____
2. _____
3. _____
4. _____
5. _____

What Is Your Vision?
Where will you be years from today and what will you be doing?

1 year _____

5 years _____

10 years _____

20 years _____

Resource Acquisition
What resources must you obtain to assist you in achieving your vision (knowledge, financial literacy, college education, professional experience, networking, etc.)?

_____

_____

_____

Action

Write five tangible steps of action that starting from *today* will assist you in achieving your vision ten years from now.

1. _____

2. _____

3. _____

4. _____

5. _____

Appendix B: Estimated Budget

MONTHLY INCOME	

GROSS MONTHLY INCOME ☐

Salary _____
Interest _____
Dividends _____
Other income _____

LESS

1. Tithe/Giving ☐
2. Taxes (fed, state, FICA) ☐

NET SPENDABLE INCOME ☐

MONTHLY LIVING EXPENSES	

3. **Housing** ☐

    Mortgage/rent _____
    Insurance _____
    Property taxes _____
    Electricity _____
    Gas _____
    Water _____
    Telephone _____
    Maintenance _____
    Cable TV _____
    Other _____

4. **Food** ☐

5. **Transportation** ☐

    Cab rides _____
    Gas and oil _____
    Insurance _____
    License _____
    Maint./repair/replace _____
    Other _____

6. **Insurance** ☐

    Life _____
    Health _____
    Other _____

7. **Debts** ☐

    Student loan _____
    Credit card _____
    Auto loan _____

8. **Entertainment/Recreation** ☐

    Eating out _____
    Babysitters _____
    Activities/trips _____
    Vacation _____
    Pets _____
    Other _____

9. **Clothing** ☐

10. **Savings** ☐

11. **Medical Expenses** ☐

    Doctor _____
    Dentist _____
    Prescriptions _____
    Other _____

12. **Miscellaneous** ☐

    Toiletries/cosmetics _____
    Beauty/barber _____
    Laundry/cleaning _____
    Allowances _____
    Subscriptions _____
    Gifts _____
    Cash _____
    Other _____

13. **Investments** ☐

14. **School/Child Care** ☐

    Tuition _____
    Materials _____
    Transportation _____
    Day care _____

TOTAL LIVING EXPENSES ☐

INCOME VS. LIVING EXPENSES	

NET SPENDABLE INCOME ☐

LESS TOTAL LIVING EXPENSES ☐

SURPLUS OR DEFICIT ☐

Appendix C: Net Worth Statement

This should be filled out twice per year. Once when you do your taxes because you are already doing paperwork. The second time in November because it reminds you of how much you shouldn't be spending during the holiday season.

Date:_____

Assets (present market value)	
Cash on hand/checking account	
Savings	
Stocks and bonds	
Cash value of life insurance	
Coins	
Home valuation	
Real estate investments	
Mortgages/note receivable	
Business valuation	
Automobiles	
Furniture	
Jewelry	
Pension/retirement	
Other assets	

Total Assets:

Liabilities (current amount owed)	
Credit card debt	
Automobile debt	
Home mortgage debt	
Personal debt to relatives	
Business debt	
Student loans	
Medical bills	
Loans against life insurance	
Bank loans	
Past-due bills	
Other debt and loans owed	

Total Liabilities:

Net Worth (total assets minus total liabilities)

Month _____ Year _____

30-Day Diary

Category	Income	Tithe/Giving	Taxes	Housing	Food	Entertainment	Debts	Miscellaneous	Clothing	Transportation	Insurance
Budgeted Amount	$	$	$	$	$	$	$	$	$	$	$
Date											
1											
2											
3											
4											
5											
6											
7											
8											
9											
10											
11											
12											
13											
14											
15											
Subtotal											
16											
17											
18											

(continued)

Month _____ Year _____

30-Day Diary

Category	Income	Tithe/Giving	Taxes	Housing	Food	Entertainment	Debts	Miscellaneous	Clothing	Transportation	Insurance
19											
20											
21											
22											
23											
24											
25											
26											
27											
28											
29											
30											
31											
This Month TOTAL	$	$	$	$	$					$	$
This Month SURPLUS/ DEFICIT	$	$	$	$	$					$	$

BUDGET
SUMMARY

Total Income	$ _____
Minus Total Expenses	$ _____
Equals Surplus/Deficit	$ _____

APPENDIX E: FINANCIAL GOALS

Date: _____

GIVING GOALS

I would like to give _____ percent of my income.

Other giving goals: _____

_____

DEBT REPAYMENT GOALS

I would like to pay off the following debts first:

Creditor   Amount

_____   _____

_____   _____

_____   _____

EDUCATIONAL GOALS

I would like to fund the following education.

Person	School	Annual Cost	Total Cost
_____	_____	_____	_____
_____	_____	_____	_____
_____	_____	_____	_____
_____	_____	_____	_____

Other educational goals: _____

LIFESTYLE GOALS

I would like to make the following major purchases (home, automobile, travel, etc.):

Item   Amount

_____   _____

_____   _____

_____   _____

_____   _____

I would like to achieve the following annual income: _____

SAVINGS AND INVESTMENT GOALS

I would like to save _____ percent of my income.

Other savings goals: _____

_____

I would like to make the following investments: Investment

_____   _____

_____   _____

_____   _____

_____   _____

I would like to provide my/our heirs with the following: _____

STARTING A BUSINESS

I would like to invest in or begin my/our own business: _____
_____

GOALS FOR THIS YEAR

Priority   Financial Goals

1   _____

2   _____

3   _____

4   _____

5   _____

Appendix F: Notes on Forming the Right Entity

Sole Proprietorship

- One business owner if that is to be you. If you have a partner, then I would not suggest this method.
- No formal documents are required in formation, so if ease of formation is your most important factor, then this could be an option.
- There is unlimited liability of the owners. There is no separation between you and the business. If someone wants to go after you, then all your personal assets are fair game.
- You are taxed on the individual level. You can take a deduction for a portion of the amount paid for health insurance to cover yourself, your spouse, and your dependents. The deduction was only 70 percent in 2002, but was raised to 100 percent in 2003 and continues to be the same. You would be liable for self-employment tax, in effect paying both the employer's and employees' shares of Social Security. You are not subject to unemployment tax.
- There are generally retirement plans available.
- You, as owner, will generally have more difficulty qualifying for other employee benefits.
- When you pass away, so does the proprietorship.

General Partnership

- Usually two or more owners.
- Not a lot of paperwork is required, but there is a little more required than a sole proprietorship.
- As with the sole proprietorship, there is unlimited liability of the owners. No separation of personal assets and business assets.
- These are pass-through entities for federal income tax purposes. You within the partnership will pay no tax, and all items of the partnership will flow through to the partners and will appear on their respective income tax returns. Usually, the general partnership can be thought of as a tax-reporting entity rather than a tax-paying entity. You are not usually eligible to receive tax-favored employee fringe benefits.
- Tax-favored retirement plans are available.
- You will have difficulty qualifying for employee benefits as the owner.

- You can usually liquidate the partnership without adverse tax consequences.

LIMITED PARTNERSHIP (usually formed as a means of raising investor capital and the popular choice for real estate syndicates where the losses can be passed down to the limited partners)

- Where there are no limited partners in a general partnership, this entity will have *at least* one general and one limited partner.
- A partnership agreement is required. This can be very tedious, not because the paperwork involved is hard to file, but because there can be *a lot* of trust issues that come into play when drafting this document. I personally did not choose to form this entity, because there is no one I trust more than myself. How the document is drafted will mean everything if there is a legal dispute and one needs to determine liability. One partner can be found liable for the others' actions when he or she had no part in the wrongdoing. However, your situation might be different.
- There is unlimited liability for the general partners, but limited liability for the limited partners. The limited liability is restricted in the amount of investment in the partnership. Limited partners can't take part in the active management of the partnership or they could be treated as general partners. In other words, if you try to act as if you are a limited partner to reduce your liability, and your actions show otherwise, you will be treated as a general partner. (Just be honest from the jump and save yourself some potential headaches.)
- This is a pass-through entity as well.
- Retirement plans are generally available.
- It's pretty hard to qualify for employee benefits as owner.
- As with a general partnership, you can liquidate without adverse tax consequences.

LIMITED LIABILITY PARTNERSHIP

- Usually two or more partners.
- You need to register under the applicable state law.
- There is limited liability for acts of other partners, employees, and agents.
- There is pass-through taxation.
- Retirement plans are generally available if you choose to form one through the entity.

- It's hard to qualify for employee benefits as the owner.
- You can liquidate without adverse tax consequences.

"C" CORPORATION

- This is good if you are planning to be *huge*. There are unlimited numbers of owners.
- This is not hard to form, but is very costly and time-consuming.
- There is very limited liability of the owners, which is why Enron and Worldcom almost got away so clean.
- There is no pass-through taxation for this entity. The corporation will be taxed, and you will be taxed at the individual level as well. There are ways to get around this taxation, however. For one, the level of tax is not as high as the individual taxation level. Another way is to *expense everything*! I mean *everything*. Expense your salary, cab rides, dinner outings, up to 40 percent of your rent if you work from home, your education costs, pension contributions, benefits, bonuses, etc. There are many books out there that can help you with this. The goal is to almost zero out your earnings and eliminate this taxation at the corporate level. Many people do it and are successful with it. However, I do advise that you operate within the legal confines of the system, and keep good records of your write-offs. This can be very tedious, but it can keep you from some fines and/or jail time when the IRS comes around (and they will come around).
- Retirement plans are generally available.
- As an owner, you will find it pretty simple to qualify for benefits.
- The life of the corporation is not affected by your death.

"S" CORPORATION (very popular among starting small-business owners)

- You will have a limited number of owners, no more than seventy-five.
- There are a number of rules and regulations that you have to abide by.
- As with the "C" Corporation, there is limited liability of the owners, so you wouldn't have to worry about being sued for your personal assets.
- Unlike with the "C" Corporation, and the most popular aspect of this entity, there is pass-through taxation. You are not taxed at the

corporate level, but only once at the individual. However, many people are unaware of the large accounting and legal costs that it takes to start and maintain the "S" Corporation. Many times they far outweigh any tax advantage that you have from forming this entity.

- As owner, you might find it more difficult to qualify for employee benefits.
- Retirement plans are available.
- As in a "C" Corporation, the life of the corporation is not affected by death, retirement, etc., of owners

LIMITED LIABILITY COMPANY (my favorite and what I chose for my company)

- You can have as many owners as you want.
- It is pretty easy to form. New York does have a publication requirement for all LLC companies. Also, LLCs are not subject to many of the restrictions of the "S" Corporations (no limits on the number of shareholders or the prohibition against corporate shareholders).
- You have a choice of pass-through or corporate level taxation. I chose pass-through, of course.
- There is some difficulty qualifying for employee benefits.
- Retirement plans are generally available.
- One can liquidate without adverse tax consequences.

ACKNOWLEDGMENTS

I WANT TO THANK GOD FOR ALWAYS BEING THERE FOR ME AND NEVER GIVING ME SO much that I cannot handle it. I am sorry that although you pushed me so hard to write this book years ago, I was too busy trying to do things my way instead of listening to your will. I am thankful that you are infinitely more patient than I am and stuck by me even though I don't deserve all of your grace. I am nothing without you.

Thanks to my mother, Carol, for being my biggest fan since day one of everything in my life, and always lending me a pair of fresh eyes to read my work. To my father, Richard, for being my motivational voice of reason and always giving me a confidence boost. To my brothers, Richard and Eric, for giving me the spiritual guidance that I need to always make sure that what I write has a strong moral compass. To my agent, Nancey Flowers, whom God sent to push me to write this book long ago, but stuck with me even though it seems as if I have ADD at times. To my friend Lory George, who was a big supporter and kept me motivated to continue to finally get this done. To Amber Morgan, who volunteered her time to help edit this book and acted as if it were her own. To all those who wrote testimonies for the book, you have all touched me in a way that words will never give justice to. Those who are fortunate enough to read your stories will definitely want to hear more, and I want to help make that happen in any way that I can. To the Optimum team for putting up with all of my crazy ideas to save the world! To my community . . . if I appear to be standing tall, it is only because you made me who I am by putting me on your shoulders and lifting me higher. There was no way that I could write my first book and not include you in it. I doubt that I will ever write a book without your involvement. I gave my life to you years ago, and consider me to be used as you wish. I love you all!

INDEX